THOMAS CARLYLE

THOMAS CARLYLE

And the Art of History

By

LOUISE MERWIN YOUNG

1971
OCTAGON BOOKS
New York

Copyright 1939 by the University of Pennsylvania Press
Copyright renewed 1967 by Louise M. Young

Reprinted 1971
by special arrangement with the University of Pennsylvania Press

OCTAGON BOOKS
A DIVISION OF FARRAR, STRAUS & GIROUX, INC.
19 Union Square West
New York, N.Y. 10003

LIBRARY OF CONGRESS CATALOG CARD NUMBER: 79-120684

ISBN 0-374-98841-2

Printed in U.S.A. by
NOBLE OFFSET PRINTERS, INC.
NEW YORK 3, N. Y.

To
R. A. Y.

"... truly the Art of History, the grand difference between a Dryasdust and a Sacred Poet, is very much even this: To distinguish what does still reach to the surface, and is alive and frondent for us; and what reaches no longer to the surface, but moulders safe underground, never to send forth leaves or fruit for mankind any more; of the former we shall rejoice to hear.... Of the latter only Pedants and Dullards ... will find good to speak. By wise memory and by wise oblivion: it lies all there."

—ANTIDRYASDUST
(*Cromwell*, I. 9)

INTRODUCTION TO THE OCTAGON EDITION

I suppose there are few who, having once written a book, would not like to have the opportunity to rewrite it to incorporate new insights and develop fleeting intuitions scared away by the overpowering influence of older scholars. This book was a sincerely intentioned attempt by a youthful scholar to open a window on a new view of Carlyle as a literary artist who chose history as his medium. It was written when the critical understanding of Carlyle had sunk to its nadir, and the sympathetic investigator was forced to work in a chill climate. The 'art of history'—Carlyle's own phrase—had been repudiated by historiographers, who had abandoned the humanities for the social sciences, as a contradiction in terms. Carlyle's belief that history was akin to epic poetry, that historical events must be intuitively seen and inwardly experienced before being successfully recreated, was not sympathetically entertained. Writing of Carlyle's conception of the historian's craft and his method of writing history in such a period required a certain boldness.

The field of early Victorian scholarship has undergone great imaginative expansion since World War II. There is no longer need to quibble over Carlyle's "misunderstanding" of his German sources—Fichte, Schelling, Herder and Goethe. He took what he wanted and needed, and absorbed the distilled essence of Herder's remarkable insights in their Goethean form. Nor is it necessary to apologize for his verbal extravagance and rhetorical manipulations. The strong emotional coloring, resourceful diction, prose cadence and facility with metaphor were the work of a controlling intelligence searching out new meanings and a poetic imagination grasping a form or symbol in which to convey them. The vivid imagery, inversions, punctuation were perfectly devised to carry the tone of the speaking voice, creating the impression of the "immediacy of the past."

In Carlyle's writing, from his earliest essays, runs a coherent manner of thinking about human existence which he sought to render intelligible. The activity of writing history emerged less in response to a premeditated plan than as a direction of attention after completion of his personal testament in SARTOR RESARTUS. The epic sweep and grandeur of the FRENCH REVOLUTION gave fullest expression to his conception of history as the "true Epic Poem"— a revelation of human destiny in a moral universe. Reconsidering Carlyle as a romantic historian, I would emphasize with greater firmness the depth of his desire to recapture the epic spirit. Copious allusions in his letters and early essays bear witness to this. He was possessed of the romantic consciousness, deeply moved by a sense of myth and the mystery of time. Consider, he wrote, "the grand peculiarity: the immeasurable one, distinguishing to a really infinite degree, the poorest historical Fact from all Fiction whatsoever . . ." The facts of history constituted "the only imaginative materials wherein reality permanently resides . . ."

Carlyle also understood the creative power of the unconscious; described his method as "keeping the whole matter simmering in the *living mind* and memory rather than laid up . . . in an inert way." Getting a "blazing radiant insight into the fact itself" was the "first and last secret of Kunst." He realized that the novel form had taken possession of the epic spirit in English literature, but saw no reason to amend his belief that "history, after all, is the true Poetry; and Reality, if rightly interpreted, is grander than Fiction; nay . . . in the right interpretation of Reality and History does genuine Poetry consist."

LOUISE M. YOUNG

Washington, D.C.
July, 1971

PREFACE

THE ONE aspect of the lifework of Thomas Carlyle which he considered most important—his attitude toward the writing of history and his practice of the craft—has been, if not generally ignored, at least insufficiently pondered. I have undertaken to consider Carlyle's philosophic approach to the materials of history and his theory and practice of what he himself designated as the "art of history" with a view to appraising his claim to a place in the select company of those who have left us an enduring record of the past. I have approached the problem by taking the broad and traditional view of history as the handmaiden of the arts, conspiring against time to rescue the past from oblivion. This study is the outcome of a belief that the moment is ripe for a fresh consideration of the controversy between Dryasdust and the literary historian.

I have relied mainly on Carlyle's own writings for the purposes of this analysis: the thirty volumes comprising the Centenary Edition and the dozen or more volumes of intimate writings, including the ten volumes of letters, the *Reminiscences*, the *Two Notebooks*. For biographic material I have depended upon David Alec Wilson's recently completed biography, in six volumes, the accuracy and encyclopedic fullness of which supersede that of Froude's *Life*. Since Carlyle's theories regarding history epitomize his social, political, and esthetic thought, my researches have led me over a wide tract of knowledge, including the philosophy of the German Renascence, the political and social thought of the late seventeenth, the eighteenth, and the early nineteenth centuries, particularly the genesis of the romantic movement, and the development of modern historiography. Direct borrowings are indicated in the Notes printed in the Appendix. The Selected Bibliography includes that portion of my reading which has proved to be most valuable. Special mention should be made here of the excellent studies of

Professor Charles Frederick Harrold, relating to certain phases of Carlyle's work as a historian. More detailed reference will be made to them later.

My special acknowledgments must begin with those to my husband, Professor Ralph A. Young, of the University of Pennsylvania, without whose sympathetic interest this work probably would never have been brought to completion. To my brother, Charles L. Merwin, I am likewise deeply indebted for assistance with the manuscript. The clarification of my ideas has been furthered by frequent discussions with interested friends, including Professor Hans P. Neisser, of the University of Pennsylvania, whose wide knowledge of philosophic writings has been extremely helpful, and Professor Elisabeth W. Schneider, of Temple University, with whom I have enjoyed a long and entirely amicable controversy, which has had the steady result of crystallizing and consolidating my views. I take particular pleasure in acknowledging my debt to Professor Edgar A. Singer, Jr., of the University of Pennsylvania, not only for the inspiration of his humane and scholarly attitude toward research but also for his specific advice and encouragement in my investigation into the precise nature of Carlyle's resuscitation of the past, recorded in Chapter Five. Most of all I am deeply grateful to Professor Percy V. D. Shelly, of the University of Pennsylvania, under whose guidance this study has taken shape, for his unfailing encouragement, interest, and scholarly help at all stages of my investigation.

L. M. Y.

CONTENTS

CHAPTER	PAGE
PREFACE	vii
I. INTRODUCTION	1
II. BACKGROUNDS	10
Rationalist Historiography	10
Carlyle's Opposition to Rationalist Historiography	14
The Influence of Herder and German Romanticism	20
The Influence of Schiller	26
English Romanticism: Scott	39
English Romanticism: Burke and Coleridge	43
III. CARLYLE'S PHILOSOPHY OF HISTORY	54
Universal History as Revelation of the Divine Idea	57
Art as Revelation of the Divine Idea	60
The Theory of Social Organization	63
The Theory of Revolution	69
The Right to Revolt	78
The Rôle of the Hero in History	81
The Theory of Right	86
The Concept of Cause	88
IV. THE ART OF HISTORY IN THEORY	92
The Story of the Time Hat	92
The Biographic Approach	97
The Development of the Biographic Method	101
History the True Poetry	110
The Historian's Function	115
History as Social Biography	119
Individual *vs.* Social Biography	128
The Theory of Evidence	131
V. THE ART OF HISTORY IN PRACTICE	138
The Creative Consciousness	138
The Process of Historical Composition	140

CONTENTS

The Secret of Being Graphic   147
Carlyle's Use of Imagery   154
Other Technical Devices   161
Carlyle's Thoughts on Style   165
The Sense of Artistic Finality   166

VI. CARLYLE'S POSITION AS A HISTORIAN   171

NOTES   187

BIBLIOGRAPHY   209

INDEX   217

I

INTRODUCTION

Few writers have commanded critical attention from as many angles as has Thomas Carlyle. His achievement in the province of prose literature is generally acknowledged. His literary criticism has won an enduring place in the history of esthetic criticism. His political and social criticism, in many respects too advanced for his own day, has been winning increasing attention as the perspective of time has revealed its constructive value. His attainments as a historian, on the contrary, have suffered a curious eclipse of critical interest, although his histories have never lacked readers. Professor Gooch acknowledges that Carlyle and Macaulay are the only historians of the early nineteenth century who are still widely read.[1] Yet Carlyle has been subjected to very little critical appraisal by the professional historiographers that is not frankly prejudiced in character. Those who judge him do so in the light of theories regarding the function and character of history which were not current in England during the early decades of the nineteenth century, and which are not necessarily any more valid than the theories Carlyle himself worked on. As a consequence, the critics' generalizations are more illuminative of present day trends in historiography than they are of Carlyle's actual beliefs and opinions. Little or no attempt has been made to understand his conception of historical writing, or to appraise his histories in the light of what he endeavored to do. The fact has been overlooked that while he was a contemporary of Ranke, his fundamental attitude places him closer to Gibbon and Schiller. A half century of time and a wide gulf in method and philosophy separated Carlyle from Gibbon; but by contrast it seems nothing to the unbridgeable abyss which lies between him and the "scientific" historians of the turn of the twentieth century whose judgment of Carlyle has been responsible for his partial eclipse. Dryasdust has had his long revenge.

In considering the case against Carlyle we have in mind the relatively moderate views of such an eminent historiographer as Professor Gooch, who described the *French Revolution* as the "most dramatic work in historical literature, the most epic of historical narratives," but a work which denied any collective life or collective aim in a people, and recognized only individuals, a generalization which we will show to be profoundly untrue.[2] Professor Gooch holds that to Carlyle, history was merely the record of a few picturesque personalities—another judgment which appears to be fundamentally wrong. This error, in particular, has been repeated with increasing emphasis by later critics, with no attempt at a closer evaluation.[3] While Carlyle's works are admittedly "supreme achievements of the creative imagination," he was "the greatest of showmen but the least of interpreters"—a generalization both inadequate and erroneous.[4] Similarly M. Eduard Fueter called Carlyle the most lyrical, most subjective of historians, without explaining what special significance these terms had except for the general inference that they implied a non-scientific attitude.[5] Or consider Professor C. R. L. Fletcher's objection, in his introduction to an annotated edition of the *French Revolution*, that "neither pictures nor portraits are history."[6]

It will be our purpose to show that such criticism of Carlyle's theory and practice of historical writing is dangerously misleading. It appears that professional critics have failed to apply the passionless objectivity, which is the canon of their school, to a critical examination of the available documentary evidence before they arrived at an interpretative judgment of Carlyle as a historian. But the eclipse of the literary historian, which the course of Carlyle's reputation epitomizes goes far deeper for its basis than a mere mistaken judgment upon a single individual. It reveals the decline of a literary mode, and its displacement, temporarily at least, by an entirely new conception of history.

Carlyle won for himself, among his contemporaries, a position of undisputed prestige as a historian. Ruskin placed him with Tacitus as one of the supremely great historians of the human soul. Emerson believed he had created a new kind of history, "a history of the mind." Mill called the *French Revolution* a work of such undoubted genius that it rose above the ordinary tests and rules and was a law unto itself. Jeffrey, Thackeray, Sterling, and Kingsley all hailed Carlyle as the greatest of English historians. His reputation mounted with each succeeding work. The *French Revolution* was the first authoritative English version of that great event, and its success assured Carlyle his public. His *Cromwell* awakened the English people to the real character of the leader so long maligned and misunderstood, and the rehabilitation of the Puritan hero placed Carlyle in the light of a public benefactor. Following *The Life of Sterling* and *Past and Present,* the monumental biography of Frederick II found a public ready and waiting and was scarcely less popular, despite its length, than the earlier works. Carlyle's wife, always one of his severest critics, pronounced it the best of his works; and Emerson called it the wittiest book ever written. Before the last volume of *Frederick* was completed, Bismarck had struck the first blows in the welding of the German Empire (1866), and Carlyle's recognition of the worth and substance of the newly emerged Prussian state seemed almost prophetic to his contemporaries. So great was his influence upon public opinion that he is credited with at least partial responsibility for England's policy of non-intervention in 1870. Carlyle's prestige as a scholar and historian with the general public remained unshaken at his death in 1881.

Then the wind changed. The success of the historical writings of Carlyle and Macaulay had given a tremendous impetus to historical study.[7] But the seeds planted by them germinated in very different soil from that in which their own ideas had grown. A new spirit, emanating from Germany, had entered into the theory and practice of historical writing. Niebuhr had laid the foundations for the science of historical criticism and published his history of Rome as early as 1811, while Carlyle was still a student at Edinburgh. Leopold von Ranke, born in the same month and year as Carlyle (December 1795), published his first great history in 1824, and the first volume of the *History of the Popes* in 1834. Although Ranke's histories established the science of historical criticism and the writing of "scientific" history on a modern footing, the new critical theories did not begin to influence scholarship in England until the middle of the century, long after Carlyle's own attitudes had been formulated and proved in practice.

In Carlyle's interpretation of the historic process and in his theory and practice of historical writing, several older streams of thought converged. He perpetuated the tradition of literary history bequeathed by the great historians of the eighteenth century. But he revitalized the tradition by introducing the leavening influences of romanticism in the several aspects represented by Herder, Schiller, Scott and Burke. To the romantic impulse he added the stimulating influence of the sociological and psychological discoveries with regard to the nature of the social organism, and the dual qualities of continuity and impermanence characterizing the historic process. Carlyle's thought remained a thing apart from other streams of thought undergoing a parallel development, such as the environmental philosophy of history of Thomas Buckle and his followers, the application of the Hegelian dialectic in the economic materialism of Karl Marx, and the new school of scientific historiography which recognized Ranke as its master. Although Carlyle's claim to distinction both as a thinker and a historian rests on a broader basis than do the claims of any of the representatives of these more specialized trends, the nature of the times obscured his significance. This fact alone would lend historical interest to any study of Carlyle's performance as a historian.

The larger issues relating to a definition of history and the true function of the historian have a contingent relationship to our problem. How far, for example, may a historian go in defining his medium and setting the limits of his task? Dryasdust currently assumes full jurisdictional rights in this province, although in Carlyle's day the license was freer. Again, what is history? An art or a science? Carlyle believed firmly that history was related to poetry, even though its method was scientific. His career may be said to bring to a close the age of the gifted amateurs, the product of whose efforts belongs as much to literature as to history.

Historiography, or the art of writing history, is a term whose content has always depended on the general intellectual environment to which it stands related, and of which it is the product. Thomas Buckle remarked that there would "always be a connection between the way in which men contemplate the past and the way they contemplate the present."[8] This fact, indeed, gives to history one of its most compelling qualities. Every age, whatever its technical equipment or philosophic shortcomings, has something authentic to give us even if it only interprets the record of the past in the light of its own ideas, and in ways acceptable to itself. The question of a general definition of history, and of those who may properly be called historians, has been debated vigorously, even acrimoniously, since the day of Aristotle and possibly even before, successive ages contributing their own specially conditioned views. The best we can do, it appears, is to admit that no wholly satisfactory definition is conceivable of so Protean a literary form; and to grant that great history, like great art, may be recognized more easily by its effect than by its form and content. One who has read Herodotus and Plutarch, Thucydides and Tacitus, Clarendon and the venerable Bede, Gibbon and Mommsen, Ranke and Carlyle, will have little difficulty in recognizing fine historical writing when he sees it, even though he may be unable to define the qualities which make the works histories and which make them great. The distance between Bede's plain chronicle and Tacitus' passionate indictment of the Empire is unbridgeable by definition. Yet that both are histories and have certain elements in common none will deny. Nor will many deny the further fact that they are read today with enduring pleasure, not merely because they are histories but because they are works of art at the same time.

Lytton Strachey defined the three essential attributes of the historian as "a capacity for absorbing facts, a capacity for stating them, and a point of view."[9] Charles A. Beard improved upon this definition by a further qualification. In his view the title of historian should be granted only to those who pursue the subject to its fullness and "try to comprehend the intellectual operations which they themselves are performing."[10] These four qualifications summarize admirably the main aspects of Carlyle's technical equipment as a historian. They are based on the assumption that the historian must have a clear conception of his task, a definite theory of his function, a specific approach to his material and a general philosophy acting as a controlling force in guiding the operation of selecting and organizing his material. It will be shown that Carlyle possessed all of these; and had, in addition, a thorough understanding of the intellectual operations he was performing.

In addition to these qualifications, however, Carlyle possessed one more, possibly the greatest of all—a qualification which Professor Saintsbury defined as the "historic sense." This quality, according to Professor Saintsbury, consists of the "power of seizing, and so of portraying a historic character, incident or period as if it were alive, not dead."[11] The imagination of the reader is excited to a degree that, even if he is convinced the thing did not happen, he sees that it might have happened. It is apparent that the historic sense is really just a special case of the poetic sense which makes of poetry an "image of man and nature . . . not standing upon external testimony, but carried alive into the heart by passion."[12] Unlike the poet, whose invention works upon the materials of his observation, the historian is constrained to remain within the limits of historical facts; but the function of the imagination is much the same in either case. The kinship of history with poetry is thus established.

It will be acknowledged at once that many excellent historians have been entirely lacking in the "historic sense." A sense for the past they almost always have and a scholar's pleasure in adding to the sum total of useful knowledge. But the quickening perception of past events and peoples, in terms not only of space and time but of subtler moral qualities lending themselves to individuation is a power of imagination granted to few. Tacitus and Herodotus possessed such power; so did Homer and Shakespeare. Among English historians before Carlyle, only Clarendon possessed it to any significant degree; while Gibbon and Scott had it to a lesser degree. Carlyle possessed it, however, to a degree equaled by "none ever before or since."[13] Saintsbury called him "one of the Deucalions of literature," who "cannot cast a stone but it becomes alive."[14] Lowell likened the figures of most historians to "dolls stuffed with bran, whose whole substance runs out through any hole criticism may tear in them," while Carlyle's are so real that "if you prick them they bleed." William Roscoe Thayer remarked that turning to Carlyle after reading most historians was like coming out of a museum of mummies into a crowd of living, breathing people.[15]

The roots of the "historic sense" lie buried deep in two primary qualities—qualities by no means peculiar to those called geniuses—a sense of the past and acute powers of observation and investigation. These qualities may be traced in an unbroken development from the earliest period of Carlyle's career. Taken together, they constitute the "historico-biographical faculty," which determined the character of all of Carlyle's writings, whether on professedly historical topics or not. His interest in the past is oddly reminiscent of the feeling of the hero in Henry James' novel that it was only when "life was framed in death that the picture was really hung up."[16] Carlyle recorded, in *Sartor Resartus,* the stirring of his infant imagination by the discovery that "Entepfuhl stood in the middle of a Country, of a World; that there was such a thing as history, as Biography; to which I also, one day, by hand and tongue, might contribute."[17] His imagination opened wide to the "grandeur and mystery of time" on the day when, as a small child, he realized that Ecclefechan burn "had flowed and gurgled, through all changes of time and fortune from beyond the earliest date of History." It was a visible link between him and the legions of Caesar who had encamped on nearby Burnswark. By means of it, all the past events which the simple brook had witnessed became part of what Croce calls the "contemporaneous present" and partook of its reality. Time was reduced to its proper significance as a mere convenience or mode of thought. The child only sensed the truth to which Kant gave him the key and a philosophic construction many years later, but the recollected experience gives us an intimation of one of the most extraordinary qualities of Carlyle's mind.

Carlyle's curiosity about the past and his parallel interest in the strange or bizarre is evidenced in what there is recorded of his early reading. From his letters and from Professor Masson's careful compilation of the books borrowed by Carlyle from the Edinburgh University Library, we can judge how wide and various was his reading up to the period when his productive career began.[18] Like Coleridge, he read every book of travels that fell within his reach. More than half of the books listed by Masson are histories and travels, and, except for his love of Scott, Shakespeare and Burns, his preference for "historico-biographic" literature was apparently ingrained. He read Smollett and Sterne and Swift; Fénelon and D'Alembert and Rochefoucauld; Voltaire and Chateaubriand; Sismondi and Montesquieu; Pascal and Montaigne and Bossuet; Millar and Roscoe and Russell; Newton and Laplace and Bossut; Hume and Robertson and Gibbon. "History in authentic fragments lay mingled with fabulous chimeras, wherein also was reality."[19]

Like Milton and Gibbon, Carlyle regarded his formal education as without significance. The true foundation of his literary career he considered to lie in his early reading. Before the Edinburgh period was finished he had managed to "furnish his young head with a considerable miscellany of things and shadows of things" out of books. He acquired an acquaintance with French and English literature of the seventeenth and eighteenth centuries, particularly humane literature, both wide and profound. Apart from his reading, Carlyle's one genuine interest during his university years was in mathematics and the physical sciences. Partly this was the result of a natural aptitude for the discipline and ingenuity required in any branch of science. Partly, too, it was the result of John Leslie's great and inspired teaching, the effect of which was unquestionably heightened by a decided partiality for his gifted pupil. In considering the future historian, too little stress is usually placed on this early prepossession for scientific pursuits as revealing the essentially pragmatic and analytic qualities of Carlyle's mind.

A final important influence on Carlyle's student years was the social and intellectual awakening he experienced in his Edinburgh environment. His hostility to the prevailing social and political philosophy was based fundamentally on its uncongeniality. Neither his economic status nor his Calvinist upbringing predisposed him toward the middle class philosophy whose prophets were Adam Smith and Jeremy Bentham, with their axioms of private property and economic individualism unqualified by social obligations. The widespread social and economic misery was acute enough to impress the most unsophisticated observer, and Carlyle's letters indicate that he was always keenly alive to it. The Industrial Revolution was taking its toll, while the inflation accompanying the slow liquidation of the Napoleonic wars bore heavily on both rural and urban working classes. Carlyle's consciousness of the injustice and inequity in the economic system probably laid the groundwork for his opposition to the bankrupt political and social ideals of the eighteenth century.

II

BACKGROUNDS

THE ENGLISH romantic movement in historiography is epitomized in the historical writings of Carlyle. Though the historical novels of Walter Scott had enfranchised the romantic love of the past a decade or two before Carlyle began writing, it was left to the latter to embody the romantic conception of history and historical writing in more significant form. Carlyle's theories were definitely romantic, but his point of departure in developing them lay not in his positive debt to Scott or to the romantic movement in England. Rather it is to be found in his positive opposition to rationalist principles. In many respects the inheritance from the eighteenth century played a more significant rôle in shaping his opinions than did the current romantic tendencies. This was true largely because the Enlightenment dominated the intellectual atmosphere in Edinburgh during his student years there; and the literature of the seventeenth and eighteenth centuries was the staple of his early intellectual diet.

RATIONALIST HISTORIOGRAPHY

Carlyle's acquaintance with historical writing was confined mainly to the French and English writers of the seventeenth and eighteenth centuries. References to the historians of antiquity in the records of his early years are infrequent enough to support the assumption that these did not influence him deeply. He mentions Thucydides several times. Tacitus he unquestionably had read and admired.[1] Wilson thinks he also was familiar with Sallust.[2] Herodotus and Plutarch were probably known to him, in translation at least. Undoubtedly the reading of his later years included the Greek and Roman historians. One recalls his urgent advice to the students at Edinburgh in the Inaugural Address to examine history, first of all the history of the Romans and Greeks. They will find, he promises, if they "read well," a "pair of extremely remarkable nations, shining in the records left by themselves, as a kind of beacon to light up some noble forms of human life for us in the otherwise utter darkness of the past ages."[3]

There is little doubt, however, that Carlyle's primary attitude toward literary history may be traced to the rationalist historians of the eighteenth century. But before we examine his specific relationships, a word should be said about rationalist historiography. Never had history attained such a vogue, nor reached a loftier level of artistic excellence than in the period from 1750 to the close of the century, when the histories of Voltaire, Hume, Robertson, and Gibbon were appearing in rapid succession. From the eighteenth century historians Carlyle derived his primary belief that a true artist and not a mere artisan was required for the writing of history; likewise the conviction that no loftier goal lay open to human aspiration than the writing of excellent histories. Carlyle believed from his earliest youth, and never ceased to believe, that history was the most elevated literary form through which the voice of a man might speak.

History as written by the eighteenth century historians was a combination of literature, learning, philosophy, and practical wisdom. Writers like Hume, Gibbon, and Voltaire brought to their readers not the results of the restricted research of a few years but the product of their entire cultural growth. They possessed broadly philosophic conceptions regarding the significance of historical events which they used freely in their interpretations. They deliberately employed every artistic resource in their power—careful selection of details, attention to form, and a polished style. Gibbon in particular possessed mastery of form and style to an unrivaled degree. His history of the greatness and decline of the Roman Empire has been superseded but never surpassed, a nice distinction among historians.[4]

Carlyle's admiration of the rationalists' conception of history as a finely serious art was offset by a corresponding hostility to their interpretation of history. The rationalist philosophy of history rejected the assumption of an all-controlling Providence, which had been the fundamental premise of the Christian philosophy of history. In place of an omnipotent God, it set up the Cartesian principles of the supremacy of reason and the inflexibility of natural laws. The Deists paid homage to an intelligent First Cause, conceived as having set the universe in motion under the control of fixed laws. What happened thereafter was a purely mechanical outcome of cause and effect relationships between objects in the universe. The Cartesian principle of immutable natural laws was extended to include the laws of human behavior, making the motives of men as individuals or in groups subject to the same unchanging influences, at all times and in all places. History must therefore reveal a uniformity and regularity of recurring phenomena. Indeed, the chief purpose of written history was defined as the effort "to discover the constant and universal principles of human nature by showing men in all varieties of circumstances and situations."[5] Such a point of view invested written history with a new and solemn dignity; or better, reinvested it with something of its ancient character. It became a corpus of instruction rather than a record of fact; "philosophy teaching by experience."[6]

This pragmatic view of history strongly affected the manner of writing it. Facts suffered constant subordination to doctrine, and except in Gibbon, there was little patience with mere accumulation of detail. At the same time the worth and significance of facts judiciously selected were emphasized. To Voltaire indeed goes the credit for the first critical inquiry into the nature and value of historical data. He was the first to insist that the historian had better work to do than dwell in courts and camps, and that history should be an exposition of the growth of national life and character.[7] His theories found little exemplification in his own work, however, and still less in the work of his contemporaries. The suggestions of Montesquieu and Turgot, writing in this period, that material factors such as climate and environment have a large bearing on the development of institutions were ignored because of the firmly entrenched prejudice that history was a record of the conscious intellectual and moral activities of mankind: fundamentally a study in ideology.[8] In tracing causal relationships, therefore, the supreme concern was with moral and not physical causes; those circumstances which operate on the mind as motives or reasons.

Contrasted with the national bias of the nineteenth-century historians, those of the century preceding had a cosmopolitan curiosity about other civilizations. Their cosmopolitanism extended to an interest in other civilizations which they regarded as "savage," because they believed that aboriginal cultures could be profitably studied as throwing light on the infancy of their own civilization.[9] In general they preferred, over all others, themes from modern history as possessing greater educative value. With the exception of Gibbon, they were reluctant to dwell on those periods, the Middle Ages, for example, when public transactions were wrapped in partial obscurity or afforded little instruction. Such unfruitful eras should be abandoned to the "industry and credulity of the antiquary." Theoretically they frowned on partisan, religious or national bias, though they frequently failed to rise above it. In fact, Hume is properly considered the father of modern party history; and Hallam and Macaulay his direct heirs.[10]

The fundamental point of view of the eighteenth century historians was thus essentially unhistorical. Their standards of critical judgment were absolute. Self-confident human reason reared itself above the mysteries which constitute the source of life and culture, attacked and discredited the organic and traditional elements of history and thereby lost all means of communication with the reality of the past. The enlightened reason in the field of historical criticism was self-assertive and limited, its sympathies were few and its judgments severe. On the other hand, it succeeded in relating, collecting, amassing, criticizing, and partly apprehending a vast mass of historical material. It gave an undeniable impetus to the dissection of the abstract material forces at work in history, even though its attempts to rationalize the spiritual phenomena of history—the origin and growth of institutions and cultures—stripped off an inalienable part of historical tradition. The romanticists were heirs of the positive achievements of the rationalist historians no less than rebels against their limitations.[11]

CARLYLE'S OPPOSITION TO RATIONALIST HISTORIOGRAPHY

To judge from his letters and from scattered references in his essays, Carlyle had a thorough acquaintance with each of the four great eighteenth century historians. Robertson probably offered him his initial taste of good historical writing. Wilson puts his acquaintance with *Charles V* in the early Annan days, when Carlyle was possibly ten or twelve years of age. It "opened new worlds of knowledge, vistas in all directions."[12] Robertson's *Scotland* he read, along with Hume's *England* and the first volume of Gibbon's *Decline and Fall* during his first term at Edinburgh (1809-10).[13] In Carlyle's opinion, Robertson's chief gift was his narrative power, the "great staple of historical excellence." While he rated him as "possibly higher than Hume or Gibbon" in "talents for general disquisition," he complained at the same time that his histories were external, mechanical, with no symptoms of having probed into the inner consciousness of the characters."[14] This charge became the common accusation he leveled at all of the eighteenth century writers. In 1824 he summed up his opinion of Robertson to Jane Welsh: "I used to find in him [he wrote] a shrewd, a systematic but not a great understanding; and no more heart than in my boot. He was a kind of deist in the guise of a Calvinistic priest; a portentous combination."[15]

Carlyle's relationship to Hume is more interesting both in its negative and its positive aspects. Probably no other English thinker exerted a greater influence on him. In addition to their Scotch origin, Carlyle and Hume had much in common. They possessed a "clear, methodic intellect," given to scientific pursuits. To both men history was a source of lifelong interest and study. Both tended to view life from a library and used the data of history as a source of authority for their speculative thought. Their philosophies stand to their histories as prolegomena, representing an organic unity. Both men approached the interpretation of history through their moral consciousness, with questions of value their fundamental concern. By both alike was history conceived as an arena wherein was enacted a perennial conflict of human wills.

Hume is usually credited with having turned Carlyle from his destined vocation in the church. But the sceptical *Enquiry Concerning Human Understanding* probably only completed Carlyle's half-formed conviction that orthodox religion was impossible of credence and belief. And if Hume did sap Carlyle's already shaken faith in orthodoxy he offered at the same time an example of sturdy strength and intellectual integrity encouraging Carlyle to "fashion his own ground plan of the universe." Hume's "honest empiricism" was consistent in asserting that the only source of knowledge was perception, excluding therefore all examination of causality, all doctrine of the "true Being."[16] Carlyle must have been impressed, too, with Hume's belief that conceptions of substance and causality are neither intuitively nor demonstrably certain, but rest on a conviction which has its roots in the emotions, a "natural belief." In the *Natural History of Religion* Hume used this principle to demonstrate how the feelings of hope and fear, of joy and terror, which are associated with the primitive apprehension of Nature contain the germ of higher forms of religious worship. Carlyle's theories are only slightly different, and whether he derived them directly from Hume or indirectly from Herder is unimportant.[17]

The negative influence of Hume's theories was transmitted through his histories. Carlyle was stimulated to open revolt against Hume's abstract and objective point of view, the mechanical causal relationships advanced as motivation. He was convinced that man was more than a bundle of vices and virtues whose personality could be appraised in terms of an aggregate of good and bad qualities. He realized that here were great histories written on premises basically wrong, and out of such a realization grew the conviction that his personal conception of history was dynamic. Stimulated by his negative reaction he formulated his own belief that without sympathetic interest in humanity, history lacked soul and significance. Without understanding and analysis of institutions, it was essentially untrue.

Carlyle set forth his objections to Hume's mechanical causality as early as 1815 in a letter to Robert Mitchell: "How odd does it look," he wrote, "to refer all modifications of national character to the influence of moral causes. Might it not be asserted ... that even those which he [Hume] denominates moral causes, originate from physical circumstances? Whence but from the perpetual contemplation of his dreary glaciers and rugged glens, from his dismal broodings in his long and almost solitary nights, has the Scandinavian conceived his ferocious Odin, and his horrid 'spectres of the deep'? Compare this with the coppercastle and celestial gardens of the Arabians—and we must admit that physical causes *have* an influence on men."[18] Carlyle deserves no special credit for demolishing the rationalist premise that human nature is the same, in all times and all places, with weapons borrowed from Montesquieu. It is important to note, however that several years prior to his introduction to German idealism Carlyle was convinced that the springs of human action lie deep and mysterious in the human consciousness, to be grasped by power of imagination rather than by reason.

If Hume had the greatest influence on Carlyle's early intellectual development, Edward Gibbon exerted the most positive influence in shaping his attitude toward the writing of history as an art. His first complete reading of Gibbon dates from the Kirkcaldy period, probably late 1817. In his *Reminiscences* he recalls with what "greedy velocity" he read the *Decline and Fall* at the rate of a volume a day. Of all books he had read he found it "the most impressive on me in my then stage of investigation and state of mind."[19] Bearing out his recollection is a reference in a letter to Jane Welsh in 1823:

Gibbon is a man whom one never forgets—unless oneself deserving to be forgotten; the perusal of his work forms an epoch in the history of one's mind. I know you will admire Gibbon, yet I do not wish or expect that you should love him.[20]

Gibbon inspired admiration but not "love," because he shared the common deficiency among rationalists of being "abundantly destitute of virtuous feeling—or indeed of any feeling at all."[21] Carlyle warned Miss Welsh that Gibbon had "but a coarse and vulgar heart, with all his keen logic, and glowing imagination, and lordly irony: he worships power and splendor. . . ."[22] He noted that suffering virtue or heroism, if unarrayed in the "pomp and circumstance of outward glory" gets little sympathy from Gibbon.

Carlyle's estimate of Gibbon in the *Reminiscences* is indicative of the strength of the indirect influence. He acknowledged how deeply he recognized and admired Gibbon's "great power of investigating, ascertaining; of grouping and narrating; though the latter had always, then as now, something of a Drury Lane character, the colors strong but coarse, and set off by lights from the side scenes."[23] Gibbon's affectation, even though majestically adapted to his subject matter, seemed to have struck an especially discordant note when Carlyle was young. He wrote to Robert Mitchell in 1818, that he was "alternately delighted and offended by the gorgeous colouring with which his [Gibbon's] fancy invests the rude and scanty materials of his narrative"; he alternately admired and deplored the bitterness of his skilful irony; and was alternately pleased and displeased by his "exuberant, sonorous and epigrammatic" style.[24] The most remarkable quality of Gibbon's style he early decided was the "species of brief and shrewd remarks for which he seems to have taken Tacitus as a model."[25] Years later in the *Reminiscences* he refers to these "winged sarcasms, so quiet and yet so conclusively transpiercing and killing dead" which had been "often admirable, potent and illuminative to me."[26]

As in the case of Hume, Carlyle was stimulated to revolt by Gibbon's philosophic approach; by the pitiless irony directed alike at the good and the bad which aroused in the reader a sense of futility and despair. Carlyle could not agree with Gibbon that history was a tragi-comedy, an exciting and colorful pageant, but essentially without significance as marking any progress in the organization of human society. Gibbon demonstrated, on the one hand, what great art could be achieved by a historical work. At the same time he showed the limitations of merely pictorial and descriptive history. His work confirmed Carlyle's fundamental conviction that imaginative insight, sympathy, and human understanding were necessary to a proper comprehension of the moral and spiritual conflicts underlying the historic processes.

While Carlyle's reflections on Gibbon show an uneasy disquietude that history so admirable should be premised on a philosophy so false, for Voltaire's point of view he has more tolerance, even admiration, and at the same time a confident awareness of its shortcomings.[27] His criticism of Voltaire's method and philosophy of history is a reasoned analysis of the rationalist's limited point of view from the standpoint of the romanticist. The essay on Voltaire, written in 1829, represents his mature thought on the subject of rationalist historiography.

Voltaire read history, in Carlyle's opinion, not with the eye of a devout seer, or even a critic, but through a pair of mere anti-Catholic spectacles.[28] The *philosophe's* deistic bias against orthodox religion so warped and distorted his view of heaven and earth that he could see neither "unspeakable majesty" nor "insufferable horror" therein. His view of the world was "cool, gently scornful, altogether prosaic"; the earth he considered merely a place for producing corn; the heavens were admirable mainly because they serve as a nautical timekeeper. As a consequence his theory of man and man's life was little; even pitiful for one who would be judged by the standards of poet and philosopher. Instead of a vision of history as a "mighty drama, enacted on the theatre of Infinitude, with Suns for lamps and Eternity as a background; whose author is God, and whose purport and thousandfold moral lead us up to the 'dark with excess of light' of the throne of God," Voltaire saw it only as a "poor, wearisome debating club dispute, spun through ten centuries, between the Encyclopedié and the Sorbonne."

Carlyle believed that Voltaire's "spiritual shortcomings" were partly temperamental, partly the result of the age in which he lived. The temper of the eighteenth century encouraged on all sides "high, all-attempting activity of Intellect; the most peremptory spirit of inquiry abroad on every subject; things human and things divine alike cited without misgivings before the . . .

tribunal of so-called Reason" which Carlyle regarded as mere argumentative logic.[29] There was a total want of the sympathetic insight and tolerance which comes from the heart and "sees farther than the head" in the reading of character. Carlyle found it only natural that the distinctive features of Voltaire's intellect should be, therefore, not depth and greatness, but the very extreme of expertness and superficial extent. Instead of the power of insight, he possessed the power of order and arrangement, both in acquisition and communication of facts; a power which comprehended the whole office of the understanding, in Carlyle's opinion. It offered the primary distinction between rationalist and romantic historiography, because the latter availed itself, at least in the opinion of the romanticists, of the higher organ of the transcendental reason.

Voltaire's method of ordering and arranging his material was the natural outcome of his shallow cause-and-effect conception of history. Carlyle did less than justice to Voltaire's ingenious theory of "filiated events," though it is perfectly true that the latter failed to interpret history consistently by means of his theory. On the whole, Voltaire accepted the Lockian premises regarding the nature of society and failed to see ". . . that the sequence or chain of causes which he fancies underlies historic processes is not properly linear but three-dimensional." History properly considered was a "tissue of innumerable lines, extending in breadth as well as in length, and with a complexity which will foil . . . the most assiduous computation."[30] Thus Voltaire's histories, "in spite of their sparkling rapidity and knowing air of philosophic insight" are among the shallowest of all histories; "mere bead rolls of exterior occurrences, of battles, edifices, enactments, and other quite superficial phenomena," a vast accumulation of "historical knowledge arranged as a museum for purposes of teaching; every object in its place, and there for its uses"; nowhere confusion or vain display; everywhere "intention, instructiveness and the clearest order."[31]

Carlyle called the spirit of such a method neither poetic nor philosophic. It was a purely business method; and the "order arising from it is not Beauty but at best Regularity." Voltaire's objects were arranged neither pictorially nor scientifically but "like goods in a well-kept warehouse" where each may be seen and come at when needed. It is interesting to observe that Carlyle used the adjective "scientific" along with "pictorial" by inference to describe a hypothetical manner of treating historical material which would be both poetic and philosophical.

Carlyle's observations on biography with reference to Voltaire's *Charles XII* are interesting. He considered it the best of Voltaire's historical writings, a judgment widely sustained by critics. As a biography he regarded it a model of graphic brevity, rivalling Sallust in its clear sketches of the strange adventures and sorrows of the Swedish king.[32] Aptly he called it a line engraving on a reduced scale "without colors, yet not without the foreshortenings and perspective observances," even the deeper harmonies, which belong to the true picture. In many respects his *Life of Schiller* was patterned after such a model.

Carlyle owed an immense debt of both a negative and a positive character to the eighteenth century historians. He owed to Gibbon a broad conception of historical writing as an art, as well as the example of patient scholarly research and wise ordering of materials. To Hume he owed the inspiration of a spirit of sceptical inquiry into the sources and limits of knowledge. From Hume also he probably learned to reject Rousseau's notion of the state of nature, which he later found to be generally held by the German philosophers, with the exception of Herder.[33] To Voltaire he owed the negative debt of a clear conception of the spiritual shortcomings and limitations of the entire philosophy of the Enlightenment as applied to history. Its virtues and defects were nowhere more obvious than in the extensive historical writings of the "great Persifleur."

THE INFLUENCE OF HERDER AND GERMAN ROMANTICISM

Romantic historiography as it developed on the Continent opposed rationalism in every particular. Its primary assumptions were the law of continuous development and the significance of tradition, in contrast with the rational idea of progress without development and consequent overestimation of the present. The mechanical concept of causality yielded to the time-honored belief in a spiritual principle controlling the destiny of man through the historic processes. At the same time the irrational and individual elements in history were given a new sort of recognition; while the doctrines of nationality and *Volksgeist* supplanted the rationalist theory of cosmopolitanism. The eighteenth century attitude toward history constituted, in effect, a denial of the historical sense. In romantic historiography, on the contrary, the historical sense was exalted to a position never before accorded it. The historian's critical consciousness became absorbed in contemplating the profound contrast between movement and stability, between creation and standard, between infinite and finite. Warm subjective interest, insurgent energy, and spontaneity replaced the detachment of the rationalists. The romantic historians turned to the past, not primarily for a corpus of instruction or data for the demonstration of first principles, but for human fellowship with those who had gone before in man's strange adventure through the universe.

The romantic revolt in historiography had its rise in the very heyday of the eighteenth century historical vogue. While Gibbon was modestly boasting that his *Decline and Fall* was to be "found on every table, almost on every toilette," a storm center destined to destroy the supremacy of the *Aufklärung* was developing in Germany. The initial impulse for the revolt from Lockian empiricism in historiography was derived from the social philosophy of Jean Jacques Rousseau.[34] A similar revolt had already taken place in German poetic theory; and when these currents eventually flowed together, the man who effectively represented the revolution in thought in all its manifold aspects in the period 1760-90 was Johann Gottfried Herder. In his nebulous and unsystematic writings, the ideas germinated by Bodmer and Klopstock, colored and amplified by powerful stimuli from Rousseau and Vico, first took form. Herder is frequently called the "gatekeeper of the nineteenth century."[35] Most of what was best in the next hundred years of Germany's intellectual history may be traced to his stimulating initiative.

In the history of literature Herder is recalled as one of the progenitors of *Sturm und Drang*. Schiller acknowledged his influence; and Goethe was an even more ardent disciple who never abandoned the Herderian principles although he progressed far beyond the romantic cult. It is here possibly that critics of the Carlyle-Goethe relationship occasionally err. Carlyle is frequently charged with misunderstanding Goethe, but what impressed him primarily in Goethe's work was the romantic pantheistic element derived by Goethe from Herder. The classical element he does not so much misunderstand as ignore. The strength of Carlyle's preference for the Herderian element in Goethe sustains the view that Herder was one of the really important influences shaping Carlyle's thought.

Herder's contribution to historiography has only recently received full recognition.[36] He adapted Vico's principle of development to the theory of the organic evolution of national life.[37] With the help of this conception he profoundly changed the methods of historical science and defined the principles of modern criticism and esthetics.[38] In Herder we find expressed for the first time the dynamic conception of *Volk* out of which grew the cult of nationalism. He discovered the *Volkslied;* probed into cultural origins. By the force of his fertile invention he suggested the vast possibilities for historical study in the fields of philology, anthropology, archæology.

History to Herder was super-personal and divine at the same time that it was individual and irrational. In the historic process he discovered a genetic purpose and a sense of continuity to which the rationalists had been blind. "Confused and incalculable as the history of man may be," he wrote, "it has a definite purpose, and that purpose is the development of humanity."[39] He denied the shallow assumption of the rationalists that history is a series of fortuitous accidents. Rather "all things rest upon one another and have grown out of one another" to form a "stream which flows unceasingly towards the ocean of humanity."

The "development of humanity" he conceived in terms of the social group, not the individual, a point on which Carlyle was in essential agreement though he developed his own variant of it. The organic unit or "nationality" possessed inherently a creative and regulative power, the "national soul," source of all culture and the true vehicle of history. This soul (the counterpart of Leibniz' monad) represented a harmony of all the active powers within the group and held the key to the secrets of history. Herder considered this strange, instinctive power, working intuitively as a living force, fashioning "organic units from the chaos of homogeneous matter" to possess the elements of growth, maturity and decay, in common with all organic life. Each national organism buds, enjoys a period of growth, matures, makes its cultural contribution, then withers, dies, making room for others which pass through the same cycle.[40]

In the *Ideen zur Philosophie der Geschichte der Menschheit* (1784-91) Herder develops a theory regarding the origin of individual nationalities which particularly influenced Carlyle. He assumed that since the individual cannot exist by himself, a higher maximum of coöperating powers forms itself with every society. In wild confusion they oppose each other until, according to infallible laws of nature, the adverse principles limit each other and a kind of equilibrium is established.[41] The group thus emerges with a definite personality, expresses itself in religion, literature, art, science and laws. The sum of these expressions is the national culture.[42] Particularly interesting is the fact that he believed that those individuals within the group who respond most sensitively to the stimuli of the national soul are its leaders, prophets, artists, and poets. Fichte and his theory of heroes owed an immense debt to Herder.

Compared with the unhistorical attitude of the rationalists, Herder had a profound sense of debt to the past. As a means of approaching it with understanding and sympathy, he formulated the "law of necessity and convenience"; i.e., power, time and place, and used it as a standard of judgment. He held that in each age everything that could blossom did blossom, each in its due season and proper sphere. The only means of approaching the past in his opinion, therefore, was through sympathetic and patient inquiry into all phases of its life. One must become a "regenerated contemporary" of ages long dead. Herder was possibly the first thinker to group under the term "history" every manifestation of the national soul, its language, literature, art, religion, customs, an idea carried to extremes by later romanticists including Carlyle. He widened the domain of history to include the entire life of the community, which Voltaire had dreamed of doing; he widened the domain of poetry to include anything relating to man's spiritual nature.

Herder had a profound influence not only on the general thought of his time but on particular thinkers such as Schiller and Goethe, Fichte and Schlegel, Novalis, Richter, and Tieck (all of whom were absorbing admirations of Carlyle). Out of *Sturm und Drang*, indeed, developed the special form of romanticism characterized by the work of Schlegel, Tieck, and Novalis with its revival of the literature of personality and individualism. In art they insisted on subjective ideals; professed contempt for form and objective classical standards. They were filled with a sense of the spirituality of the universe; of a personal relationship with an immanent God which rubbed out the boundaries between the real and the unreal, between the past and the present, between poetry and prose. It is apparent what import such theories had when applied to a conception of history.

The magnitude of Herder's influence on Carlyle is still further demonstrated when we consider Carlyle's express reaction to him as revealed in the *Notebooks*. He mentions him first in 1822. Goethe, Schiller, Richter, Novalis and Klopstock he knew well by this time, but his acquaintance with the speculative thinkers was just beginning. Herder is the first he mentioned; the only one he noticed with steady satisfaction. In one place he copied a long passage from the mystical *Fragmente;* an allegory on sleep and death and their common relation to night, wherein one sees "the shining books of Immortality" which time, "the all-destroying may never smite."[43]

Again he referred approvingly to Herder's controversy with Kant whose new philosophy Herder hated and "wrote against . . . bitterly." Carlyle's uncertainty on the Kantian issues and his later criticism of the Kantian elements in Schiller's thought admit a preference for Herder's side in the dispute. He particularly agrees with Herder in the view that nature does not give people "dim intimations of true beauty and just principles in Art," as the Kantians held.[44] Temperamentally he was opposed to the rational deductive quality of the Kantian logic. The theory of individual psychology which he had adopted by this time did not permit the belief that abstract intellectual principles are capable of universal apprehension, and in this he was sustained by Herder.

In a later reference he mentions having read the *Ideen;* calls it "an extraordinary book." He gets to the heart of Herder when he notes the emphasis on "circumstances and organization: *Er war was er seyn konnte.*"[45] He notes further that Herder holds this world sufficiently explainable without reference to another, making immortality merely something to be hoped for, a degree of optimism which Carlyle's Calvinism never permitted him to share. He was warmed by Herder's general point of view, however, because the latter "loves all men and all things, and this means much. . . . Herder's very descriptions of animals and inanimate beings are animated, cordial, affectionate; much more so, those of man in their varied Thun und Treiben."[46]

A final aspect of Herder's thought which Carlyle found especially congenial was his strong belief that writing history was vastly more important than speculating about it. Herder's contemporaries were busying themselves energetically constructing tight *a priori* systems of historical interpretation with a general indifference to the facts of history. Fichte, Hegel, Schlegel, Schelling, even Kant and Schiller, thought they could force the living data of history into procrustean beds of preconceived principles. Except for Schiller none of them practised the art of historical narration. Herder fulminated against such nonsense. He saw clearly, as Carlyle did later, that the philosophy must emerge from the facts, and not vice versa. Out of this grew his suggestions for enlarging the domain of historical study to include all of the humanistic sciences, philology, anthropology, archæology, and sociology. Possibly his greatest discovery was this of the inner relationship of all the parts of the historical process: what we call today an historical mode of thought.

Only Schiller among those whom Carlyle would call "metaphysicians" comes off as well in the letters and *Notebooks* as Herder; and in a sense Herder and Schiller complemented each other. It was in Herder that Carlyle discovered those ideas, raised to the level of general principles or suggested hypotheses, which he found so congenial in Goethe, Novalis, Richter, Tieck, and Fichte. The tendency of critics to emphasize the importance of Fichte and ignore Herder's influence has probably resulted from the generally delayed recognition of Herder except in the field of historiography; partly also from the parallel fact that relatively few persons have been interested primarily in Carlyle as a historian.

THE INFLUENCE OF SCHILLER

In 1788, when Gibbon's last volume was appearing in England, Friedrich Schiller published the first part of a grandly conceived historical work dedicated to the celebration of human freedom, *Geschichte des Abfalls der Vereinigten Niederlande von der Spanischen Regierung*. "In my hands," he wrote to his friend Körner, "history is becoming something in many respects different from what it has been."[47] His remark was more significant than he realized. His histories, dwarfed as they are today by his dramas and poetry, mark the point where the swelling tide of romantic historiography moved into the channels marked out for it by the speculations of Jean Jacques Rousseau. Schiller was more profoundly influenced by Rousseau than were any of his fellow countrymen; he was the first historian properly to apply the principles of the Genevan to historiography.[48] In a sense he transformed the writing of history just as Rousseau did the novel by effecting a fundamental change in the approach to his material.

Historians, from antiquity to the Enlightenment, while varying greatly in the uses to which they put their data, had shared a generally objective point of view. Schiller introduced the romantic principle of subjectivism, a departure as radical as Herder's new theory of the social organism. The apprehending of historical material was conceived to be an emotional as well as an intellectual process. The "man of feeling" displaced the dispassionate analyst of the eighteenth century. It was discovered that individual men and women emerged from the impersonal and fragmentary data of history when viewed with genuine subjective sympathy. As a consequence, personalities displaced abstractions in historical narratives. The materials of history, moreover, were found to constitute a quarry for novel and drama as well as for purely historical narration, a truism in Shakespeare's day but rediscovered with immense results two centuries later. Scott and Schiller seized upon this old truth, developed it in different directions, and established the fundamental principles of the romantic re-creation of the past.

Schiller was perfectly aware of his iconoclasm when he set out to prove that art was as important as scholarship in historical writing. He was convinced that fidelity to facts could be maintained through careful selection, without sacrifice of dramatic or picturesque artistry.[49] He made constant use of the classical adornments of broad generalizations, analogies, dramatic climaxes. In fact, he deliberately exploited his materials to the end that his histories might read like novels; might conclude with a dénouement as artistically inevitable as that of a tragic drama. In a letter to Karoline von Beulwitz, written in the historical period, he comments:

I shall always be a poor authority for any future investigator who has the misfortune to consult me. But perhaps at the expense of historic truth I shall find readers, and here and there I may hit upon the other kind of truth which is philosophic. History is in general only a magazine for my fancy, and the objects must content themselves with the form they take under my hands.[50]

It is apparent that he believed his histories derived a higher value from the fact that through art he might occasionally arrive at the "truth called philosophic."

Schiller exercised the historian's prerogative of choosing themes best designed to accomplish his aims. Like his favorite historian and model, Plutarch, he particularly enjoyed the celebration of valorous deeds and vanished heroes.[51] The periods covered by the *Revolt of the Netherlands* and the *Thirty Years' War* were revolutionary epochs in which whole peoples rose to levels of heroism; and majestic figures such as Philip II, Gustavus Adolphus, Wallenstein, Egmont, and William of Orange occupied the stage. Even with such materials to engage him, he confined himself to those phases which best exemplified the splendid conquests of the spirit of freedom. If occasionally he distorted the materials, or altered his characters the better to fit his prearranged design, his intuitive judgments were for the most part deep and sound.[52]

The influence of Schiller and Herder tends to overshadow that of the rest of the Germans in the development of Carlyle as a historian.[53] From Herder (and Burke) he derived the most important elements of the political and sociological beliefs which largely shaped his historic judgments. Schiller he echoes in the theory and practice of historical writings and in his conception of the historian's mission. Striking dissimilarities exist, of course, because while Schiller's approach to historical materials made him a pioneer in romantic historiography, his interpretation of history was a composite of the classical and the romantic elements, a fact which Carlyle clearly saw and pointed out in the *Life* as well as, more forcefully, in the later essay on Schiller.

Carlyle's first acquaintance with Schiller came through the offices of Mme de Staël. In a letter to Mitchell in early 1819 he called attention to the "brilliant work of Mme de Staël; *Considerations sur quelques Evenemens de la Révolution.*"[54] Whether he was yet acquainted with *l'Allemagne* is not clear. Wilson assumes that he was. At any rate it was probably Mme de Staël who stimulated him to a serious study of German literature; and it was undoubtedly she who first introduced him to the work and personality of Schiller.[55] It was an unfortunate circumstance that her portrait of Schiller as the "supreme exemplification of intellectual nobility," a man whose moral perfection, purity of soul, and idealized love of liberty made him inhumanly perfect, should have been impressed upon Carlyle before his own independent judgment could be formed. He did not escape from the cold grip of Mme de Staël's conception of Schiller's character until after the *Life* was completed, a fact which greatly affected his manner of treatment though it did not seemingly diminish his enjoyment of Schiller's work.[56]

Schiller, Goethe, and Klopstock were among the first of the Germans he read after learning the language in late 1818.[57] Early in 1819 he confessed to "living riotously in Schiller, Goethe and the rest. They are the greatest men at present with me."[58] Schiller impressed him much more deeply than Goethe in this early period. He urged his new acquaintance, Jane Welsh, to read Schiller and Goethe so that together they could enjoy them. Never yet had he met "anyone to relish their beauties; and sympathy is the very soul of life."[59] His first gift to Jane was a copy of *Don Carlos*. To Edward Irving, not yet converted, he wrote reassuringly in 1821: "Schiller . . . most certainly you would like. He has all the innocence and purity of a child, with the high talents and strong volitions of a man; a rare union. . . ."[60]

Carlyle's relation to Schiller offers many parallels with that of Coleridge to Schiller a quarter of a century earlier. From the standpoint of interpreting Schiller to the English reading public, Carlyle picked up Schiller where Coleridge had dropped him. While he did no translations as remarkable as Coleridge's famous version of *Wallenstein*, the review public had no rounded and complete interpretation of Schiller's writings and personality until Carlyle gave it to them, first in the *Life of Schiller*, later in the essay published in *Fraser's* in 1831.[61]

Like Coleridge, Carlyle came to Schiller's writings in a period when he was peculiarly susceptible not alone to the intellectual opinions but still more to the moral example of Schiller's personality and career. It is customary to assign the credit for Carlyle's emergence from the spiritual crisis recorded in *Sartor* to the intellectual influence of the Transcendental writers. Too little credit is given the more intangible moral influences, of which Schiller's was probably the greatest.[62] He was unquestionably one of the "Fire Pillars" in Carlyle's dark pilgrimage, representing in sublime form the "embodied possibilities of human nature," and coming opportunely at a time when the way ahead was most obscure and doubtful.

In view of his influence, nothing could have been more appropriate than that a biography of Schiller should initiate Carlyle's serious literary career. In late 1822, Edward Irving recommended Carlyle to Taylor, proprietor of the *London Magazine,* as a likely person to do the first of a series of "portraits of men of genius and character." The *Life of Schiller* was to be the first of the series. Carlyle set to work in the spring of 1823 and had the first instalment ready for the October issue. What was intended as a single essay grew to be a substantial biography in three instalments. The following winter the entire work was revised and issued in book form under the title, *The Life of Schiller, Comprehending an Examination of His Works.*[63] But Carlyle thought so little of the volume that he let it appear anonymously.

The *Life of Schiller* was both good and conventional enough to win its author considerable favorable attention; a result which probably would not have occurred had he succeeded in doing it in what he already considered his "natural vein." Welcome as the favorable notice was to him, he felt a deep dissatisfaction with his efforts and realized that he had not penetrated to the heart of Schiller. Seemingly unaware of the fact that his normal subjective approach was obstructed by the fixed intellectual image acquired from Mme de Staël, Carlyle saw Schiller only as a moral giant constantly preoccupied with the image of perfection he found in his own heart.[64] "Intellectual nobility" of such immeasurably heroic proportions was not possible to grasp in terms of ordinary human values.

The notebook jottings of the period are full of self-criticism and dissatisfied comment. He realized that the work was not going as it should; he seemed aware that it was because his imaginative faculty had not been stirred, but apparently he did not perceive any deeper reason for it. In November 1823 he wrote in the *Notebooks:* "*Schiller* is in the wrong vein. Laborious, partly affected, meagre, bombastic; too often it strives by lofty words to hide littleness of thought."[65] By this time the first instalment was out and the second in preparation. Part II "likewise is very bad," he decided after he had sent it off to London.[66] While engaged on the third part, he confessed again that *Schiller* is not in his "natural vein." "I am scribbling, not writing *Schill-*

er," he wrote, "my mind will not catch hold of it; I skim it, do as I will, and I am as anxious as possible to get it off my hands."⁶⁷

The biography of Schiller is so altogether unlike Carlyle's later work that critics usually gloss over it with a few vague or embarrassed comments on its immaturity or its hack work character. The same critics forget seemingly that the essays, too, were essentially hack work, or at least were so regarded by Carlyle; and even the first of these, "The Metrical Legends of Joanna Baillie," *New Edinburgh Review* (1821), is Carlylean in tone and style. From the special point of view assumed in this study, the *Life of Schiller* is almost as interesting by virtue of its limitations as by its positive qualities. It constitutes Carlyle's first serious effort to deal with historical data, and judged by his own standards, it is more or less unsuccessful.

Early in the *Life of Schiller* Carlyle gave initial expression to what became one of the cardinal principles of his esthetic doctrine: "the grand secret of moving others is, that the poet be himself moved."⁶⁸ But the poet can only be moved and his imagination stirred through a subjective apprehension of his material. Such apprehension enables him to penetrate to the heart of his subject and discover an informing principle around which to organize his materials. With a historian whose approach is subjective the process differs only in the nature of the data. When Carlyle records that his "mind will not catch hold of" what he is doing, he is describing somewhat loosely a situation in which the subject-object identification has been obstructed, in this case by an intellectual preconception. He has not apprehended Schiller as an individual personality, but rather as an abstraction symbolic of moral perfection much as a rationalist historian would have done. In contrast with the highly successful subjectivism of his later historical writing the result is extremely revealing.

Interesting as the biography is because of its faults, it is still more valuable as a confession of discipleship to Schiller as historian and man of letters. Carlyle's development had reached a stage where he found it easy to see in Schiller the prototype of himself. In the extended analysis of Schiller's preference for histories and historical dramas, for example, he is really rationalizing his own preferences. The elements of Schiller's technique which he admired are those which most nearly resembled his own; those which he disapproved are the classical qualities which were in conflict with his romantic beliefs. His discussion of Schiller's philosophy of history is fairly good, considering that he knew Kant only superficially, and that the only approach to Schiller's thought is through Kant.[69] Carlyle's philosophy of history differed from Schiller's, because the latter's was fundamentally rationalistic; but he was perfectly aware of the more striking ideas they shared in common.

By the time Carlyle was engaged on the *Life of Schiller* he had arrived at a point where it was manifestly necessary to make a clear choice among the various alternatives open to him. He was more or less committed to a literary life, dark as the way seemed; and he was determined on doing something creative. "Literature" was what he eagerly aspired to write, and "literature had nothing to do with the magazine fare" on which he was compelled to subsist.[70] Review writing offered neither scope for his ambitions nor decent material comfort. He discharged his mounting bitterness against the book world in a half dozen highly personal paragraphs prefaced to Part II of the *Life*. "Except the Newgate Calendar," the biography of authors is "the most sickening chapter in the history of man."[71] With naïve candor he admitted that the literary life, on the face of it, should be "the most enviable which the lot of this world affords." Instead it is the "most thickly beset with suffering and degradation." He warned that "literature is apt to form a dangerous and discontenting occupation even for the amateur." Still more fearful are its perils for one "who does not live to write but writes to live." The "Man of Letters" is too often a pitiful object, "dissatisfied with his best performances, disgusted with his fortunes," spending his "weary days in conflict with obscure misery . . . the victim at once of tragedy and farce; the last forlorn outpost in the war of Mind against Matter."

Carlyle's extravagant vision of himself occupying the "last forlorn outpost" is symptomatic of the critical moment in his career. He had chosen literature, but beyond its being creative, he still had to choose a genre suitable for his abilities. History and the novel apparently were the only forms that ever seriously attracted him, and of these history was incomparably the more important. It could almost be said of him, as Gibbon said of himself, that from his earliest years he had aspired to write history.[72] It is recalled that his first paid efforts, except translations, were the biographical sketches for Brewster's *Edinburgh Encyclopedia* (1819-20).[73] The first original project recorded in the *Notebooks* in 1822 was for a "series of historico-biographical portraits" of the chief personages of the Puritan Revolution.[74] His next original project was an elaborate proposal to edit a "Literary Annual Register," the scope of which betrayed his romantic notion of what constituted history.[75] In the meantime he did the commissioned biography of Schiller and the translation of *Wilhelm Meister*.

Probably it was a mixture of opportunism and deliberate choice which finally turned the scales in favor of history. The early biographical sketches, the *Life of Schiller*, the abortive *History of German Literature*, the critico-biographical essays all belonged to the historical genre and at the same time had their form dictated by external circumstances. Not until *Sartor Resartus* did Carlyle have a clear choice; and there it is possible that had *Wotton Reinfred* not proved so bleak a failure, we should have had a philosophic novel like *Wilhelm Meister* in the place of autobiographic romance. There is abundant evidence that Carlyle viewed history as possibly the highest form of prose literature, even though he had an early hankering after something more inventive. He turned to it, however, from the standpoint of the artist and not the antiquarian. In this he had Schiller as prime exemplar.

Considerable importance must be attached, therefore, to Carlyle's analysis of Schiller's reasons for turning to historical writing as a relief from poetry and fiction, particularly tales of horror such as the "Geistersehr." First of all, Schiller's talents were best suited to historical writing because his greatest source of strength lay in his intellect; and while his imagination was strong, it was not particularly inventive.[76] Compare this with Carlyle's self-criticism in the *Notebooks:* "I am far too much of a critic; too little of an *artificer* in all points; always asking how? Or only saying thus."[77] The second reason Schiller was drawn to history was that it was "grounded on reality"; because the "mighty revolutions and commanding characters that figure in it would present him with things great and moving" about which to write. This emphasis on reality was always a cardinal point with Carlyle. He discussed it, significantly, in the first of his critical writings. "Though poetry is an imaginative art," he wrote in "Joanna Baillie," "its productions must be founded on reality" to yield us the greatest gratification. "The idea that what we are contemplating did actually take place . . . that the characters before us were in fact real inhabitants of this earth . . . adds a wonderful vivacity to our impressions." The third and fourth reasons Schiller turned to history, according to Carlyle, were that it required the "greatest possible cultivation of the intellect," and "could not fail to be delightful to one for whom human nature was a matter of most fascinating speculation." No one is likely to dispute that these qualities also drew Carlyle to the writing of history.

Discussing Schiller's specific method in the *Revolt of the Netherlands,* Carlyle took pains to call our attention to the fact that Schiller's realization of the limitations of the "clear but shallow" histories of the *Aufklärung,* particularly Watson's *Philip II,* first stimulated him to undertake his own version of the Dutch revolt in order to invest the "dry bones of history with nerves and tissue." Schiller acknowledged his desire to "extend and render permanent" the enthusiasm and excitement aroused by Watson's history; because he realized that his stimulation had come less from the book than from the particular form which his imagination had imparted to the materials. It was these "powers of imagination" which he "felt desirous to render permanent" by communicating them to others.[78]

When Carlyle described the *Revolt* as possessing all the common requisites of orthodox history, and many others which were peculiar to itself, he threw light on what he considered the truly philosophic method of writing history. Schiller makes no effort, he said, to provide a continuous narrative. The information he conveys is minute and copious; we have all the circumstances set distinctly before us; "yet such is the skill of arrangement, these are at once briefly and impressively presented," not by means of continuous narrative but "gathered up into masses, which are successively exhibited to view," minor facts grouped around some leading one to which, as the central object, our attention is chiefly directed. This method of "proceeding from eminence to eminence, and thence surveying the surrounding scene," was, in Carlyle's opinion, "undoubtedly the most philosophical of any."[79] He admitted the perplexities of such a method, its rigorous demands on the author in selecting his materials and determining his point of view. The historian who chooses it selects the hardest way and increases his eventual responsibility; unsuccessful, it is "intolerable." Schiller "accomplished it in great perfection, however."

What, in Schiller's opinion, is the "truth that is philosophic?" Carlyle summarized it by saying that the business of history "is not merely to record but to interpret." It "involves not only a clear conception and a lively explanation of events and characters, but a sound, enlightened theory of individual and national morality, a general philosophy of human life whereby to judge them and measure their effects."[80] Such a historian "stands on higher ground, takes in a wider range" than the eighteenth century historians. If the facts of history are merely raw materials to the "philosophic" historian, their importance, in Schiller's view, depends on their relation to the intellectual formula that would explain them. The seeming capriciousness and chaos in history challenges the logical mind to introduce a rational principle of order and significance. This principle he believed to be the evolutionary progress and emancipation of the human race. Schiller derived his rational ideal of political freedom from Condorcet, Rousseau, and Kant. It bears no resemblance to the ideal of the spiritual enfranchisement of humanity of which Herder and later Carlyle dreamed.[81]

The rational character of Schiller's philosophy of history

probably accounts for Carlyle's contemptuous reference in his *Notebooks* to Schiller's "blarney about history." The latter held the eighteenth century belief that history paints a vast progress from barbarism to an apex in his own enlightened age. He acknowledged the irresistible impulse to trace events to a general law of development and to determine the idea from which they flow as their generating principle.[82] Viewed thus, phenomena cease to seem lawless or to be the product of chance. They become an "harmonious element in a concordant whole . . . an intellectual perception." Schiller borrowed his teleological principle from Kant and indirectly from Hume. Carlyle was unimpressed by it because of its essentially rational character.

Carlyle did derive from Schiller, however, the useful idea of history as a stream flowing through time, bearing only those facts which have an incontestable relationship to the present constitution of society. It is the mission of the historian to retrace for his fellows the "first design of the existing whole, to seek the rules of this mechanism, the unity of this combination, the laws of phenomena, and to trace the work back to its first outlines."[83] Schiller had a curious theory of how man's deeds earned the right to find their place in the stream of universal history, a theory compatible with his general system of morality. Carlyle arrived at the same theory by a different process of reasoning, though he was unquestionably influenced by Schiller. In an impressive passage in the *Philosophical Letters* Schiller describes how man

. . . works up, smooths and fashions the rough stones the times bring to him. If the personages which coöperated actively in bringing about this event, were only not unworthy of the great work to which they were unconsciously subservient—if the powers which aided in its accomplishment, and the single actions out of whose concatenations it wonderfully arose, were but intrinsically noble powers, and the actions beautiful and great, then is the event grand, interesting and fruitful for us, and we are at liberty to wonder at the bold offspring of chance, or . . . offer up our admiration to a higher Intelligence.[84]

Carlyle also borrowed from Schiller the belief that great blanks exist in universal history; the events of many ages are irrevocably forgotten. Hence universal history can never be more than an aggregate of fragments; it can never aspire to be a science. Such facts as do exist require careful selection, with the principle of selection, noted above, based upon an essential incontestable relationship with the present constitution of society, the welfare or misery of the generations now living. This idea connects the past with the present both as cause with effect and as means with purpose, and makes of history a morally elevating object of study. As Schiller stated it, the domain of history is so "fruitful and comprehensive that the whole moral world is embraced within its boundaries."

Carlyle had no patience with Schiller's cosmopolitanism and theory of perfectibility. While admitting the philosophic spirit which rises above the "poor and little aim" of writing for one nation, Carlyle (echoing Herder) felt that nature herself, no doubt wisely, partitioned us "into kindreds and nations and tongues." He reasons on the basis of a sounder psychology than Schiller's that we "require individuality in our attachments; the sympathy which is expanded over all men will commonly be found so much attenuated by the process that it cannot be effective on any. And as it is in nature, so it is in art, which ought to be the image of it." Universal philanthropy is powerless as a rule of conduct; while the theory of perfectibility and "progress of the species is unfitted for deeply exciting the imagination. It is not with freedom we can sympathize, but with free men. . . . Perhaps, in a certain sense, the surest mode of pleasing and instructing all nations is to write for one."[85]

Not until he wrote the essay on Schiller did Carlyle grasp fully wherein lay the profound differences between his approach to history and Schiller's. There he admitted that the fundamental charge against Schiller is his lack of spontaneity. His poetry as well as his prose "is the labored product of certain faculties rather than the spontaneous product of his whole nature."[86] Such a genius is reflective rather than creative; philosophical and oratorical rather than poetic. As a consequence he tends to keep his gaze fixed "aloft rather than around him"; his speculations are concerned with the dignity and destiny of man, rather than the common doings and interests of men. In his histories he "looks abroad on the many-coloured stream of life as if from a college window, dwelling altogether on the abstract and systematic, on romantic love, on old conventionally noble themes, on the effect of constitutions, of religious and other such high, purely scientific objects." Even his heroes seem inhuman as they tower aloft, "far-shining, clear, and also cold and vacant, as a sea beacon."

As an artist Schiller brought the scenes of his histories and dramas before us with great fidelity, not alone the outward or surface movements but the mechanisms of his characters. "There is action enough in the plot, energy enough in the dialogue ... but throughout a certain stiffness and effort. . . . The characters do not, as it were, verify their human nature, by those thousand little touches and nameless turns, which distinguish the genius essentially dramatic from the genius merely poetical; the Proteus of the stage from the philosophic observer and trained imitator of life."[87] Carlyle points out that Schiller's plays and histories are only moving when he is portraying grandly tragic or majestic themes, which recalls Coleridge's interpretation of Schiller as master of the "material sublime." Incapable of the "intense drama of passion," the "diffused drama of history" alone gave him scope for his varied powers.[88]

Carlyle shared with Schiller, however, the belief that the function of poetry, and indeed of all art, is to bring harmony into existence, though Carlyle's understanding of harmony was a unity effected by an emotional and intellectual reconciliation which provided man with a balance between thought and action. The highest art reaches a plane where the dualism inherent in man's nature, the dichotomy between feeling and thinking, between inclination and duty, is resolved in the realm of the ideal. Carlyle believed man was able in such moments to glimpse the reality behind appearance; identify himself with it. The mission of art was exactly that. It was on these grounds that he objected to Schiller's constant idealization of the common and particular in an effort to elevate it to the universal and sublime. These qualities lifted Schiller's works beyond the reach of the ordinary sympathetic mind that stood to gain most from his artistic message.

In no sense did Carlyle approve of Schiller's esthetic philosophy of life, strongly as he was influenced by his idea of the poet (as we shall see later). The sphere of the esthetic was a means to an end with Carlyle, never an end in itself, even if conceived on such a lofty moral plane as Schiller's. In his *Notebooks* Carlyle remarked that Schiller's pursuit of the Beautiful and representation of it in suitable forms "operated as a kind of religion in his soul." He considered the esthetic a necessary means of improvement among political societies; but Carlyle suspected that his efforts in this cause "not only satisfied the restless activity, the desire of creating and working on others, which forms the great want of an elevated mind, but yielded a sort of balsam to his conscience; he viewed himself as the apostle of the sublime."[89] "The desire of creating and working on others," in Carlyle's opinion, was the true basis of the artist's motivation.

ENGLISH ROMANTICISM: SIR WALTER SCOTT

A recent writer, surveying the transition period from rationalist to romantic historiography, holds that the chief stimulus provoking the development of a new conception of history was the romantic revival in literature and that Sir Walter Scott was the connecting link.[90] It seems obvious that both literature and history partook of certain influences in common—the revival of primitivism and medievalism in the eighteenth century; the resuscitation of folklore and balladry; the democratic impulse in Burns and Crabbe; the pervasive nostalgia for the past. All of these influences had to do with the interest in and love for the past, the enlargement of the domain of the imagination to include history as the material of literature. The philosophy of romantic historiography is a thing apart in origin and derivation.

Sir Walter Scott's gift to romantic historiography was its outward dress. It will be recalled that the original source of the romance, with its record of wonderful events believed to have happened in the past, lay in history; while the earliest essence of the novel, with its imitation of real life and manners, lay in the fabliau. Both prose forms had undergone a considerable independent development in English literature, but each lacked important esthetic elements the other possessed. To Scott goes the credit for blending the two forms in the historical prose romance, combining the interest arising from descriptions of men and manners with the more universal quality adhering to history.

Scott availed himself of the Aristotelian dictum that men, when they believe something has happened, are always ready to believe in an imaginative account of how it happened. He brought to his task a memory stored with the exciting, picturesque legends and historical anecdotes of his native Border country, an inexhaustible storehouse of partly true, partly fictitious materials. Thanks to his wide knowledge and observation of living men, he was able to invest his ideal *dramatis personæ* with the bright colors of reality by means of intimate details of manners and costume. Over it all he cast the spell of a genuinely profound love of the past.[91]

It was Scott's good fortune to satisfy a general craving in the society of his day for an ampler range of thought and action. As Carlyle points out in his essay on Scott, the latter's success was attributable mainly to his age's need of him. The bankrupt period after the downfall of Napoleon was "at once destitute of faith and terrified at scepticism." By enlarging the sphere of fiction to include history he rediscovered a veritable El Dorado; and the effect of his discovery spread rapidly over continental Europe. In every nation in which historic tradition was vivid men began to revive the memories of the past. The fact that the old life of men could be resuscitated not as a dead tradition but as a "palpable presence" was a quickening revelation.

No one has done fuller justice to the importance of Scott's service to historiography than Carlyle himself in his essay on Scott published in the *London and Westminster Review* in 1838. The indefinable sense of a living past which was Scott's most valuable possession (just as it was Carlyle's) enabled him to go far beyond Schiller's pioneering efforts in subjective historical writing. As Carlyle says, writers of history hitherto had been "unaware that the bygone ages of the world were actually filled by living men, not by protocols, state papers, controversies and abstractions of men. "Not abstractions were they, not diagrams and theorems; but men in buff . . . coats and breeches, with colour in their cheeks, with passions in their stomach and the idioms, features and vitalities of very men." The faint hearsays of history as philosophy teaching by experience must exchange themselves everywhere for "direct inspection and embodiment." This and this only will be counted "experience." "It is a great service, fertile in consequences, this that Scott has done; a great truth laid open by him." History will henceforth have to take thought of it.[92]

The "great truth" laid open by Scott was the rediscovery of an old medium of literary art lost to the world for two hundred years. There are two primary methods of seizing and expressing the image of life through literature. One is through imaginative apprehension; the other through direct observation. Scott blended these media with a result often described as romantic realism. The means he used to accomplish the fusion lay wholly in his exploitation of the past. He brought to the large stores of historical legends with which his memory was richly furnished an antiquarian's love of minute details regarding manners, costumes, speech. He gave us realistic actuality clothed in the glamorous atmosphere of the romantic past.

He strengthens our convictions of actuality in his selection of *dramatis personæ*. His heroes are usually drawn from history, sometimes under thin disguises, and are commonly agreed to be what Carlyle called them: mere "mechanical cases" of men and women with the souls left out, not "created and poetically alive" but only "deceptively enacted."[93] While these characters carry along the action and sustain the epic interest, the main burden of the tale's human interest is borne by the earthy, humorous peasants with whom they are associated. The latter are not in any sense historical creations. They are simply Scott's contemporaries drawn from his own experiential knowledge; the observed characters of his everyday Scotch existence.

Carlyle's criticism of Scott for fashioning so many of his characters from the skin inwards rather than from the heart outwards is a sound criticism of the chronic weakness of the "local color" method. Historical realism, except in the skilful hands of a Shakespeare, is too frequently inclined to stop short with the "mechanical case." Mere pictorial effects, the stage scenery and costuming of the past are substituted for the fusion of reality and ideality which only a creative imagination can accomplish. The criticism has even been advanced in some quarters that the "local color" technique of historical realism is, in strict sense, anti-historical.[94] Its attempt to lend past events the vividness and intimacy of contemporaneous happenings tends to destroy all sense of historical perspective.

Coleridge seized upon Scott's use of local color as containing the secret of his "felicity" and sustaining interest. "The language, manners, etc. introduced," he says, "are sufficiently different from ours for poignancy, and yet sufficiently near and similar for sympathy."[95] And again, because the author speaking and reflecting in his own person, "remains still . . . in sufficient keeping with his subject matter, while his characters can both talk and feel interesting to us as men, without recourse to antiquarian interest. . . ." Coleridge's indifference amounting to aversion for anything partaking of the antiquarian did not prevent his giving a characteristically acute analysis of the effect of Scott's method.

Scott demonstrates the limits beyond which a mere technique of recapturing the past cannot go. Fundamentally he is lacking in the highest order of historical imagination. Like Macaulay a generation later, he is too minute a copyist; too decided a moralist; too literal a judge. We agree with Coleridge in forgiving Scott's trifling historical improbabilities, inaccuracies of date, anachronisms of speech and costume.[96] But the "moral anachronisms" which form a constant pattern are another matter. The men and women who address us from the carefully set stage of the past are really Scott's contemporaries in thought, feeling, and taste. Scott's own "intellect supplies the place of intellect and all character in his heroes and heroines, and *representing* the intellect of his readers, supersedes all motives for its exertion, by never appearing alien, whether as above or below." Taine says that Scott was incapable of the "great divinations and the wide sympathies" required to unlock the door of the past.[97] It is remembered to his credit, however, that he revived a vogue for historical narration. He educated the reading public to appreciate the historical best sellers of the coming generation.

ENGLISH ROMANTICISM: BURKE AND COLERIDGE

Viscount Morley once remarked that the date of a man's birth was the most significant fact to be known about him. Carlyle was born in 1795, a year made memorable by the "whiff of grape shot" which brought to a close the main phase of the French Revolution. The generation which arrived at maturity during the final liquidation of the revolutionary struggle included three writers—Byron, Shelley and Carlyle—the patterns of whose thought were as distinctly dominated by that event as those of Burke, Coleridge, Wordsworth, and Southey, their intellectual progenitors. The Revolution was only a tradition to them, not a personal experience; yet they preserved in a sense the original passion of the revolutionary spirit. They revolted against the conventions and controls of the reactionary social order, the corruption and hypocrisy which flourished unheeded on all sides. Shelley and Byron went further and revolted against the principle of authority itself, arriving at a sort of political anarchy not unlike Schiller's moral anarchy. Byron holds a mediate position between the fiery social bias of Shelley and the equally fiery but opposite social bias of Carlyle.

Shelley and Carlyle interpreted for their generation the antithetic points of view held a generation earlier by Godwin and Burke. Shelley courageously accepted the failure as well as the glory of the Revolution as part of the appointed order of the world.[98] Bolstered by his Godwinian theory of perfectibility, and has own illimitable confidence in human nature, he endured the isolation resulting from his confidence that the final victory would be decisive, even though remote. Probably the most constructive visionary in the annals of English literature, certainly the most sublime apostle of revolution, he believed that mankind was capable of guiding its own destiny—not through the power of human reason, significantly, but through the possession of loving hearts.

Carlyle, on the contrary, stands in the line of succession from Burke through Coleridge. Compared with the minority opinion voiced by Shelley, Carlyle gives voice to the majority opinion. The French Revolution had been the epochal event in the lives of Burke, Wordsworth, Coleridge, and Southey. It was a thing they had "dwelt with, openly or privately, ever since" their youth.[99] They had interpreted it as "the suicidal explosion of an old, wicked world, too wicked, false and impious for living longer"; in Wordsworth's words

> a terrific reservoir of guilt
> And ignorance filled up from age to age.[100]

When Southey conveyed his gratitude to Carlyle that a strong voice had at last expressed that meaning, and delivered a salutary bit of "scriptural exposition" to the world, he was a representative spokesman for this entire group.

Carlyle's choice of the French Revolution as the theme for his first great history seems both symbolic and inevitable in view of this relationship. He gave final and artistic form to the judgment on the Revolution of his intellectual forbears. In addition, the Revolution's "admonitory glow" possessed for him personally a unique value.[101] His record of it must be joined with *Sartor* as a profound confession of philosophic beliefs. The later histories contain the same beliefs implicitly. No other of his writings, however, came "so direct and flamingly from the heart" as *Sartor* and the *French Revolution*.

It will be recalled that the immediate reaction to the events of the French Revolution in England was far other than that voiced by Carlyle half a century later. In 1789 there was deep satisfaction at the downfall of a corrupt and despotic government, one which in addition had been a traditional enemy of the English people. Many believed it the realization of the eighteenth century dreams of perfectibility. Others saw it as a proper extension of the principles already established in England by the Glorious Revolution of 1688. Edmund Burke stood practically alone in vigorous dissent. He undertook to prove the difference between such constitutional reforms as the Revolution of 1688 effected and the present violent overthrow of existing authority. In his arguments he advanced far beyond the particular to the general principle and developed a reasoned attack on the whole theory of social change by means of revolution. His *Reflections on the French Revolution* (1790) was both powerful and cogent enough to alter the entire drift of English opinion.[102]

From our special point of view, the valuable part of the *Reflections* is Burke's treatment of the general method and justification of political change, involving a wider consideration of the ultimate nature of human society. He opposed the current Lockian conception of society as an association of individuals bound together by a contract for certain definite purposes.[103] Like Herder, he was stimulated by Rousseau to develop a conception of society as a living organism whose character is determined by its history, and whose members are bound together by unseen mysterious forces.[104] Though a weighty protest against the mechanical view of society had been advanced earlier by Montesquieu, it was Burke who finally overthrew the Lockian supremacy in political thinking.[105] Against the omnipotence of the individual, he set the collective reason; against the claims of the present, he set the accumulated experience of the past; for natural rights he offered social rights; instead of liberty he advocated law.

Burke conceived society as a partnership between all men in all ages, past, present, and future. It was created; not constructed. Its development was a growth rather than an elaboration. It possessed the unity and continuity of life rather than the fortuitous mechanism of an invention. He lifted political theory out of the Lockian category of law and placed it in the organic category where it has remained ever since. He is remembered not only for one of the greatest defenses ever offered for the theoretical basis of conservatism; but his declaration of the principles of continuity, solidarity, and evolution has caused them to take their place as essential elements in conservative political thinking.

Burke derived from the French Revolution his conviction that neither theoretical considerations nor conscientious intentions could create vital political institutions, and he bequeathed it to Coleridge and Carlyle. Herder had seen long before the Revolution that institutions had their origin in a vital need and grew unconsciously in the course of historical development. The experience of the Revolution bore him out. While Burke probably had no knowledge of Herder or Vico, he came to precisely the same conclusions in his reaction to the French Revolution. In history—and history to him was a reservoir of the accumulated experience of the past—resided a secret wisdom superior to human perspicacity. The highly complex, minutely differentiated organization constituting society with its institutions, ideas, sentiments, and habits sending their roots deep into the past is subject to mysterious, non-mechanical forces. He considered it a monstrous usurpation that any man or association of men should presume to reconstruct *de novo* such an organism at any given time.

At the same time Burke held firmly to the "great law of change" as necessary for the conservation of human society; but he conceived it as an organic principle working itself out according to the "Divine Tactic," without need of help from presumptuous human intellects.[106] He perceived clearly that violent political overthrow from below not only destroyed the existing authority but created a condition antagonistic to any kind of political stability. In violent change, he believed, the power inevitably gravitated to the most undisciplined elements. We shall see how Carlyle used this conception as the framework of his analysis of the progress of the French Revolution.

Burke's theory regarding the nature of human society is the first of two of wide import on which his whole system may be said to rest. The second is his belief that man is a moral and religious as well as a political animal; and that the course of history is guided by the Providence of God. This, like the first, Carlyle fully shared. Burke believed that the destiny of nations and the constitutions of states are ultimately the result of spiritual forces beyond knowledge. While he belongs in the ranks of the great inductive historical thinkers in his constant appeals to the experience of men and nations, yet in the final analysis his method is deductive, and his political philosophy, firmly grounded as it is on historical method, rests ultimately on his deep-rooted theism.

Like Herder, Burke believed that religion constituted the basic fabric of society. "We know, and what is better, we feel inwardly, that religion is the basis of civil society, and the source of all good and of all comfort."[107] Referring to Christianity, he wrote, "on that religion, according to our mode, all our laws and institutions stand as upon their base." He felt strongly that an "element of mystery lay in the cohesion of men in societies, the sanctity of contract; the whole fabric of law and obligation which is the sheltering bulwark between civilization and barbarism. When history and reason had contributed all they could to the explanation, it seemed to him as if the vital force, the secret of organization ... must still come from the impenetrable regions beyond reasoning and beyond history." It was these qualities which led Lord Morley to conclude that in Burke, despite all his political and practical sagacity, lay fundamentally a "certain mysticism."

In the *Appeal from the Old Whigs to the New* occurs a passage which perhaps best expresses Burke's religio-political creed.[108] He urges the conservative doctrine that the situation of the individual, far more truly than his choice, is the arbiter of his duties. Only a few lines need be quoted for its striking resemblance to Carlyle's later thought:

I may assume that the awful Author of our being is the Author of our place in the order of existence; and that, having disposed and marshalled us by a divine tactic, not according to our will, but according to His, He has in and by that disposition, virtually subjected us to act the part which belongs to the place assigned us. We have obligations to mankind at large, which are not in consequence of any special voluntary pact. They arise from the relation of man to man, and the relation of man to God, which relations are not matters of choice. . . . Dark and inscrutable are the ways by which we come into the world. The instincts which give rise to this mysterious process of nature are not of our making. But out of physical causes, unknown to us, perhaps unknowable, arise moral duties which, as we are able perfectly to comprehend, we are bound indispensably to perform. . . .

Burke's protest against rational individualism led him into opposite errors. In reverencing the past, he became in a sense its slave. His respect for inherited tradition blinded him to faults in the social structure; led him to oppose with horror the mere suggestion of novelty. Like Carlyle, Burke's religious temperament induced him to promote the rôle of religion from its sound place as a buttress of the social order to an exaggerated position as its very foundation. In the final analysis the moral relations and duties of man represent only one angle of an equilateral triangle, with the economic and intellectual relations holding equivalent stations.

In his theistic idealism, Burke is the immediate forerunner of Coleridge. It will be recalled that Coleridge, along with Wordsworth and Southey, was an ardent sympathizer with revolutionary principles and practices during the early phase of the French Revolution. The philosophic defense of the new artistic principles advanced by the Lake poets was really only an extension of the same principles embodied in the Declaration of the Rights of Man. Freedom of invention in the sphere of art was transformed into a metaphysical theory which demanded for the individual the right to dispense with rules of all kinds. This involved a cutting loose from all historical continuity, from all tradition and authority in the practice of art. To these esthetic principles Coleridge remained a firm adherent.

It was quite otherwise with his political and social beliefs. Disillusioned by the excesses of the Revolution, Coleridge became an avowed disciple of Burke and in time outstripped his master in philosophic conservatism. While he represents the connecting link in English thought between Burke and Carlyle, and the latter might be said to have been a disciple in a mild way in his early years, their eventual positions were miles apart. Lord Acton is said to have remarked that he had no need of Carlyle because he had read Coleridge first; but such a judgment, beyond being based on an admitted ignorance of Carlyle, reflects the superficial resemblance in their general theistic outlook. To both men atheism was mere intellectual presumption, reverencing neither the past nor the present, the good nor the bad. They agreed in believing that the most heinous spiritual sin was claiming to explain the world by the methods of science and rejecting that moral and spiritual part of life which could not be so explained.

Coleridge and Carlyle shared certain Transcendental beliefs in common; the theory, for example, that every institution has an underlying Idea whose essential nature does not change from age to age but whose external form must undergo constant modification to meet the changing needs of the time.[109] It is the duty of thinkers and statesmen to reinterpret the idea from generation to generation. This belief is parallel, of course, to Schiller's theory of the mission of the poet, Fichte's idea of the vocation of the scholar, and Carlyle's theory of the rôle of the hero. Developing from it is the axiomatic conviction that the highest truths are not within the reach of all people. Effective government must be by the select, therefore, and not by the democratic machinery which was currently enfranchising the middle classes whose interests could not be identified with those of society at large.

Coleridge's aristocratic bias is as different as possible from Carlyle's. The latter called him "deficient in sympathy for concrete human things . . . rubbing elbows with us on this solid Earth."[110] He was not so much indifferent as unaware of the social group *per se*. He believed that even though the people constitute the lifeblood of the state, they are not capable of preserving that organism. "What does history show," he contended, "but the story of noble structures raised by the wisdom of the few, and gradually undermined by the ignorance and profligacy of the many?"[111] He particularly believed profound social danger lay in the growth of cities, with their vast populations likely to become mobs in the hands of selfish demagogues, though the urbanization movement was an inevitable corollary of industrial development and so recognized by his more critically minded contemporaries. Such a confusion of symptoms with causes is typical of Coleridge's social criticism.

The strongest elements in Coleridge's mature thought were the sense of the complexity of the world's problems, speculative and practical, and a negative conviction of the incapacity of the ordinary mind to solve them by its own resources. Such conclusions were not strange in the latter phases of so frustrate a destiny as Coleridge's. In a sense, however, they were also the conclusions of his generation, a generation which saw the sun rise on the most hopeful period the world has ever seen and set again on a scene of general confusion, despair, and disillusionment.

By nature Coleridge was a thinker with a passion for first principles. In *The Friend*, first published in 1809, he laid the philosophic basis for Tory views on an even surer foundation for the conservation of society than Burke had offered. Later in the *Idea of Church and State* he defended the established order on philosophic premises. The hereditary aristocracy had been the traditional repository of the learning and culture of the past, and on it should fall the burden of controlling the masses below it. The aristocracy, in turn, must acknowledge reverence for the Established Church.[112] As firm a believer in Divine Government as Burke, Coleridge vitiated the force of his metaphysical ideas by grafting them on the moribund body of orthodox dogma. Partly the weakness was personal; partly it represented the spirit of his generation.

Carlyle had little patience with Coleridge's surrender to such worn-out institutional clothes as the Established Church. The "half-contemptuous, half-compassionate" tone of his chapter on Coleridge in the *Life of Sterling* is sufficient testimony of the facts. He marveled at the "sublime secret of believing" which enabled Coleridge, "after Hume and Voltaire had done their best and worst with him" still to "profess himself an orthodox Christian, and say . . . to the Church of England . . . *Esto Perpetua.*"¹¹³ Coleridge acknowledged, of course, that the Church was "tragically asleep," sunk under the influence of materialism and deism. But he was confident that it could be revived to a state of pristine vigor by lifting the interpretation of dogma above the sphere of understanding into the higher sphere of the reason. His "fatal delusion" in seeking a bulwark for his principles in an idealized conception of existing institutions probably was in part a want of moral courage in denying tradition, and lack of will to grapple with his problems. A third element seems even more important to the present inquirer: Coleridge's curious propensity for living, not in the actual world of space and time, but collaterally in a world of his own making. Carlyle, like many others critical of their own age, found support for his convictions by turning to the past. Coleridge, on the contrary, could not give substance and reality to his institutional conceptions by means of historical perspective because the past had no actuality for him. This temperamental lack of historic judgment, or more narrowly the historic sense, may account in part for Coleridge's compromise.

With his customary acuteness, Coleridge revealed his awareness of his peculiarity in an inimitable comparison of himself with Scott:

Dear Sir Walter Scott and myself were exact, but harmonious opposites in this;—that every old ruin, hill, river or tree called up in his mind a host of historical or biographical associations,—just as a bright pan of brass, when beaten, is said to attract the swarming bees;— whereas, for myself . . . I believe I should walk over the plain of Marathon without taking more interest in it than in any other plain of similar features. Yet I receive as much pleasure in reading an account of the battle in Herodotus as anyone can. Charles Lamb wrote an essay on a man who lived in past time:—I thought of adding another to it on one who lived not in time at all, past, present or future, —but beside or collaterally.¹¹⁴

Coleridge's lack of a sense of reality in time, whether past, present or future, throws light on many elements that seem inexplicable in his social philosophy. The statement, for example, in the *Idea of Church and State* that while the reading of history inevitably disposes a man to satire, the "science of history, history studied in the light of philosophy, as the great drama of an ever unfolding Providence . . . infuses hope and reverential thoughts of man and his destiny."[115] As representing a Coleridgian point of view this is meaningless; an unassimilated bit of Transcendental dogma. Consider rather the wistful acknowledgement in *Table Talk:* "If men *could* learn from history, what lessons it might teach us. But passion and party blind our eyes and the light which experience gives is a lantern on the stern, which shines only on the waves behind us."[116] Not "passion and party" are altogether to blame for blinding Coleridge's eyes, but the want of historic judgment which is able to perceive events and institutions in time realistically, and not out of it ideally.

Coleridge had read widely in history, but his appreciation seems to have been limited. What he cared for and what he sought was a sense of personality in the maker of the record; and more important still, the "principles" to be evolved. "I have read all the famous histories," he said in *Table Talk*, "and, I believe, some history of every country and nation that is, or ever existed; but I never did so for the story itself as a story. The only things interesting to me were the principles to be evolved from and illustrated by the facts. After I had gotten my principles, I pretty generally left the facts to take care of themselves. I never could remember any passages in books, or the particulars of events, except in the gross. . . ."[117] The ancient historians he admired more than the moderns, but with the exception of Herodotus he does them scant justice. Consistent with his attitude toward history, he judges them in terms of broad generalizations, often illuminative but never wholly true. The sole object of Thucydides, for example, he took to be the delineation of the ills arising from the conflict between democracy and oligarchy.[118] Tacitus, on the other hand, had no other object than to "demonstrate the desperate consequences of the loss of liberty on the minds and hearts of men."[119] When we contrast these observations with the accuracy of his usual generalizations about poetry and drama, it seems apparent that he did not approach historical writing with the same subjective attitude. If there were need to add further support to a point already labored, we could refer to the harsh criticism of Gibbon's *Decline and Fall*.[120] Allowing his primary complaint against Gibbon's "detestable style" to be critically permissible from Coleridge's point of view, one could search far in his writings for a more unhappy interpretation.

This extensive and perhaps too specialized criticism of Coleridge is intended merely to establish the quality of his relationship with Carlyle. Their fundamental premises may be freely compared; but the logical structures reared on the basis of those premises are mainly diverse. Coleridge caught the torch of romantic political theory from the hands of Burke and passed it on to Carlyle; but at the point of contact the relationship ceases to be significant. The same is true of their mutual relationship to German idealism. Carlyle picked up the German poets and philosophers where Coleridge had dropped them a decade or two earlier. He did not merely add to Coleridge's interpretation. He reinterpreted them in a way that made the German Renascence a leavening force in English thought. However much more qualified Coleridge was by temperament and training to grasp the philosophic principles involved, there seems no question today that Carlyle's was the greater interpretation in point of influence.[121]

III

CARLYLE'S PHILOSOPHY OF HISTORY

MAZZINI once said that he would willingly "undertake to declare the personal feelings of any historian, after reading twenty pages of his history."[1] Allowing for a degree of exaggeration, there is a large element of truth in this generalization. In a sense, historians cannot narrate the simplest fact without having determined its importance on the basis of a preconceived theory regarding the meaning of the historic process. In other words, history has no objective but merely a subjective existence, from the interpretative standpoint.[2] The methods of the historian, whatever his attitude, may be reduced finally to these: the collection of facts; the arrangement of these according to sequence of time and causation; the criticism by which the value of the facts is determined; and the interpretation in accordance with the results of arrangement and criticism. In carrying out these processes, however, the human equation is so important that it altogether determines the result. In the place of an objective series of events, objectively arrived at, history becomes a subjective entity, dependent on the "cast of mind" of the historian. Fustel de Coulanges may assert: "It is not I who speak, but history which speaks through me"; but his view is balanced by the opposite and equally extreme view that history is created, not by the characters and events, but by the historian.[3] The product of the process of historical inquiry thus depends for its selection and arrangement of materials on the historian's philosophy of history, no less than its form depends on his power of expression.

Carlyle's philosophic views on history and history writing are scattered through the entire body of his writings. There is a constant intermingling of the abstract and the concrete, the theoretical and the practical, the eternal and the temporal in the purely historical writings no less than in the early speculative and critical writings. The so-called speculative phase of his career began with the first published essay ("Joanna Baillie") in the *New Edinburgh Review* in 1821 and is usually regarded as ending with the publication of *Sartor Resartus* in 1833. The first half of this period is notable mainly for the *Life of Schiller*, in which he analyzed Schiller as historian and artist in terms equally applicable to himself. The latter half is the period of the great critical essays, culminating in *Sartor*, and dominated by the philosophic principles of Transcendental idealism. While these twelve years are commonly regarded as yielding sufficient data for a thorough notion of Carlyle's philosophic and artistic beliefs, the truly speculative phase was completed only with the *French Revolution*.[4] In the latter work may be found his theory of the process of historic change in its most significant and only complete form. The book is no less remarkable as the historical narration of an event in time than it is as an investigation of the process of change itself. Carlyle's mind was too analytic and fundamentally pragmatic to be satisfied with a metaphysical theory of the general purport of history. He was equally interested in the process of historic change.[5]

Carlyle was one of the most absorptive of thinkers; and one of the least systematic in the arrangement and display of his possessions. With a due expenditure of time and energy, the student of Carlyle's writings is rewarded by the discovery of authentic glimpses of Kant, Herder, and Fichte; of Goethe, Schiller and Richter; of Novalis, Tieck, and the Schlegels; of Vico and Spinoza; of Schelling, Hegel, and Comte; of Coleridge, Burke, and Hume; of Burns and Scott. Such a list reveals merely that he was affected by many of the currents of the romantic movement, particularly the esthetic, ethical, and political. Possibly the most remarkable feature of his philosophic premises was the passion for unity which enabled him to force the potent new wine of Transcendental and romantic thought into the old skins of his Calvinist inheritance.

Like Burke, Carlyle constructed no formal metaphysical system by which we can conveniently label him. He had, as Goethe discerningly remarked, certain "unborrowed principles of conviction" by which he tested the world from earliest childhood. They were derived partly from his Calvinist background; partly they were the natural possession of an earnest and strongly pragmatic mind. When in late youth he came in contact with the congenial metaphysics and epistemology of German Idealism, he read his way into it so completely that it ever after colored his thought and expression. But what he borrowed from the Transcendentalists, with the exception of the artists among them, was mainly the categories of thought, esthetic and philosophic. These categories he filled with possessions already acquired, either by inheritance or by early acquaintance with the writings of the English and Scottish schools of moral philosophy.

Carlyle probably shares with Burke the distinction of being the most inveterate foe of theories and theorists in English literature.[6] Both men had a highly articulate aversion for the "thick darkness of metaphysics" and the "metaphysical knights of the sorrowful countenance" who wander therein. Henry James reports Carlyle as saying once: "Poor John Mill is writing away there in the *Edinburgh Review* about what he calls the philosophy of history! As if any man could ever know the road he is going, once he gets astride of such a distracted beast as that!"[7] He referred more than once to the "disease of metaphysics"; and he believed the "mere existence and necessity of a Philosophy is an evil."[8] Like Burke again, however, he possessed the generalizing type of mind, based on inherent rationality and penetrative insight, which compelled him to press back from events to principles, and lift even ordinary incidents into the realm of great ideas. However much he disclaimed the possession of a philosophy of history, no one can read him long without being struck with the persistence with which he theorized upon historic processes.

In a perfect state all thought would be action, in Carlyle's view. Philosophy, except as poetry and religion, would have no being. He conceded, though, that formulating some theorem of the universe is an unescapable necessity to man, "standing in the center of Nature, his handbreadth of Space encircled by Infinitude; his fraction of Time encircled by Eternity."[9] He impatiently dismissed as futile the "blarney about history" which emanated from Germany and the pens of Hegel, Schelling and Schlegel, because it was divorced from the practice of historical writing.[10] Yet he wrote no history himself until his thought and purpose with regard to it were fixed and explicit. Nor did he ever consider a historic document without bringing to it the full powers of his interpretative insight.

UNIVERSAL HISTORY AS REVELATION OF THE DIVINE IDEA

Carlyle's philosophy of history is based on the Transcendental conception of the universe as a revelation of the Divine Idea. This fundamental conception, as old as the Hebrew religion, was rejected by the rationalists, but was reëstablished by the revival of idealism. In the view of the Transcendentalists, material creation was merely an appearance, a shadow in which the Deity manifests Himself to men.[11] Not only has the unseen world reality; all else has unreality. Consider the passage in *Sartor*:

So that this solid-seeming World, after all, were but an air image, our Me the only reality; and Nature, with its thousand-fold production and destruction, but the reflex of our own inward Force, the "phantasy of our Dream"; or what the Earth-Spirit in *Faust* names it, the *living visible Garment of God*.[12]

Such a conception of the Divine Principle is the primary basis on which Carlyle erects his system of thought. It matters little whether his God was the God of the Scottish Kirk or the pantheistic God of Goethe and Spinoza. His temperamental Calvinism and Transcendental idealism were merged into a single identity.

The Divine Idea finds finite revelation in two primary forms. One of these is the living world of nature, including man and the institutional symbols which give form and pattern to his existence. The other is the invisible world of spirit which is universal history, or the collective destiny of man. The highest visible embodiment of the latter invisible world is in art, broadly conceived, because it sums up the history of the spirit from age to age. Carlyle's philosophy, like Hegel's, may be reduced to a single conception of the historic principle, the idea of development which finds a systematic elaboration in the entire material of history.[13]

The idealists were in fundamental agreement on the existence of a higher organ of knowledge named reason. They differed variously in their atempts to prove the sovereignty of the Divine Idea as conceived by reason. Some appealed to the philosophic proof; others to faith; still others to experience or history. Carlyle joined Hegel, Fichte and Schelling (to name only a few) in the latter category. Universal history became to them not only the sublimest revelation but the most indubitable proof of a reasonable, purposeful Deity working with the plastic force of the collective destiny of man. Carlyle never wavered in his conviction that the Divine Idea behind the veil of nature and of universal history was reasonable and just; and possessed thereby a key to the truth and meaning of the historic processes. The ways of the "incomprehensible All" may be inscrutable to the individual, "his doings and plans manifested in completeness not by the year or by the century, on individuals or nations, but stretching through Eternity and over the Infinitude which he rules and sustains."[14] From the standpoint of historic perspective they can be understood as possessing cause and purpose; they can be seen to be leading man up to the "dark with excess of light" of the throne of God.

Beneath the Miltonic metaphor, Carlyle concealed an advanced evolutionary conception of history as a slow progress toward a better life for humanity. Eighteenth century thought had been fairly well impregnated with a general idea of progress but the conception did not attain philosophic completeness until the scientific advances of the late eighteenth and early nineteenth centuries.[15] The evolutionary hypothesis probably entered Carlyle's thought through his early scientific pursuits and remained to become an organizing principle in his speculative thinking.[16] In *Signs of the Times* he explicitly declares his optimistic faith in the imperishable dignity of man, and in the "high vocation to which, throughout this his earthly history he has been appointed. However it may be with individual nations, whatever melancholic speculators may assert, it seems a well ascertained fact, that in all times . . . the happiness and greatness of mankind at large have been continually progressive."[17] And in *Sartor* he expresses much the same thought:

> Find mankind where thou wilt, thou findest it in living movement, in progress faster or slower; the Phoenix soars aloft . . . filling the Earth with her music; or, as now, she sinks . . . and immolates herself in flame, that she may soar the higher and sing the clearer.[18]

Carlyle's conception of universal history was all-inclusive. His writings are sprinkled with half-poetical, half-philosophical aphorisms on the "Tissue of History" which inweaves all Being as a "God-written Apocalypse" whose figures and events possess the "somnambulism of uneasy sleepers." The universe is a "vast symbol of God," and history is its representation or text; a "book of celestial hieroglyphics whose lexicon is in heaven, in which only the prophets may read, and they only here and there a line."[19] This conception of universal history as a vast, spiritual force with an existence independent of the mere facts of recorded history broods over the entire body of Carlyle's writings. He shared it with many others in the heyday of idealism's supremacy; Richter, for example, with his "Infinite Spirit, who with Nature and History legibly writes to us"; and Novalis who wrote of the "all-presence of the Spirit of History." Likewise the Earth-Spirit in *Faust:*

> 'Tis thus at the roaring loom of Time I ply
> And weave for God the garment thou seest Him by.

To Carlyle this conception of universal history was no mere poetic figure of speech. In emphasizing the apocalyptic nature of history he subscribed fully to Schiller's aphorism: *"Die Weltgeschichte ist das Weltgericht."* The spirit of universal history is a court of judgment qualified to decide the truth or falsity of men and events and their right to become a part of living history. As a repository of facts as Carlyle defined them, of the living tissue of reality behind appearance, it is one of the instruments through which the Deity shapes the destiny of men. Carlyle tended to identify universal history with destiny. The wide canvas of historical events is linked with the larger movement of which events themselves are but a part. Rightly considered, no fragment of history can be understood without referring to all the rest; the humblest department is informed with the idea of the whole, and only in the whole is the partial to be discerned.

ART AS REVELATION OF THE DIVINE IDEA

The clearest visible emblem of the Time-Spirit in its revelation of the Divine Idea is in art; and here Carlyle derived as much of his thought from Herder as from Fichte. In defining works of art he exercised to the utmost the romanticist's privilege and included both written and "acted poetry." Universal history itself may be likened to a poem: "epic in its continuous flow, tragic from its ever-recurring catastrophes, and lyric as an anthem of praise to God."[20] Schelling's similitude just cited may be taken as typical of the romantic idealists; but while Carlyle would agree and possibly use the same figure, his fundamental point of view was somewhat different from theirs. In their conception history is the process by which God attains self-consciousness and realizes Himself. Carlyle, on the other hand, believed that history pertained to man, not God. Man is the hero and protagonist. It is man's discovery of the divine principle within himself, his realization of a personal relationship with the absolute which comprises history for him.

The function of art, as Carlyle understood it, is not only to bring harmony into existence through a reconciliation of the antagonistic elements of man's dual nature as Schiller conceived it, but to render in palpable form the Divine Idea beneath the show of things that all men may share in the revelation. In articulate poetry, as he defined it, whether a play by Shakespeare, a poem of Dante's, or a heroic life as lived by a Luther or Cromwell, all men may recognize the Invisible embodied concretely in the visible. Thus in a nation's acted and written poetry, rightly considered, may be discerned the grand spiritual tendencies of each age, "the national physiognomy, in its finest traits, and through its successive stages of growth."[21] Carlyle developed this idea at length in the *Historic Survey of German Poetry,* and concluded that the history of a nation's poetry, properly written, would constitute "the essence of its history, political, economic, scientific, religious." The record of a nation's highest aims and enthusiasms from age to age would contain the living principle around which all the detached facts and phenomena would shape themselves, "all the separate characters of poems and poets, [would] fashion themselves into a coherent whole."

Then there is the mass of "inarticulate poetry" which must have its due place in the vast body of universal history. This is to be found lying buried in popular mythology, in all the traditionary and spiritual possessions of a people. In a sense it is the most important part of universal history, from the standpoint of romanticist historiography, because only through it can the daily lives of the masses be comprehended. In *Sartor* Carlyle gives explicit expression to this when he describes the chief results of men's activity and attainment as "aeriform, mystic, and preserved in Tradition only." Such are man's forms of government; his customs or fashions both of "Cloth-habits and of Soul-habits"; much more his collective stocks of handicrafts, the faculty he has acquired of manipulating nature."[22]

It is apparent how such a conception of universal history as the primary spiritual revelation of the Divine Idea, finding in poetry broadly conceived its loftiest visible emblem, will shape Carlyle's ideas of such secondary media as written history and historians. Deferring a detailed consideration of these until the next chapter, we will set forth here the other primary manifestations of the Divine Principle as it finds embodiment in the experiential world of nature. In nature, strictly speaking, Carlyle had less interest than his fellow idealists. He shared with them the pantheistic feeling that external nature was "unspeakably beautiful" because she represented "not dead hostile Matter, but the veil and mysterious Garment of the Unseen ... the Voice with which the Deity proclaims himself to man."[23]

But this generalized love of nature did not approach the sensitive awareness of Novalis, for example, who possessed what Carlyle describes as a "peculiar method" of viewing nature: "rather in the concrete, not analytically and as a divisible aggregate, but as a self-subsistent universally connected whole."

Carlyle agreed rather with Goethe that man is the divinest of the natural symbols of the Godlike. "What is this Me?" he asks in *Sartor* ". . . an embodied, visualized Idea in the Eternal Mind." To the eye of pure reason man is a "soul, a Spirit and divine Apparition." "Where else," demands Teufelsdröckh, "is the God's-Presence manifested not to our eyes only, but to our hearts, as in our fellow man."[24] As a corollary, the loftier the acted life, the more sublime the emblem of the Infinite. The noblest works of art are the lives of the "heroic, god-inspired men." Again and again he likens a heroic life to a poem in which nature appears in her sublimest vesture.

Man has both an individual and a social significance as a symbol of the Divine Idea. The institutions which give form and pattern to his existence constitute the final symbols through which the Invisible is clothed in visible form. Man lives and has his being in and through the institutional symbols. In them lies an element both of concealment and of revelation; concealment of the mystery with which we are surrounded, revelation of the infinite in finite modes through which we can find existence possible in the "prose domain of sense." While the acted and written poetry of a national group theoretically offers the historian his sublimest materials, we shall see that Carlyle was equally interested in the institutional materials.[25]

The unity with which Carlyle fused his conceptions rises to the level of an organizing principle. What is all science, history, poetry, of whatever sort, but a right naming of reality? What is man, society and its institutional framework but a visible emblem of the Divine Principle at work in the universe? What is the rôle of the individual but discovering wherein lies his right relation to the universe and from that point finding his realization in the Aristotelian dictum of action, not in thought? What is the ultimate rôle of the prophet, the poet, the king, the priest, but interpreting in more or less intelligible terms the reality beneath appearance for the sustaining guidance of those not endowed with the intuitive power to apprehend reality? What is the true interpretation of universal history but the palpable rendering of the great men and great events —the Reformations, Swiss Revolts, Cromwelliads, French Revolutions, no less than the lives of the Luthers, Dantes, Mahomets, Knoxes, Burnses, Miltons, Shakespeares, that comprise the "inspired text of that Divine Book of Revelations, chapters of which are completed from Epoch to Epoch and called history?" These conceptions make plain one of the sources of Carlyle's biographic approach to history. In the lives of heroes the essence of history is most easily apprehended; in other words, the inexhaustible significance of the hero is his poetic value.

THE THEORY OF SOCIAL ORGANIZATION

The pragmatic quality of Carlyle's mind disposed him to a fundamental awareness of the connection between psychology and an adequate philosophy of history. Hume may have influenced him in this connection, though he disagreed with Hume's premises. Probably from Burke he derived a more congenial theory of the fundamental laws, powers, and affections of the human mind and character. It is doubtful whether he knew the contemporary French philosopher, Cousin, who is generally credited with first designating the science of history as properly a psychological science. In Cousin's view, historical analysis may supplement but cannot be substituted for psychological analysis.[26] Cousin presented his theory of history first in 1828, in a series of lectures given in Paris. Since Carlyle's opinions were well developed by this date he apparently arrived independently at theories similar to Cousin's, the originality of which has received little recognition.

Carlyle's theory of society is posited on the psychological assumptions of irrationalism. In his view the springs of human action lie buried deep in the primitive subconscious, whereby we partake of the essence of the Infinite. The primary principle of life, therefore, is mysterious, anti-rational and anti-mechanistic. Its inner sanctuaries lie in the "domain of the Unconscious, by nature infinite and inexhaustible," an "abyss of mystery and miracle" where alone it can creatively work. From that mystic region, and from that alone, "all wonders, all Poesies and Religions and Social Systems have proceeded."[27]

Carlyle believed that a theory of individual psychology was the heart of all other social, economic and political theorizing; that the latter, indeed, was merely the "finite, modified development" of it.[28] The only theory of psychology which in his opinion adequately accounted for the primary, unmodified forces and energies of man, the mysterious springs of love, fear, wonder, enthusiasm, poetry, and religion, ignored intellectual cognition in favor of an emotional basis buried deep in each individual nature. Carlyle called his theory of individual psychology the "science of Dynamics" to distinguish it from the Utilitarian "science of Mechanics" with its Lockian psychology. Since Carlyle's true philosophic interests were bounded by the limits of moral philosophy, his theories really comprise a system of morality grounded on feeling, reminiscent not only of Burke but of his predecessors in the English group of moral philosophers, notably Shaftesbury. The influence of the latter, in fact, he felt not only through the medium of English thought but through the work of Herder and Schiller, both of whom had been powerfully affected by Shaftesbury's "universal optimism."[29]

The "science of Dynamics" is the key to Carlyle's critical and historical analysis. By means of it he interprets the lives and works of men in terms of psychological motivation. His entire body of writings, critical and historical alike, is dominated by the conviction that no mechanical formula, no profit and loss calculus, no rational ideology of any sort, ever availed as a means of understanding the inmost motives of men which compose the living tissue of history. The grand agents in moving men to "deep, all pervading efforts" for some "invisible and infinite object" are and have always been the primary, unmodified forces of religion, fear, love, enthusiasm—all of them indefinable, ideal, even mystic in nature. At the same time he recognized fully that the dynamic and mechanical points of view are not really opposed but complementary. Undue cultivation of the inward or dynamic province is almost as evil in the long run as excessive cultivation of the outward or mechanic province. The former leads to idle, visionary courses and eventually to fanaticism; while the latter ultimately destroys moral force, the parent of all other force, by drying up the emotional springs whence it comes.[30] If Carlyle carried historical subjectivism to its logical extreme, he did so with complete knowledge of what he was doing, as well as an extraordinary understanding of the psychological processes which he undertook to interpret.

Carlyle's notion of the social organism suggests Shakespeare's lines:

> There is a mystery . . . .
> . . . . in the soul of state;
> Which hath an operation more divine,
> Than breath or pen can give expression to.[31]

In "Characteristics" (reminiscent of Shaftesbury in more than its title), he sets forth his theory of society and the individual from the standpoint of the primary forces constituting the "Chaos of Being." The principle of life, the highest mode of being, is mystery; to begin to know oneself and express oneself is to decline from that mode. But the life principle, before it can do its appointed work in the world, must struggle up from its residence in the unconscious or emotional nature through the "outer mechanical rind of the conscious." By consciousness Carlyle means the effort to explain the nature of being in terms accessible to the understanding. The all-important function of consciousness is to control and canalize the vital force residing in the subconscious. Thus sensibility and understanding are not two different sources of knowledge but only different stages of the same living activity. All the ideas by which the individual advances, step by step, from consciousness of its immediate environment to knowledge of the universe are innate within the subconscious as internal powers. This vital unity of man's psychical life is a conception Carlyle derived directly from Herder.[32]

The doctrine of "self-consciousness" which Carlyle used as his chief weapon in social criticism developed naturally from the foregoing. Wherever or in what shape vital powers are at work, the test of their working well or ill lies in the degree of silence or unconsciousness in their life element. "Silence is the element in which great things fashion themselves together; that at length they may emerge . . . into the daylight of Life, which they are thenceforth to rule."[33] Thought will not work except in silence; neither will virtue work except in secrecy.

It is evident that Carlyle's theory of the social organism is far removed from the rational theory of contract which underlies the varying theories of Hobbes, Locke and the English school, or Rousseau, Kant and Fichte. Like Burke and Herder he believed that the institutional pattern of society was really composed of the visible symbols of the same primary, irrational forces to be found lying in the individual subconscious. Society has its origin wherever two or three men come together. It becomes an organism superior to the individual organism, with its own identity and principles of growth. "I have strange glimpses of the power of spiritual union, of association among men of like object," he records in his *Notebooks*.[34] The true elements of religion, of government, and of the economic machinery of a state have their bases in this psychic organism called society.[35] The reason is, of course, that the indestructible qualities in man are of the spirit. Properly speaking, "man is a spirit: invisible influences run through society, and make it a mysterious whole, full of life and inscrutable activities and capabilities. If our individual existence is a mystery; our social is still more so."[36]

Unlike Burke, who could not bring himself to posit social origins and believed we had to draw a "sacred veil" over the beginnings of governmental and social institutions, Carlyle was eager to analyze the process from its primitive beginnings. He followed Herder not only in believing that the origin of all institutions lies deep in the primal chaos, but also in the satisfying conviction that the primal unconscious is informed with the laws of order and righteousness which partake of God's nature. His thought is similar to Herder's again (also Hume's and Vico's) in considering the institution of religion as the first collective manifestation of the Divine Idea in the social organism. The religious principle is a compound of love, fear, and wonder, which taken together form the basis of worship, the capacity for reverence, the acknowledgment of authority, the aptitude for coöperation: all social virtues whatever. Furthermore, the religious principle is not only most deeply bedded in the primal psychological processes, it is the repository of whatever moral force resides in the organism, and, as we have already pointed out, Carlyle believed that moral force was the parent of all other force. Religion is the "inmost pericardial and nervous tissue, which ministers life and warm circulation to the whole of society," while the economic processes comprise the "muscular and osseous tissues" and the body politic the mere outward skin, holding the whole together and protecting it.[37]

Obviously religion as Carlyle defined it was something quite different from the orthodox dogma to be found in "cathedrals and chapter houses." It resembled Herder's doctrine of a vital relationship between God and man, a relationship made manifest through successive revelations of God from age to age. These revelations take the shape of a spiritual principle (compare Ranke's *Zeitgeist*) which determines in large measure the quality and character of a nation's achievements. This revelation or "spirit of the age" has a dual aspect. In one sense it is determined by the age's capacity to receive a profound revelation of God. In another sense it itself is accountable for the responsive or non-responsive character of the age; in short, it is self-determined.

This involves a conception of periodicity or rhythm in the historic process which is, indeed, one of the fundamental premises on which Carlyle erects his philosophy of history. From whatever source he derived his conviction that the process of historic change can be analyzed in broad terms of successive ages of critical and organic activity, his thought bears marks of the influence not only of the Kantian group and of Herder and Goethe but of St. Simon, from whom he borrowed the systematic elaboration of the principle.[38] The idea proved extremely fruitful in Carlyle's analysis of social change, and he anticipates modern sociological tendencies in his use of it.

The theory of periodicity is developed at length in "Characteristics" and in *Sartor*. In the former he writes that all ages may be distinguished as being in one or another of two main categories. Either they are ages of belief or unbelief; of faith or scepticism. Either they are creative or critical; dynamic or mechanical. Once their fundamental quality has been determined, the historian may proceed in his detailed analysis of particular events rendered explicable by the primary characteristic of the period. In *Sartor* he puts it in somewhat more Hegelian and at the same time metaphorical terms. Every conceivable society may be represented in terms of the current status of its religious institutions as in one of three states: first, the period of struggling to find an articulate voice; second, the creative age, in which the church is audibly preaching; third and finally, the age in which the church has grown old and dumb, ready for dissolution. In the last period society, properly considered, is practically extinct. Not social ideas but mere gregarious feelings and inherited habitudes hold the world from dispersion, national and domestic wars.[39] In all of his discussions of cyclical change, Carlyle assumes that the process is self-generative, a matter of organic growth and development. Ages of faith, for example, contain within themselves the causes of their own eventual downfall; likewise in the case of ages of criticism. The process is rhythmic, ever recurring and tending to spiral slowly upwards toward a vague goal of spiritual realization, with which in the final analysis Carlyle has little concern or interest. His ultimate concern is with the problems of the present and how the experience of the past can best be made to serve in solving them.

Social institutions constitute the normal channels through which cyclical change takes place. Carlyle's conception of them is strictly functional, a mingling of Hegelian and Herderian elements. Institutions arise to serve a social need, and possess vitality only so long as they minister to that need. He likens them to the houses wherein our lives are led, and like all human habitations they require constant adaptation and repair.[40] In a world of "continual growth, regenesis and self-perfecting vitality" even the "very Truth must change its vesture from time to time." No institutions retain their vitality and usefulness forever in this so changing world; eventually they become as deserted edifices: "the walls standing, no life going on within but that of bats, owls and unclean creatures." Such institutions must then be pulled down if "they stand interrupting any thoroughfare." The periodically recurring epochs of decadence and unbelief, when "no Ideal grows and blossoms, only cant and false echo," when old and worn-out forms must be divested for new, are the revolutionary epochs in history.

In this phase of his thought Carlyle departs widely from Burke and Coleridge and shares the position of the revolutionary political thinkers on the continent, notably Herder and Schiller. It will be recalled that the English thinkers believed the fabric of society underwent constant modification and mutation to suit altered needs: the so-called "law of change" enunciated by Burke. But the latter, for all his sense of historical perspective, permitted the past to define the limits of the present. No matter how deserted the edifice became, to use Carlyle's figure, nor how effectively it blocked the thoroughfare, time had put its sacred stamp on the symbol and man had no right to lay violent hands on it. Coleridge, likewise, with his lack of historical perspective, would let the deserted edifice stand in the hope that it might again miraculously be filled with life. This brings us to Carlyle's conception of revolution.

THE THEORY OF REVOLUTION

The primary quality of the social organism is its constant mutability. The historic process may be likened to a ceaseless conflict between innovation and conservation, waged in the "daemonic element" that lies deep in all human beings. Constantly present is an indestructible hope in the future, but opposing it is an equally indestructible tendency to persevere as in the past. "The law of perseverance is among the deepest in man," Carlyle wrote in *Sartor:* "by nature he hates change. Seldom will he quit his old house till it has actually fallen about his ears."[41] In the *French Revolution* he named this conservative quality "indolence." Meanwhile, innovation, like Enceladus, must move whole Etnas to gain the smallest freedom. Yet all human beings are in constant movement, working forward by action and reaction, phase after phase, by unalterable laws toward an appointed goal. The seed sown must grow, ripen, wither. "What changes are wrought, not by Time but in Time," he exclaimed in *Sartor;* "cast forth thy Act, thy Word, into the ever-living, ever-working Universe: it is a seed-grain that cannot die." The beginning holds in it the end, and all that leads thereto.

The process of regenesis is thoroughly dynamic, but it is almost never effected without struggle and conflict of a greater or less catastrophic degree. The fire consummation and rebirth of the phoenix of society is not accomplished without sparks flying. Upwards of a century or two, and some millions of men, are frequently needed to light the funeral pyre of a moribund social order, or are licked into its high eddying flames.

Carlyle's analysis of the spirit of revolution relates it closely to his general philosophy of the blind, elemental nature of social forces. The discussion of it is the whole burden and purport of the speculative portions of the *French Revolution;* making the latter a veritable natural history of the "Revolution prodigy," a case book for sociologists and social psychologists.[42] Carlyle's contemporaries, with the exception of Emerson, made little of this aspect of his history, mainly because his moral message was more adapted to their needs and tastes. It is unfortunate, however, that their interpretation made so deep an imprint on the general consciousness that the more permanently valuable phase of Carlyle's profound and understanding record of the process of change in social institutions has been overlooked by modern readers to whom such problems are of immediate and vital concern.

Every man holds confined within himself a madman; still more society, Carlyle says in the *French Revolution.* This madness buried deep in the hearts of all men is invisible, impalpable, yet a true reality, a dæmonic quality held in check only by sound government and social order. In our fixed system of habits lies the unwritten constitution of society. And even though unwritten, it is the only one society dare not disobey. Written constitutions are, in fact, merely "solemn images" of this. The unending struggle between written constitutions and changing habit patterns is the source of the "world-shaking and world-making chaotic revolutions."[43] It is one of the "mights of men" that each of us has the right to crush the lies that oppress us, though Carlyle warned that woe shall be ours if we replace those lies with new ones, based on injustice and dishonesty.

When a bankrupt society becomes finally a "World solecism," with ineffective institutions, with authority grounded on mere habit, with enormous physical misery the inevitable corollary of moral evil, then the "dæmonic element" may be expected to break out in violent irruption. Not until shams and delusions become body-killing as well as soul-killing will a people become endowed with sufficient moral force to arise and shake off the incubus of a moribund society. For it is "not hunger alone . . . but the feeling of the insupportable, all-pervading Falsehood which had finally embodied itself in hunger" that has been the soul of all the just revolts of men.[44] The basic condition of the French people, for example, was "emptyness of heart, pocket and stomach." Thus "endowed with ferocity grounded on appetite, strength grounded on hunger," they rebelled against an oppressive social system and discovered that what they had considered an ordinance of nature was a mere ordinance of art. No mere economic, political, or religious institutions can resist the force with which men are endowed under such circumstances.

Carlyle is preëminently the historian of revolution. His three major histories, *French Revolution*, *Cromwell*, and *Frederick*, are concerned with periods of social and political convulsion when old forms are in process of destruction and replacement. Modern European history offers no more chaotic epochs than those chosen by him for resuscitation. His selection of such themes did not depend altogether on their revolutionary setting, however, as it did with Schiller. The basis of his choice lies much deeper—in the heart of his theory of individual and social psychology, of the nature and growth of institutions, of the character of the historic processes themselves.

There is no novelty in the choice of such periods; only in the reasons for the choice. Historians from Herodotus to the present have found the inspiration for their efforts most commonly in the spectacular and catastrophic epochs. History, like epic poetry, begins in the description of notable events and cannot depart widely from the grandly moving themes if it is to find readers. But for Carlyle, as for Tacitus, there was another element besides the heroic which interested him in such periods. That was the opportunity they afforded for the analysis of human character in terms of motives. Tacitus tells us that he deliberately passed over eight centuries of Roman history rich enough in glory, to settle on the Imperial epoch, a "period rich in disasters, terrible with battles, torn by civil struggles, horrible even in peace" because the souls of men were laid bare.[45] The most profoundly psychological and individualistic of ancient historians, Tacitus was interested primarily in human motives, the "ultimate matter of history." Both Tacitus and Carlyle were less concerned as historians with the events themselves than with the springs of human action behind the events. These could best be seized when the historic process was abnormally speeded up as in the violent overthrow of a moribund society. Peaceful mutation from moment to moment becomes sensible only from epoch to epoch and offers the historian less workable materials than does the speedier change of revolution. "Happy is the people whose annals are vacant"; a history of such a people is neither necessary nor possible.

Carlyle defines this "revolution prodigy, unfolding itself to terrific stature and articulation by its own laws and Nature's," as a break in the historic continuity of causally connected events, an eruption of elemental forces through the hard crust of formalism which characterizes institutions in their mature and decadent phases.[46] "All things are in a state of revolution, strictly speaking, in change from moment to moment in this Time-World of ours. In fact, there is nothing else but revolution and mutation, the former merely speedier change."[47] The speedier change of the revolutionary epochs is excellently adapted to the historian's purpose because it affords a microcosmic view of the entire process of institutional growth and decay.

Quite clearly Carlyle limits revolution to the period of "open, violent Rebellion and Victory of disimprisoned Anarchy against corrupt, wornout Authority." He devotes himself to explaining how anarchy breaks forth from prison, "bursts up from the Infinite Deep and rages uncontrollable, immeasurable, enveloping the world in phasis after phasis of fever frenzy; till the frenzy burn itself out and what elements of new Order it held (since all Force holds such) developing themselves, the uncontrollable be got . . . harnessed and its mad forces made to work toward their object like sane regulated ones." Carlyle's ultimate philosophic concern is with the process or mechanism of change. In a revolutionary period when normal mutation has attained great velocity, the workings of the mechanism are palpable enough to be seized in terms of single lives, or single great events. Thus the life of Cromwell, in conception at least, is a microcosmic history of the human soul. The life of the French people, as protagonist and hero of the French Revolution, is a microcosmic history of a social organism. The great revolutionary event itself is the best instance offered by universal history in which the process of change can be caught and fixed in a single image.

From the standpoint of revolution, Carlyle's three major histories form a single pattern. Two of them are concerned with the "revolution prodigy" itself. The *French Revolution* is a veritable Epos of the spirit of revolution conceived as a resistless force set in motion by elemental energies rising out of the instincts of men and eventually working themselves out to a level of law and order. *Cromwell* was originally conceived as a revolutionary Epos, but resolved itself into a case study of a perfect revolutionary leader. In a sense, Cromwell *was* the Puritan Revolution. The life of Frederick merely pushed back the boundaries of the investigation begun in the *French Revolution*. Warning symptoms of the oncoming revolutionary era lay in the political decrepitude of the great European nations in the seventeenth and eighteenth centuries. The Holy Roman Empire was a phantom, its machinery rotten and crumbling; yet it claimed dominion over a large portion of Europe.[48] By giving it a death-dealing blow, Frederick really paved the way for the events of 1789.

As always in the case of true revolutions, the seeds of the French Revolution had been planted centuries before. Royalty once had possessed the principle of life; had grown mysteriously, subduing all things and assimilating what it needed until it became a main fact of social existence. But the institution of monarchy had found its origin in serving a social need; had grown, ripened, withered as all institutions eventually do. When Louis XVI ascended the throne he represented a "Solecism incarnate," a lie doomed to die by the "cloud-capt spectre of Democracy" which had been installed as the "major of the palace" by the "*philosophe* prophets of the paper age." French society had become a wretched spectacle, founded on lies and corruption. No social bonds held these people together, since in reality they had no religion, no belief, no king. But spiritual bankruptcy had long been tolerated, and even the rottenest society will hold together for generations through custom and force of habit if not roughly handled. It was economic bankruptcy which induced the final ruin, reducing the oppressed masses to elemental emotions of hunger and fear and encouraging them to try conclusions with their oppressors.[49]

Carlyle has been criticized, particularly by professional historians, for failing to stress the economic and social causes of the French Revolution.[50] Yet it is apparent, if the foregoing analysis is valid, that his theory of the social organism and the process of change revolves around the central idea that social cataclysms can never be either unaccountable accidents or the work of one or more isolated individuals, however "heroic." By their very nature their sources lie in those institutional factors which he is criticized for ignoring. It is true that he begins his account of the French Revolution with the calling of the Estates General in 1789, but it appears sufficiently plain to the careful reader that his express purpose to deal with the "revolution prodigy" alone has much to recommend it both from the standpoint of art and of analysis. The authority of his entire conception depends on the idea that the sources of the revolution lay, not in the events of 1789 or of the years immediately preceding, but in the whole process of organic growth of the institutions of religion, monarchy and privileged nobility which characterized French (and European) civilization.

He also was perfectly aware, and it fitted neatly into his general theory, that actual conditions in France were considerably better the last decade or two before the overthrow than they had been under the two previous Louises. The kingly authority had been well-intentioned, even kindly, benevolent. Taxes had been lessened, and honest attempts made to lighten the burdens of the people through administrative economies. Plenty of pacific plans for revolutionary reforms had been proposed by Turgot and Necker, and approved by the king, even though they were overridden by the blind stubbornness of the nobility. "The sceptre of the sword was struggling hard to become the sceptre of the pen"; but it was these symptoms of "passive inertness" among those able and fit to govern which Carlyle believed offered the true signs of imminent downfall. The stillness was not that of "unobstructed growth" but the languid hush before the storm. Hope and paper promises always usher in a revolution.[51]

It should be emphasized here that Carlyle did not consider revolutions an inevitable and necessary part of the process of historic change. He held firmly to the aphorism developed in "Characteristics": "The healthy know not of their health, only the sick." The growth of institutions and states is more normal and rapid when it progresses by steady, silent persistence; and a lack of self-consciousness is a quality of healthy states no less than of healthy peoples. While the elements of potential revolution are constantly present, a healthy social organism is never afflicted by a violent overthrow of its established institutional structure. Such upheavals are the penalty of persistent disobedience to the laws of normal growth, the stagnation of moral forces, the disruption of those elemental energies working silently in the subconscious life of the masses of people. Like Burke he saw in revolutions a strong retributive element, but while Burke believed that the violence and tragedy were punishment for the immoral act of rebellion, Carlyle took the more philosophic view that it was the just penalty for denying the fundamental moral laws governing human behavior.

Carlyle introduced an interesting theory to explain how a social organism may undergo peaceful mutation indefinitely by constant adaptation of its institutional structure. In all societies there are institutions or "chimneys" through which explosions may come. The revolutionary principle tries every avenue of escape offered by these chimneys before breaking a new crater. In England, for example, revolution is evident in the constant fluidity of government, in the frequent change of ministries, and in a law-making body responsive to the public will even if not always to the social needs.[52] These qualities were not merely manifestations of modern democratic machinery but have characterized English government for centuries, except in the Stuart period, when the Time-Spirit required a Cromwell and drastic measures. Other periods have witnessed plenty of channels for expressing the constantly changing temper of the times. The course of English history, he believed, supported his theory that a society's growth is most rapid, its people's welfare best served, when the necessary and normal institutional modifications were accomplished without the necessity of a violent disruption of the natural flow of events.

In France, on the other hand, the revolutionary spirit, nursed on the *Contrat Social* and the *Rights of Man*, tried the law parliaments as the first avenue of escape. The blind court gave no heed. A second effort at escape was made through the convocation of the Estates General. This time the courtiers found the "touchhold for the well-charged explosive" in refusing to acknowledge the deputies, even ordering them home. The people found their organic significance, and the Third Estate was suddenly endowed with life.[53]

Carlyle believed that some sort of "preternatural machinery" usually sets in motion the "Epos of the Revolution," although he contends there is no real necessity for it. In the case of France it was undoubtedly the starving brigands with whom Paris was overrun who incited the "great dumb beast of St. Antoine" to become one of the moving forces in loosening the ties binding the rotten social structure. Suspicion, dark rumor, and fear galvanized the proletariat into an elemental force, irrational, irresistible and terrible, its mysterious potency as incalculable to itself as to the enemy it was bent on destroying. Tacitus may have inspired Carlyle with the original notion of the mob as an elemental force of nature, though the former usually treated the mob as a senseless, brutal aggregate of human beings reduced to the bestial level through propinquity with so many of their own kind and capable of infinite mischief in the hands of a dominating personality. To Carlyle a mob was less terrible than it was awe-inspiring, even in its most destructive moments. To the historian in particular, he thought, few phenomena could be more portentous; a mob is a genuine outburst of nature, issuing from and communicating with the mysterious depths of consciousness where the principle of life resides. All social explosions have in them "something mad and magical which all life secretly has." They ripen like dumb dreadful forces of nature, yet they are human forces and we are part of them. None of us but possesses the daemonic element of the potential revolutionary.[54]

The "art of insurrection" Carlyle believed to be practically an invention of the French people; though Tacitus claimed the same distinction for the Romans. The vehement Latin temperament, both historians would have agreed, was perfectly adapted to mob expression.[55] Certainly a French mob as Carlyle paints it is one of the liveliest phenomena in history; rapid, audacious, inventive, clear to seize the moment, instinct with life to its finger ends. Here is a true reality, a sincerity deserving the recognition of the poet, and it is as the poet that Carlyle portrays it. Unlike modern battles, which are wearisome to him because they are so mechanistic, Carlyle likened the mob battles, such as the insurrection of women, to the ancient heroic battles of which Homer sang.

The heart of the French Revolution, then, in Carlyle's opinion, lay not in the conduct of the noblesse, nor in the failure of the National Assembly, but in the head and heart of every violent-speaking, violent-thinking French man and woman, impelling and impelled. To a people, compounded of credulity and incredulity, it does not matter greatly what forces set their imaginations to working. But once the revolution prodigy has unfolded itself to terrific stature and articulation, by its own laws and nature, not by formulas or abstractions, it has become unintelligible and incredible to Reason, "the waste chaos of a dream." Since the French Revolution was in a sense leaderless, the unchained forces were left without direction and control to work themselves "lighter and lighter," until they had released what they possessed of "physiological irritability," and perfected themselves "into vitality, into actual vision, and force that can will."[56] For social chaos, in Carlyle's view, always has two elements: one of potential development, and one of ruin. Battle between these two forces is the revolutionary principle.

Had Mirabeau, or even Danton lived, the course of the Revolution might have been different: "a real man might have tamed this chaos, but only time and men, wanting a hero."[57] Not the power of reason but moral force alone avails in guiding and controlling so elemental an organism as an insurrectionary people. This introduces the hero in one of his most typical rôles, but before we discuss the problem of the hero, a brief discussion is needed of the morality of revolution.

THE RIGHT TO REVOLT

Goethe effectively summarized Carlyle's views on the morality of revolution when he said to Eckermann: "A great revolution is never the fault of the people. In fact, revolutions are utterly impossible so long as government is just and vigilant. If the need for revolution exists, however, God is with it and it prospers."[58] Goethe was no friend of the French Revolution, and by nature hated violence and disorder, yet he saw in the rottenness of a social structure the extreme necessity for reform, by violence if peaceful evolutionary means should fail. He did not agree with many of his contemporaries, however, that revolutions constituted a short cut to the millennium. In the end they prove the longest way to accomplish the desired end. It might be mentioned here that Goe-

PHILOSOPHY OF HISTORY

the was probably responsible for certain special aspects of Carlyle's point of view. From him came the fruitful hint that the Diamond Necklace incident marked the real beginning of the revolutionary period. Carlyle seems to have deliberately worked himself into the revolutionary setting by the two trial flights, "Diamond Necklace" and "Cagliostro." It was probably Goethe who made it clear to him that a society so easily duped by an archadventuress and by the prince of quacks was rotten to the core; and that those incidents were not only intrinsically interesting but possessed great value and significance as symptoms of a diseased organism. Carlyle resembles Goethe in being more interested in symptoms than in causes, in diagnosis and prognosis rather than therapy.[59]

In addition to Goethe, however, Carlyle found congenial doctrines regarding the morality of revolution in various other sources. Most of the literary and philosophic writers of the German Renaissance agreed that the revolutionary principle has within it an element of right. They generally agreed, too, that without the power of right, no great revolutionary struggle ever was endowed with the power of might, though the Spinozistic doctrine was found in its most uncorrupted form in Herder and Goethe.

Carlyle, however, did not need to look to the radical political thought of the eighteenth century for the germ of the idea that sovereignty ultimately rests with the people. Man's right to revolt against unjust or wicked rulers had been established not merely as theory but as a practical issue two centuries before by John Knox in his native Scotland. The right of resistance and deposition was elevated to the level of formula by a fellow Scot, George Buchanan, in *De Jure Regni*, a work which constitutes a landmark in the history of political thought.[60] Knox in turn derived his political beliefs from John Calvin, while the latter mainly restated the principles of Thomas Aquinas.[61] It seems unquestionable that such beliefs were a fundamental part of Carlyle's inherited convictions. John Knox was still a lively and potent tradition, particularly among the independent dissenting peasant farmers like Carlyle's parents; and his history of the

Reformation in Scotland probably ranked with the Bible as a staple of popular reading.

Briefly stated, the Calvinist view held that all function and authority come from God. The ordinances of God are the unchanging moral laws of truth and justice, binding upon all men in all times and all places. Earthly laws must be conformable with these natural laws; so, too, must the constitutions of states, and the contracts between sovereigns and peoples. The principle was firmly established that the rulers did not represent the authority of God; on the contrary the highest authority resided in God's laws. Second to them were the people as the source and author of earthly laws. Third were the earthly laws as finite embodiments of God's ordinances. Fourth in order was the sovereign, subject to the laws, to the people as the author of the laws, to God as the author of all. George Buchanan added to this theory of the sovereignty of the people the axiomatic corollary that the many are wiser than one. Here lies the germ of the principle of revolt as Carlyle understood it. The multitude, with deep intuition, is the ultimate judge of the morality of its own acts. Hence, revolt to be morally justified must be a spontaneous expression of a group incited to unpremeditated action.[62] The volition moreover, must come from the instinctual level; it must be a natural act on the moral plane. Given these elements the revolution is morally justified and destined to succeed.

So far has Carlyle advanced beyond the position of Burke. Positing the same sort of social order based upon authority, the same theory of institutional origins based on irrational premises, the same theory of individual psychology, the same theistic belief in the ultimate reality of truth and justice, he yet held that a man's rights are within the ultimate limits of his judgment to determine. Society has the moral right to revolt against outworn institutions from which reality has fled; those which have outlived their functional justification. Society has not only a right but a duty to do this; a mandate laid upon it by the Time-Spirit to refuse to live a lie if it would retain its spiritual birthright. How clearly it hears the mandate and is able to avail itself of the moral might with which the Time-Spirit has silently invested it, depends in large part upon the nature of the leader whom the crisis calls forth. It is at this point that Carlyle's theory of heroes enters his philosophy of history. The hero theory has a dual aspect. As the heart of his biographic approach to history, the theory of heroes will be treated in the next chapter on Carlyle's method. Here we are concerned with the social and political significance of the hero in the interpretation of history.

THE RÔLE OF THE HERO IN HISTORY

In Carlyle's conception the hero constitutes the link between "acted" or universal history and recorded history. It will be recalled that he understood universal history as a process of change whereby the Divine Idea is made manifest to men. Its identity is absolute; its existence independent of humanity. It is coterminous with time; in a sense, it is time, or the Time-Spirit. While the whole meaning and significance of man's life is derived from his relation to the processes of universal history, he is seldom aware of it as an individual.[63] There are occasional individuals, however, endowed with superior moral and intellectual powers who sense the transcendent relationship. They are intuitively aware of the Divine Idea beneath appearances; and have an intimation of the significance of the universal processes going on behind the curtains of prosaic existence. Such individuals are the geniuses, the inspired heroes of history.[64] In their comprehension of the Divine Idea, universal history discovers a crevice through which to reveal itself.

Carlyle developed an embryonic hero theory early. It will be recalled that the first project recorded in the *Notebooks* was a series of biographic and analytic sketches of the leaders of the Puritan Revolution. "How was it such noble minds were generated in those times?" He already suspected that sternly exacting periods call forth heroic qualities, a conviction which grew steadily and became a fixed part of his conception of the nature and quality of the heroic. This independent conception of the hero was nurtured by his reading in German literature. The romantic conception of the hero or genius as an exceptional individual with a plenary inspiration beyond analysis is constantly pervasive in Transcendental literature as well as in the writings of Coleridge and Burke. The hero's power is naïve, God-given, unconscious of itself and capable of varied forms of effective expression. In *Heroes and Hero Worship* Carlyle writes: "For at the bottom, the Great Man, as he comes from the hand of Nature, is ever the same kind of thing: Odin, Luther, Johnson, Burns . . . these are all originally of one stuff."[65] The truly great man could be all sorts of man. He assumes diverse forms, depending on "the kind of world he finds himself born into," the critical nature of the times and his reception by his fellows.

The particular mark of genius is insight, the intellectual power to comprehend reality. When the man of genius possesses in addition sufficient clarity of judgment to base his volitions upon this insight, he is a potential hero, only awaiting the stamp of the time to be transformed into a prophet, a poet, a king, or a warrior. And while Carlyle admits the possibility that many a potential hero is a buried Enceladus, no man ever rises to heroic stature without the peculiar gift of apprehending the reality beneath the show of things. In Schiller's theory of genius he found this congenial reconciliation of the moral and intellectual aspects of genius as different forms of the same essential quality. Carlyle believed it a gross calumny on human nature to say that there ever was a "mind of surpassing talent that did not surpass in capability of virtue; and vice versa."[66]

The hero, whether he be poet, prophet, or king, is conceived of essentially as a man of action. It is everywhere apparent that Carlyle extols action and not thought as the end of man; indeed, in action alone will man find the "certitude which can allay the curse of reflection and its consequent disquiet of mind." All human talent, he says, and especially all deep talent is a talent to do, and is intrinsically of silent nature: "inaudible, like the Sphere Harmonies and Eternal Melodies of which it is an incarnated fraction. All real talent . . . would much rather, if it listened only to Nature's monitions, express itself in rhythmic facts than in melodious words. . . ."[67]

Human talent is a force, a mysterious force emanating from that "thousand-fold complexity of Forces" which is the universe outside ourselves. Call it genius, inspiration, or merely long patience, it has both the power of Reason to comprehend the reality behind appearances, and the "free force direct out of God's own hand" to shape its original thoughts into words or actions, thus awakening the "slumbering capability of all into Thought."[68] The great man is a "portion of the primal reality"; "direct from the Inner Fact of things," he lives in constant communion with it. The Divine Idea reveals itself in many ways, but never more sublimely, more commandingly than in the lives of heroes.

The appearance of heroes in a social organism such as Carlyle assumed is an inevitable corollary. The existence of the indestructible primary qualities of love, fear, religion, wonder, and enthusiasm implies an object of worship. Thus it is the instinct of hero worship which creates the heroes, or at least makes possible the emergence of heroes as a social phenomenon, and not vice versa. Although Carlyle undoubtedly derived his idea of the hero's mission in large part from Fichte, it was from Burke also that he acquired the notion that the individual instinctively subordinates himself to declared authority; finds freedom and security in so doing.[69] "By instinctive eternal ties a submissive respect of what is greatest is rooted in the hearts of all men, even the lowest." In the process of historic change, particularly the upheaval of societies, this faculty of admiration and obedience is the ultimate foundation upon which new and better structures are built. Carlyle's appeal is not to reason but to history; not to a social contract but to expediency. In this phase of his thought more than any other, perhaps, has Professor Cazamian the right to call him the "supreme utilitarian"; a utilitarianism founded on will and instincts, not on understanding.[70]

What part do heroes play in determining the course of history? Certainly a less decisive rôle than many of Carlyle's critics have commonly assumed. In a sense it is unfortunate that Carlyle yielded to the pleadings of friends and to a degree of economic necessity in giving the lectures on heroes. Their publication was inevitable; but it seems not unlikely that Carlyle would have been dismayed if he could have known that in a century his volume on heroes would be more widely read than the *French Revolu-*

tion; and that his name would be practically synonymous with "hero worship." Essentially the idea of heroes and hero worship is only a corollary of his vastly more important theories of the social organism and individual morality. Mere repetition in the volume on heroes, in addition to its strikingly obvious and even picturesque character, gives it a weight out of all proportion to its intrinsic importance in his theories.

The chief value of the hero in the historic process is to define the quality of the age from epoch to epoch. Heroes are the spokesmen, the leaders who have both the power and the vision to articulate what meaning the "primal reality" has for their generation. They do more than openly articulate what all men dimly feel. That is the work of the lesser Voltaires, Scotts. They frequently emerge in periods of social upheaval, when critical dangers call forth the heroic qualities in all men and permit the assumption of power by a true hero. Such heroes appear in the guise of saviors of their epochs, a Luther, or Cromwell, or Napoleon.

More often the heroic force is unable to find expression in the field of action and must be transmuted into the sphere of thought; then the hero becomes a Dante, a Rousseau, a Shakespeare, a Burns. There is no question but that Carlyle puts a higher premium on the hero as a man of action than as a man of thought, partly because of his strongly ethical nature, and his conception of the universe as force; partly because such heroes are rarer and the work they do much more measurably significant from the standpoint of the historian. The achievement of a Dante or a Shakespeare transcends the material limits of written history, possibly is ultimately more significant in acted history, therefore, but has less use for the historian.

While Carlyle comments on the irony of a world in which a Burns found nothing better to do than gauge wine, and a Shakespeare managed a theatre, he relates the work which the hero as poet accomplishes to the silent invisible forces at work in the world, which in the final reckoning are among the mightiest. If the greatest forces working in acted history are the silent ones, then the work of Shakespeare in creating a great tradition whereby far-flung Anglo-Saxon peoples are held together by invisible bonds will last throughout history.[71] Men understand not what is among their hands; therefore it is true that the weightiest causes of historical transactions are likely to be mainly silent. Though as a historian he would find it difficult to so treat it, Carlyle is certain that in universal history Goethe is greater than Napoleon.

Thus it is that the true heroes of history must be distinguished from those who merely made a great noise in their own age—the Tamerlanes, Charles Vs, Voltaires. The verdict depends upon what truth resides in them, a verdict which posterity with sound instinct can always render. In the essay on Voltaire, Carlyle criticized the weakness of historians for "conquerors and revolutionists," whose mere amplitude in recorded history strikes the investigator as signifying a mighty influence. On the contrary, "there is no class of persons creating such an uproar in the world who in the long run produce so slight an impression on its affairs."[72] Johannes Faust and his movable types were vastly more significant in universal history than twenty Tamerlanes. In Carlyle's opinion Voltaire offered an excellent instance of the great agitator often confused by historians with a great man. Voltaire was emphatically a man of his century; uniting in his person whatever spiritual accomplishments were most prized by that age but wanting the depth to perceive its ulterior tendencies. His greatness and his littleness alike fitted him to produce an immediate effect. He railed at the abuses of the Church, for example, and in attempting to destroy it, had no intimation that the entire social structure would inevitably fall with it. In his polemics he merely led "whither the multitude was of itself dimly minded to run," and kept the van not less by skill in commanding than by cunning in obeying.

It seems apparent, then, that the heroes of history are neither the makers of history nor altogether the products of history. It is a case of mutual action and reaction. Nor is their appearance at the proper moment a certainty. Plenty of ages have called loudly for a hero and have gone down to ruin and despair because he did not appear.[73] Such an age was that of the Revolutionary era.

Other ages, on the contrary, have failed to recognize their heroes, the Burnses and Shakespeares who with mighty intellects and incalculable powers of insight and moral force found no active sphere for the use of their energies in their own age.

Carlyle conceived the wide canvas of historical events as linked with the vastly greater movement of which the events themselves are but a part. His real concern as a historian was with the fate of social groups and not of individuals.[74] The heroes of the epic, whose actions and passions offer the historian his primary material, are really borne along on a tide of events to which they are virtually subordinate. The hero's destiny is never self-woven, therefore, as it is usually considered to be by the tragic damatists. It is woven by forces beyond his control and even beyond his knowledge. Yet inasmuch as the group is only to be seen in the named individuals who represent it, there is an instant tendency on the part of the historian to follow the traditions of drama.[75]

THE THEORY OF RIGHT

Wherein lies the might of a Cromwell, a Luther, a Shakespeare, of all who conquer in whatever province? It lies in a balance of moral force. Man's history makes it manifest to the dullest "that mind is stronger than matter; that mind is the creator and shaper of matter; that not brute Force but only Persuasion and Faith is the king of this world."[76] Or again, "it is ever to be kept in mind that not by material but by moral power are men and their actions governed."[77] Carlyle's conception of the primacy of the human will regards it as the cement which holds the social fabric in place. The hero possesses both the will and the vision to use his moral force effectively. In this sense he possesses a divine right to rule, and upon lesser men is imposed the duty of obeying him.

From Goethe and indirectly from Spinoza Carlyle derived the axiom that in a moral universe, right and power are one and the same. Every man or cause receives from nature for working purposes exactly as much power as he has right. Spinoza argued that the natural right of nature as a whole, and therefore of every individual thing contained in nature, extends only so far as its power. Therefore, what any single man does by the laws of his nature he does in virtue of an absolute right, and his right over nature extends as far as his power.[78] With Spinoza this doctrine is based ultimately on expediency, and rigorously excludes all questions of moral obligation or duty. Burke interpreted Spinoza's political doctrine to admit of those primary ideas of humanity, truth, and justice, which for reasons of logic had been excluded.[79] In Burke's view expediency can only be understood in the light of a large number of other ideas and instincts, religion, tradition, reverence for the past and the unconscious desire to perpetuate it in the present.[80]

Transcendental thought was thoroughly impregnated with the doctrine that might should and must reside in right. Coming down from Kant through Fichte we find the clearest and most explicit expression of the might of right in the *Staatslehre*. There Fichte writes:

> To compel men to adopt the rightful form of government, to impose Right on them by force, is not only the right but the sacred duty of every man who has both the insight and the power to do so. There may even be circumstances when the single man has this right against the whole of mankind; for as against him and Right, there is no man who has either rights or liberty.[81]

In him lies the compulsive power ordained of God.

Carlyle held the same theory of imperious individual authority and pushed it to extreme limits in attacking the idols of liberty and democracy current in his day. It is not, however, to be confused with the Nietzschean theory of the superman, as it so often is. Nietzsche's doctrine was based on individualism, with anarchy as its logical ultimate. He placed the individual in the center of his system, permitted the individual's ego to spur him to activity of which he is both the cause and effect, the beginning and end. The sole mission of the individual ego is to acquire the power and knowledge necessary to realize his latent possibilities. Professor Cazamian, in contrasting Carlyle and Nietzsche, calls Carlyle's doctrine "moral collectivism," the very opposite of

Nietzschean individualism.[82] The hero is not an end in himself, but an instrument of the transcendent will. Realizing his possibilities is less a harmonious development of his whole being than the successful transmission of the divine inspiration he possesses. The source of the hero's force ultimately is not within but without himself. The sincerity and selflessness which constitute the strict conscience of the hero, an inalienable attribute of his heroic quality, guarantee his awareness of the superhuman control to which he in turn is subject.

The disintegration of modern governmental authority and the rise of a dictator class Carlyle would probably regard less as a vindication of his theories of authority (though they are that), than as a fulfillment of his prophetic warnings regarding the shortcomings of democracy. His emphasis on the rough instinctive forces at work in human society, the blind processes of nature which must somehow be reconciled with the eternal course of the divine will, leaves room for the working out of such a phenomenon as the contemporary dictator. His sympathetic and admiring portrait of Dr. Francia is further evidence that the utilitarian aspects of his hero theory would measure the value of the dictator in terms of his tangible success. If the dictator brings order out of chaos and imposes a fruitful authority upon the people whom he governs, he is succeeding because there resides in him enough moral force to justify success. "I will allow a thing to struggle for itself in this world," Carlyle wrote, "with any sword or tongue or implement it has, or can lay hold of ... very sure that it will, in the long run, conquer nothing that does not deserve to be conquered. What is better than itself it cannot put away, but only what is worse. In this great Duel, Nature herself is umpire, and can do no wrong: the thing that is deepest rooted in Nature, what we call truest, that thing and not the other will be found growing at last."

THE CONCEPT OF CAUSE

In the foregoing discussion we have shown Carlyle's philosophy of history to comprehend the world not as a-being but as eternally becoming, in the words of Goethe. The historic process as a causal whole or unity within the limits of time possesses two fundamental characteristics, continuity and change. It is not a series of endlessly recurring cycles, as the Greeks conceived it; nor a drama with a climax in the appearance of the Messiah and a dénouement in the destruction of the world, as the Hebrews and later the Christian theologians conceived it. It is a ceaseless process of action and reaction, through phase after phase, spiraling slowly upward toward a better realization of man's latent capacities.

Such an interpretation of collective behavior assumes some theory of motivation. What underlies the dialectic process of action and reaction, growth and decay, creation and criticism which characterizes the historic process? Conflict, said Carlyle; conflict in the arena of human will. The idea of conflict as the dynamic force underlying the mutability of the social mechanism is as old as the Christian philosophy of history, where it is dramatized as a perpetual battle between God and Satan for the soul of man. In rationalist theory it is discovered as the intellectual conflict of ideas seeking domination, only to be dominated in turn by new ideas. In romantic and Transcendental historiography it was held by Schiller to be a conflict between tyranny and freedom; in Kant a conflict between social interests with selfish ends to serve, working toward a perfect government. In Hegel we have conflict as the motivation of the historic process, and stemming from Hegel the modern Marxian dialectic.

Carlyle visualized the conflict which underlies the continuous becoming of the historic process in terms both of the individual and the group. With the individual the struggle is plainly the ancient one between necessity and free will. The "ring of necessity" is forged of the unescapable moral laws within whose scope the free will struggles to assert itself. The free will, parent of all volitional activity, is grounded in the primary instincts no less than the innate ideas regarding the moral laws. The meaning of life is freedom, voluntary force, yet it is compassed round with sternest necessity. To each of us is given a certain inward talent, and outward environment of fortune. In these we find the maximum of capability, the limit of freedom. To those who accept the categorical imperative, the divine law of duty, as their gospel of freedom, a fruitful and productive harmony of powers results. Carlyle held to the logical truism, so pervasive in the thought of his day, that complete obedience to moral law contains the maximum of freedom.

In the sphere of the social group, the conflict is waged between the institutional forces which are still alive and those no longer fulfilling their functional purpose: the "ceaseless conflict between Innovation and Conservation." In this larger conflict the individual is lost in the group and is mainly unaware of the mysterious forces which control his social volitions. These larger mass movements are the true stuff of the historic process. Volition therefore is both voluntary and involuntary. In individual behavior it appears voluntary within definite limits. In social behavior it is mainly involuntary. Thus the movement of "free human minds" becomes a "transcendent fanaticism," a "raging tornado of fatalism, blind as the winds."[83] "Strange," Carlyle wrote in the *French Revolution*, "the man's cloak seems to hold the same man, yet the man is not there, nor the source of what he will do or devise. Instead of the man and his volition there is a piece of fanaticism and fatalism incarnated in the shape of him." The incarnated fanaticism goes his road; he cannot be helped, nor can he help himself. Carlyle is speaking here, of course, of the volitional state in a period of social upheaval, but the difference is only one of degree in more peaceful times. "To such heights of miracle can men work on men; the Conscious and the Unconscious blended inscrutably in this our inscrutable life; endless Necessity environing Free-Will."

Civilization is only a wrappage through which man's savage nature can occasionally burst. The world of nature, of which man is a part, has an "Infernal in her as well as a Celestial." The struggle of the celestial to free itself from the infernal, or better to tame and regularize the infernal, is another aspect of the conflict motivating the historic process. Out of chaos is born the world of order. In the French Revolution Carlyle saw "dim chaos . . . struggling through all of its elements; writhing and chafing towards some creation." This constituted his solution of the problem of theodicy.

Sterling once remarked of Carlyle: "I find ... his fundamental position is, the good of evil: the idleness of trying to jump off one's shadow."[84] Certainly Carlyle's theory of sin was founded on a fundamental optimism. "No matter how evil a thing is; in it is some good trying to free itself; an Ideal struggling to come forth out of dark Chaos; live its day, then depart."[85] "Without evil," he declared in *Sartor*, "there was no good." This paradox dawned on him slowly, as he records in *Sartor*, but became a fixed principle from which he never departed. For a ratification of his belief he again turned, not to faith or to reason, but to history. The witty but caustic remark of his friend Henry James is recalled in this connection. Carlyle was forever under the dismal necessity "to ransack the graves of the dead, in order to find some spangle, still untarnished, of God's reputed presence in our nature."[86]

In summary, Carlyle grasped the essence of the traditional dualism in history, which was sharpened to a point of open conflict in the nineteenth century, and reconciled the antithetic points of view more impressively than any historian before or since.[87] On the one hand was the living independent value of the historic event which occurs but once and is determinate in itself. On the other was the abstract law—the generic concept of change in time—which emphasized not the individual form but the social life and its historical development from the point of view of modern scientific developments. "In this aspect the essence of the historical view of the world has been by no one so deeply grasped ... and warmly set forth as by Carlyle."[88]

IV

THE ART OF HISTORY IN THEORY

"THE STORY OF THE TIME HAT"

IN 1833 Carlyle wrote to his brother: "My mind would so fain deliver itself of that 'Divine Idea of the World.' I want to write what Teufelsdröckh calls the Story of the *Time Hat;* to show forth to the men of these days that they also live in an Age of Miracles." Universal history offers humanity both the sublimest revelation and the most indubitable proof of the existence of the "Divine Idea." Recorded history, when written by one who has the key to the "engraved Hierograms" which are the facts of history, is an inspired text wherein we may find revealed the meaning of existence in terms of a moral universe based on unchanging laws of truth and justice. The present age is always so restricted and even blinded by the modalities of space and time that the perspective and discernment needful for a realization of the grand mysteries of existence, of human life and personality is wanting in all but its great men, its poets and thinkers. Carlyle believed that no miracle approached this of "clapping on the Time-Hat"; of conversing face to face with Paul and Seneca in the first century, and also conversing face to face with other Pauls and Senecas buried in the depths of future time.[1] While all art, properly considered, embodied this insight into the ultimate realities behind appearances, the writing of history ranked first because its materials contained the most authentic repository of truth and reality.

Carlyle wrote his brother in 1832 that his "trade" is to "write truth while I can be kept alive by so doing, and to die writing it when I can no longer be kept alive."[2] *Quid est Veritas?* Like many another artist, Carlyle believed he had an answer to Pilate's question. Truth, he believed, is the reality behind the veil of appearance, the soul of fact, the inexhaustible attribute lending meaning and dignity to man's life, the imperishable element in art, in religion, in history. Truth is ever to be sought and never wholly discovered. Each succeeding age sets out on the quest afresh and deposits what it can discover in its art, in its religion, in its manner of living. Truth, like its correlative, beauty (with which Carlyle identified it) is not a separate entity but an attribute with which the human mind invests certain aspects of its experience. It is a subjective value; a value without meaning except in terms of human judgment.

In his conception of truth, Carlyle epitomized the whole meaning and purpose of art as he understood it; and, in addition, summarized his principles of literary composition. After evolving his principles, he turned to history to find them exemplified; since, by his own definition, he had made history the repository of facts possessing the twin attributes of reality and vitality. What was his conception of the "art of history" and how did he arrive at it?

Carlyle did not turn to the past to escape from the uncertainty and confusion of the present, as Henry James would have us believe.[3] On the contrary, he turned to the past for the sake of the present. Seizing the truth, as it lies embalmed in the past, is not easy; but Carlyle believed it to be infinitely easier than discovering it in present events. A critical discontent with his own age was a fundamental quality of Carlyle's, possibly the primary motive animating his writing; but he sought to admonish it, not to escape from it. He observed once to his brother that he had a "deep Ernulphus curse" to pronounce on "gigmanity" before his work was done. John Sterling told him his nature was "political"; and Carlyle acknowledged in mid-career that the oracle had verified itself beyond expectations. He had the subtle gift of the born historian of thinking himself into another age and sharing its thoughts, emotions, conflicts. At the same time he never forgot that he was writing for the nineteenth century. While writing *Cromwell*, he wrote to Emerson: "For my heart is sick and sore on behalf of my own poor generation . . . thus do the two centuries stand related to me, the seventeenth *worthless* except precisely insofar as it can be made the nineteenth; and yet let anybody *try* that enterprise!"[4]

A still more important reason for turning to history to discover the Divine Idea behind appearance is the imperishable quality of truth. A certain distance in time permits the untruths to be winnowed out while the age's real leaders and most significant happenings gradually come to the surface. As we pointed out earlier, Carlyle believed that men and their actions are governed by moral, not material, power. The so-called "chain of causes" controlling the sequence of events is not a *superficies* but a solid, and is not discernible at all except from a distance. To prove this, Carlyle cited his favorite example of faulty historic judgment. Tacitus was the wisest, most penetrating man of his time, but so superficial was his insight into the importance of a nearly contemporary event that he dismissed in a sentence the "baneful superstition" of "that class, hated for their wickedness . . . called Christians." The same "uncertainty, in estimating present things and men holds more or less in all times . . . for human society rests on inscrutably deep foundations; which he is of all others the most mistaken, who fancies he has explored to the bottom."[5] The onlooker tends to estimate importance by mere magnitude, by the degree of noise and tumult raised by the "conquerors and political revolutionists," while the true forces governing the world are precisely those silent ones working deep beneath the surface of everyday events.

A third reason drawing Carlyle to the writing of history was the esthetic nature of historical material. The records of the past are among the most malleable of imaginative materials because they are endowed, without effort on the part of the artist, with a quality of esthetic objectivity, a quality which some psychologists call "psychic distance."[6] They possess both spatial and temporal separation, and by means of this separation the artist's personal emotional experiences may be projected and made esthetically valid. The artist can actually attain a more intimate and personal relationship with his audience by filtering his ideas through distance and lending them a strange beauty and impressiveness. Carlyle recognized this quality in the material of history, and accounts for it on the grounds of the poetic value residing in reality, as we shall see later. It is the fundamental source of his conviction that history and poetry may be identified, and the basis for a conception of history as the "highest kind of writing, far higher than any kind of Fiction even of the Shakespeare sort. For my own share," he declared, "I now enjoy no other Poem than the dim, shadowy as yet only possible *Poem,* that hovers for me in every seen Reality...."[7]

Although Carlyle's profound interest in historical literature dates from his earliest youth, and he seems always to have regarded orthodox history as the "highest of the arts," the working definition he finally gave to the business of the historian was original and arbitrary, and at the same time a consistent part of a closely reasoned theory. The writing of formal history *qua* history presumably interested him less than the employment of the poetico-historical medium for representing in authentic and comprehensible terms his psychologic insights into the springs of human behavior. Wilson believed he wrote history, not because he was academically interested in uncovering and preserving the past, but because he had to write something, and could not lose himself sufficiently to write fiction or drama.[8]

As a matter of fact, up to the completion of *Sartor,* it is quite possible to imagine Carlyle fashioning some form of the novel as a catch-all for his social criticism, his speculations, and his humane interests. *Wotton Reinfred* was an attempt at a "didactic novel" and admittedly not promising. But *Sartor,* also called a "didactic novel" by its author, was historical in method and autobiographic in content.[9] In form it pointed the way to the historical romances, *The Diamond Necklace* and *Cagliostro,* in which Carlyle was deliberately experimenting with a "poetico-historical" narrative technique. These writings only hint at what Carlyle might have accomplished, had he chosen, working with historical materials but using the flexible novel medium. The heyday of the novel had not yet arrived, of course, and Carlyle was handicapped further by a temperamental prejudice against "fictioneering." He was conscious, moreover, of a want of invention; but this difficulty, if it had proved a real one, would have been largely overcome by the use of historical materials.[10]

The student of Carlyle as a historian is tempted to sigh a little over the irony of the widespread disparagement of his histories on the ground that they read like novels. If he had adopted some form of the philosophic novel, it is probable that his final output would not have been greatly different in artistic value, truth to nature, and impressiveness of intellectual and moral worth. He would have used his great gifts for the same essential ends, and by trespassing on the spirit but not the letter of the jealously guarded province of Dryasdust, he would have been spared the shafts and darts of "envious calumniators."

Miss Thrall suggests that *Fraser's* encouragement of an exploratory and inventive attitude toward literary forms and methods gave scope and stimulus to Carlyle's biographic tendencies.[11] Emphasis on biographic treatment was a fixed policy of *Fraser's;* but Carlyle had his biographic predilections before his association with the magazine began. Their strengthening may have been partly the result of *Fraser's* policies; partly, too, it was a normal development. An influence even stronger in this direction than that exerted by *Fraser's* came from Carlyle's friendship with John Stuart Mill, most valued of his early London acquaintances. Mill's father was a historian of respectable attainment.[12] Mill himself was collecting the materials for a history of the French Revolution when Carlyle was in London in 1831; and the pressure of other duties induced him to offer his resources to Carlyle, who was already keenly interested in the revolutionary period.

From the moment when Carlyle first fixed his attention seriously on the project of writing on the Revolution, he began whipping into form his practical theories regarding history and historical writing, most of which had their genesis earlier but did not take specific and practical shape until he had a definite project in his eye. The essay "On History," written just before the London visit alluded to above, drafts a theory of historical writing which no man could hope to apply. But the later essay, "Biography," outlines a practical scheme for a new and unique kind of social history.

THE BIOGRAPHIC APPROACH

Carlyle's evolution from an ambitious youth with more or less undefined yearnings toward literature, to a historian with a well-formulated theory of his craft, was a slow spinning of inclinations and aptitudes into a single strand which might be termed the biographic interest: a psychologic concern for the fundamental motives underlying human life and behavior. He set forth the elements in historical research which particularly attracted him in a letter to Mill in 1833. Having just read Thiers' *Histoire de la Révolution Française,* he reported that Thiers overlooked the most important aspect of the matter: i.e., the "private-biographic phasis; the manner in which individuals demeaned themselves, and social life went on, in so extraordinary an element . . . for the 'thin rind of Habit' was utterly rent off; and man stood there with all the powers of Civilization, and none of its rules to aid him in guiding these. There is much I would fain investigate farther in this sense. . . ."[13] This was precisely the aspect of the Revolution which Carlyle's history did investigate.

The "unspeakable delight in Biography" which Carlyle attributed to "man's sociality of nature" is a generalization based on his own profound preferences. "Man is perenially interesting to man," he wrote in "Biography," "nay, if we look strictly to it, *there is nothing else interesting.*"[14] Emotionally and intellectually he was committed to the belief that knowing our fellow creatures is the beginning and end not only of literature and criticism, but of all art, science, morality and religion.

> How inexpressibly comfortable to know our fellow creature; to see into him, understand his goings-forth, decipher the whole heart of his mystery: nay, not only to see into him, but to see out of him, to view the world as he views it; so that we can theoretically construe him, and could almost practically personate him; and do now thoroughly discern both what manner of man he is, and what manner of thing he has got to work on and live on!

The pervasive and deeply rooted humane interest evidenced in this and similar passages characterized Carlyle from his earliest youth. It largely guided his early preferences in literature; and had a shaping hand in the molding of his theories of art and history.

When Carlyle came to develop his esthetic theories he grounded them on the biographic interest. The "business of biography" is practised and relished in nearly all phases of man's daily life. Our common speech, for example, is almost altogether biographic; so is our art. Even our interest in and enjoyment of art is mainly of the biographic sort. Thus the biographic interest is the source not only of the artist's inspiration but of his appeal.

In the Art we can nowise forget the Artist; while looking on the *Transfiguration*, while studying the *Iliad* we ever strive to figure to ourselves what spirit dwelt in Raphael; what a head was that of Homer, wherein ... that old world fashioned itself together, of which these written Greek characters are but the feeble though perennial copy.

Had the *Transfiguration* been painted without human hand, a lichen picture on a rock, for example, it would afford us nothing like the esthetic pleasure it does because the biographic interest would be wanting; and "pitiful Littlenesses as we are," we turn always to worship at man-made shrines.

Of history Carlyle believed the whole purport to be biographic; although the "feast of widest biographic insight" which our appetite hungrily anticipates most often proves to be a "mere Ossian's feast of shells." In any case, we bring to the reading of history the perennial hope of "gaining some acquaintance with our fellow creatures, though dead and vanished ...; how they got along in those old days, suffering and doing; ... how, in short, the perennial Battle went, which men call Life, which we also ... with indifferent fortune, have to fight, and must bequeath to our sons and our grandsons to go on fighting,— till ... the Volume of Universal History wind itself up." Even the whole class of "Fictitious Narratives" from the highest category of epic or dramatic poetry down to the lowest of "froth Prose," contains nothing but mimic biographies, endeavoring to deliver the "grand secret wherewith all hearts labor oppressed:

the Significance of Man's Life." Carlyle conceded that the highest of these, the work of Homer, Shakespeare, and Goethe, for example, is a reality no less than the truest history.[15] It partakes of the same qualities of insight, of verisimilitude, of power to compel belief.

In analyzing the biographic element in art and what qualities in it excite our interest, Carlyle decided that it had both "poetic and scientific" aspects; a scientific aspect, because everyone has the problem of existence set before him, and derives instruction from the biographic expression of others' experience. A poetic interest inheres still more; for precisely the "same struggle of human Free-Will against material Necessity, which every man's Life . . . will more or less victoriously exhibit,—is that which above all else . . . calls the Sympathy of mortal hearts into action; and whether as acted, or as represented and written of, not only is Poetry, but is the sole Poetry possible." Thus each individual whom we encounter in acted or written poetry is a "mirror both scientific and poetic . . . both natural and magical;—from which one would so gladly draw aside the gauze veil; and peering therein, discern the image of his own natural face, and the supernatural secrets that prophetically lie under the same."

Carlyle's treatment of the biographic interest is placed in an interesting light when compared with Emerson's position on the same issue. "We are always coming up with the emphatic facts of history and verifying them here," wrote Emerson. "All history becomes subjective; in other words, there is properly no history, only biography. Every mind must know the whole lesson for itself; must go over the whole ground. What is does not see, what it does not live, it will not know."[16] Thus Emerson develops his fundamental conviction that the "world exists for the education of each man." The facts of the past are a tremendous educational force, particularly when "dissolved in the shining ether of poetry." But they are more than a means to an end; they are also an end in itself. To appreciate them fully, man "must attain that lofty sight where facts yield forth their secret sense, and poetry and annals are alike."

Carlyle's thought was not dominated by an optimism so unqualified as Emerson's. The latter epitomized the attitude of a youthful civilization, rich in possibilities beyond the dreams of any but its philosophers. In a country like Emerson's, boundless in resources and hope, it was safe to assume a universe of transcendent moral goodness and order; even to identify nature with God. That the world existed for the education of the individual was a possible assumption when there were not more individuals than could reasonably expect to make a decent showing in the process. The uses of history were to instruct, therefore; to guide; to elevate.

Carlyle's universe was both grimmer and more human. The sheer struggle for existence in an overcrowded arena was one phase of man's battle; the other was the conflict between necessity and free will in his own soul. History was the loftiest of the arts in serving both of the primary human needs. It offered instruction in man's struggle for existence, as Emerson believed; but even more important, it offered sympathy, encouragement, and inspiration in the dark conflict man wages in his own soul. The human life is too brief to show evidence of the purpose and design which Carlyle believed underlay reality. One must turn to history for convincing and irrefutable proof that the universe is a moral universe grounded on the fundamental laws of truth and justice.

Carlyle's theory of the biographic purport of art and of history as occupying a supreme place among the arts does not neglect the nature of the esthetic response. He seems to have been wholly committed to the belief that the esthetic experience is volitional in character.[17] It is based on an act of will whereby the subject identifies himself with the artist; sees with his eyes; understands with his mind; shares his feelings. This theory, resembling in many respects the modern theory of empathy, was based on the assumption that the artist differs from other men only in degree. His perceptions have a heightened quality; his insights are more penetrating; his judgments more valid. But his audience is capable of sharing his perceptions, his insights, his judgments. Depending on the degree of their talents, the pleasure they take is "streaked with the same strange joy" the artist experienced in creation. "A vein of poetry resides in all of us, and each becomes a poet when he reads a poem well."[18] The imagination which "shudders at the Hell of Dante, is the same faculty, weaker in degree, which called that picture into being." The poet and the artist are present to us; "we partially and for the time become the very Painter and the very Singer, while we enjoy the Poem and the Song."

THE DEVELOPMENT OF THE BIOGRAPHIC METHOD

The decade of Carlyle's great critical essays is extremely important in any study of the development of the later historian. In it we witness the formulation of his theories of history and historical writing, and the development of the biographic method. The biographic approach to literature and art received gradually increasing emphasis as it became more and more the fundamental method in his critical writing. His critical theory was predicated on the assumption that the artist's mind and his work represent an organic unity and that the one cannot be understood without knowing the other. In criticism, as later in his histories, Carlyle always displayed the keenest curiosity in discovering an inner harmony between a man's life and his works. He declared his purpose, as early as the *Life of Schiller*, to be the ascertainment by "what gifts and what employment of them [Schiller] reached the eminence on which we now see him; to follow the steps of his intellectual and moral culture; to gather from his life and works some picture of himself. It is worth inquiring, whether he who could represent noble actions so well, did himself act nobly. . . ."[19]

The early essays formulate the same theory of a biographic approach to the problems of criticism. Critic and historian must search for answers to the same questions: "What manner of man is this? How shall we interpret, how shall we even see him? What is his spiritual structure, what at least are the outward form and features of his mind. . . ?"[20] Likewise the highest function of criticism (and of history) is to "grasp the soul and spiritual existence by which alone the body and its movements can be informed with life."[21] Neither the critic nor the historian is interested in the mechanism whereby Addison struck out similitudes, but in the far more mysterious mechanism whereby Shakespeare organized his dramas; gave life and individuality to his characters.

The critic's problem became identified more and more with the biographer's as Carlyle's historical tendencies gained ascendancy. In the first essay on Goethe he wrote that the chief question for the critic is "not only what were these works but how did they originate." In the succeeding essay on Burns he phrased the problem altogether from the point of view of the biographer, intent on probing the "inward springs and relations" of his subject's character: "How did the world and man's life, from his particular position, represent themselves to his mind? How did co-existing circumstances modify him from without; how did he modify these from within? . . . What and how produced was the effect of society on him; what and how produced was his effect on society?"[22] Carlyle conceded that these exacting specifications "furnish a model of perfection in biography," but he added that if a man is great enough to justify a biography of any sort, he deserves one patterned over such a model.

In biographical criticism a premium is placed on lives lived and events completed in the past, with a parallel tendency to under-rate the work of the present. But what constituted a fault in criticism was a gain in history. As Carlyle's essays became more and more biographic, they tended to become less and less critical.[23] The essays in the period after 1830 show a steadily increasing emphasis on the historical interest, even when treating professedly literary themes such as Johnson, Diderot, Mirabeau, and Scott. Carlyle revealed a parallel tendency to write on non-literary themes, though there his choice was partly speculative, partly critical, partly historical. The purely literary interest did not so much wane as become merged with the historical interest; and finally it was completely absorbed. Carlyle seemed scarcely aware of the gradual substitution of historical for literary standards, because at all times his fundamental, acknowledged interest was in the man, and the man's work was considered primarily as a medium for approaching the man. The tendencies which finally became paramount were latent in the earliest essays.

The year 1830 is not only a convenient dividing line between the early literary essays and the later biographic essays, but also seems to have been the decisive year in Carlyle's development. In that year he finished the first draft for *Sartor,* the long essay called *Thoughts on Clothes*. In the same year he wrote "certain abstruse Thoughts on History." This brief essay indicates that Carlyle's thoughts were turning seriously in the direction of historical writing as a medium of creative expression. It may be recalled that he had scattered his opinions on the writing of history freely over his writings before elaborating them in the essay "On History." Indeed, there is little in it which he had not expressed, or hinted at, earlier, particularly in the *Life of Schiller* and the essay on Voltaire. But the essay is worth examining for the general principles he considered it necessary to set forth. The tone is self-conscious and critical, with little of the impressive force and self-assurance which marks the essay "Biography" as the greatest of his speculative essays.

History is the root of all science and the "first distinct product of man's spiritual nature."[24] A talent for it is inborn; in a sense all men are historians; the whole frame of existence may be conceived to be historical. By means of history men war against oblivion; uniting themselves with the future as well as the past. This sense of looking both before and after, the intimation that the coming time waits, unseen, yet definitely shaped, in the time come, gives to human life some of its most prized qualities—security, hope, immortality, for example. Thus history unites with prophecy.

Written history, Carlyle acknowledged, has always ranged among the highest of the arts. But it has taken on a new character since the days of Herodotus. Instead of minstrel and story teller, it has become a "school Mistress"; more than that, a "free emporium" where all kinds of "belligerents peaceably meet and furnish themselves." Sentimentalist and utilitarian, sceptic and idealist, all urge us to examine history and there find the proof we need and desire. Yet Carlyle considered it dubious that "historical philosophy" has yet furnished a clear answer to the real problem: "What the aim and significance of that wondrous changeful Life it investigates and paints may be." What is the course of man's destiny; or is it really guided forward by an unseen, mysterious wisdom? These altogether fundamental questions have been glanced at "only dubiously and from afar," because two almost insurmountable difficulties lie in the way. "Before Philosophy can teach by Experience, the Philosophy has to be in readiness, the Experience must be gathered and intelligibly recorded."[25]

At this point Carlyle arrived at the heart of the historian's problem as he saw it. Forgetting the philosophy for the moment, he said: "Where can we find the experience gathered and intelligibly recorded? The current of human affairs is too intricate, unfathomable, to be fully understood by any man, even if the true representation of it were possible. Social life is the aggregate of all individual lives, but which of us is able to render intelligible even our own biography? If we do not understand ourselves and our own age, how much less may we know of other ages and other lives, the inward condition of which was not only unlike our own but the outward record of it faultily or inadequately preserved.

The record of battles and wars, of laws and political constitutions does not represent "our Life, but only the house wherein our Life is led . . . whose essential furnitures, the inventions, and traditions, and daily habits that regulate our existence" are the work, not of the men whose names are preserved in the record of history, but the nameless innovators, the "long forgotten train of artists and artisans; who . . . have been jointly teaching us how to think and act, how to rule over spiritual and physical nature." It was part of Carlyle's central conviction that the enormous opulence of life in this universe surpasses comprehension. Shakespeare might easily have remained silent. Cromwell, "the best king we ever had," narrowly missed spending his days as a grazier at Ely; while Luther, likewise, missed by only a little living and dying as an obscure Dominican. "Wherever I go or stand," he once wrote Sterling, "I find the *inarticulate* dust of

Poets (of Makers, Inventors, great struggling souls ...) and I say to myself, 'There have been millions and millions of poets and hundreds of them have been Shakespeares.' ...."[26]

Carlyle emphasized the fact in 1830 that recorded experience is inevitably imperfect and will always be so. The real features of an historical transaction are never committed to the record; but at best "some more or less plausible scheme and theory of the Transaction."[27] There is always a fatal discrepancy between our manner of seeing events and their manner of occurring. Observation is limited by space-time coördinates; it must be successive, while the events occurring were simultaneous. In the "ever-living, ever-working Chaos of Being," occurrences are never so simply related to one another as they appear in our observation. For all action must be figured as three-dimensional, extending in length, breadth and depth; while observation and its record in narrative is necessarily linear or two-dimensional. It is apparent that the historian capable of solving these problems has never appeared ; and is not likely to appear.

The unfathomable nature of history leads to the necessity for a distinction between the two great classes of workers who delve in that quarry—the artist and the artisan. The need for both sorts is readily observed, though Carlyle laments the tendency current in his day to cope with the infinite nature of history by mere division of labor, aggravating the already strong "mechanical tendencies" of the age. The men who "labour mechanically in a department [of history], without eye for the whole" are the artisans, the simple husbandmen who are not to be blamed for disregarding the inscrutable and infinite mystery of man's destiny except when they deny its existence. The artist-historian, on the other hand, "informs and ennobles the humblest department of history with an Idea of the whole." He must be aware of the "mighty tide of Thought and Action" that rolls on its course away from scenes in senate-houses or king's antechambers. The time has come, Carlyle believed, when the historian, to deserve the name, must depict "not the outward condition of man's life but the inward and spiritual."[28]

The findings of the essay *On History* may be seen to be largely negative. Carlyle assessed the difficulties and impossibilities of writing what he conceived to be the ideal history. He urged the necessity of a new, subjective approach to history. At the same time he acknowledged that such history would require a philosophy for its interpretation, and intelligibly recorded experience for its material, neither of which had ever been available hitherto. And even if the philosophy were in readiness, and the experience legibly recorded, there would be a final difficulty of expression because historical action is three-dimensional, while ordinary historical narrative is merely linear. The essay ends on a note of philosophic defeat.

Two years later Carlyle recurred to the problems of historical writing in the essay prefatory to the critical review of the Croker edition of Boswell's *Johnson*. This essay, entitled "Biography," and the attendant train of speculative thought apparently had been touched off by a careful study of Boswell's great biography in an effort to determine what qualities made it so compelling as history. His general opinions on Boswell had doubtless been formulated long before, but it seems a plausible assumption that the solutions he had found by 1832 for many of the theoretical problems nagging him in 1830 were suggested, at least in part, by a restudy of Boswell. Certainly he realized that he had a model for historical narrative satisfying even his exacting requirements. The portrait of Johnson is three-dimensional; it is alive; it is credible; and it offers the reader a deep view, not only of the outward condition, but the inward and spiritual life of eighteenth century England. It is pleasant to imagine that the encouragement of Boswell's example stimulated Carlyle to formulate the positive theories of historical writing toward which he had long been tending.

The groundwork of Carlyle's formula as he developed it in "Biography" is built upon the primary importance of the biographic interest, not only in history but in all art. The artist derives from the biographic element the means of seizing and delineating facts; while at the same time the reader finds it the source of his esthetic enjoyment of the finished work. Carlyle attributed this dual rôle of the biographic element to the psychological power of reality to compel belief. Thus the historian's materials may and probably will be faulty and inadequate, but if he properly *possesses* those materials and conveys them in terms of three-dimensional poetic reality, the reader will have an insight into the "inward life and spiritual condition" of the time portrayed.

Carlyle arrived at the conclusion that not the "material, not the susceptibility" were wanting for the creation of literature that would partake of reality; the thing wanting was the poet to work on these.[29] By exploiting more and more the sphere of reality, call it history or poetry, and searching for its inexhaustible meanings, the artist might restore to literature the transcendental qualities of poetic beauty and truth it possessed in the great creative ages of the past. Such a mission he believed to be open to the one who would endeavor to write history on the basis of the subjective principles of philosophic interpretation and poetic re-creation of the lives of past peoples.

In May 1833 Carlyle published the third and last of his speculative essays on the writing of history. In this brief paper, entitled "On History Again," he advanced still further along the road toward a constructive theory by establishing a realistic basis for the selection of historical data. Since history consists of all we speak and do, and properly considered includes all other studies, the perfect history is clearly an impossibility. Yet since history is the "Letter of Instructions, which the old generations write and posthumously transmit to the new . . . the only *articulate* communication . . . which the Past can have with the Present," our "shred of a letter" is "unspeakably precious."[30] With considerable ingenuity Carlyle then analyzed the process whereby the "magic Web" of universal history weaves itself forward, by a mixture of "philosophic insight and indolent neglect," out of the "ravelled immeasurable mass of threads and thrums, which we name *Memoirs*."[31] By *Memoirs* Carlyle designated the entire output of the "historic organs" with which Nature has endowed man in order that this same "Letter of Instructions" might reach us in "boundless plenitude"—the miraculous faculties of speech and of writing. Clearly, he decided, the historical inquirer can never want pabulum, or the raw materials of such.

The problem is not scarcity of output at all, but the right

principles for the selection and compression of the "autobiography" of mankind which accumulates daily. Here again Nature has been kind in endowing man with an unconscious talent for forgetting as well as a like unconscious talent for remembering. "Memory and Oblivion . . . like all other contradictions in this strange dualistic Life of ours, are necessary for each other's existence: Oblivion is the dark page, whereon Memory writes her light-beam characters, and makes them legible." The noisy transactions of the day are partly effaced by the new clamors of the morrow, and "in the immeasurable conflict and concert of this chaos of existence, figure after figure sinks . . . what cannot be kept in mind will even go out of mind; History contracts itself into readable extent."

Carlyle admitted that the entire wisdom of such a system of "contraction and epitome" was open to question. The events worthiest to be known are frequently the ones least spoken of; "it lies in the very nature of such events to be so." A "moral Pancirollus" could find plenty of material for a "mournful Book of Virtues Lost," reciting the lives of noble men, "doing and daring and enduring, whose heroic life, as a new revelation and development of Life itself, were a possession for all, but is now lost and forgotten, History otherwise having filled her page." Nevertheless, "by a natural tendency alone, and as it were without man's forethought, a certain fitness of selection" does inevitably occur. Men permanently speak

> only of what is extant and actively alive beside them. *Thus do the things which have produced fruit, nay whose fruit still grows, turn out to be the things chosen for record and writing of; which things alone were great and worth recording.* The Battle of Châlons, where Hunland met Rome, and the Earth was played for, at sword fence, by two earth-bestriding giants, the sweep of whose swords cut kingdoms in pieces, hovers dim in the languid remembrance of a few; while the poor police-court Treachery of a wretched Iscariot, transacted in the wretched land of Palestine, centuries earlier, for "thirty pieces of silver," lives clear in the heads, in the hearts of all men. Nay moreover, as only that which bore fruit was great; so of all things, that whose fruit is still here and growing must be the greatest, the

best worth remembering; which again, as we see, by the very nature of the case, is mainly the thing remembered. Observe, too, how this "mainly" tends always to become a "solely," and the approximate continually approaches nearer; for triviality after triviality, as it perishes from the living activity of men, drops away from their speech and memory, and the great and the vital more and more exclusively survive there. Thus does Accident correct Accident; and in the wondrous boundless jostle of things (an aimful Power . . . dwelling *in* it), a result comes out that may be put up with.[32]

Carlyle's conviction that the untruths and the trivialities tend to be canceled out in the process of weaving the web of universal history is a corollary of his Goethean belief in the imperishable nature of truth; that the deeds and thoughts of men are planted in the "seed-field of Time," to live and grow there with what vitality is in them. Ultimately the belief rests upon his fundamental conviction that the universe is grounded upon moral laws of order, truth, and justice. It is an essentially optimistic theory which dares to hold that men tend to remember only those things which are greatest and best worth remembering. To justify it Carlyle had recourse to still another of his psychologic insights into the nature of the human consciousness. Men tend to hold in memory only that which is still bearing fruit in the world, because the act of remembering ultimately depends upon the act of believing; and men cannot believe, at least not for long, that which is not credible, which does not accord with their concrete experiential world.

This brought Carlyle to his concept of history as the "true Epic Poem," and the facts of history as the only imaginative materials wherein poetic reality permanently resides. "The significance, even for poetic purposes," says Sauerteig, "that lies in Reality is too apt to escape us; is perhaps only now beginning to be discerned."[33] Carlyle felt the necessity of a harmonious union between the imagination and the understanding to create belief. "All Mythologies were once Philosophies; were *believed;* the Epic Poems of old time, so long as they continued *epic,* and had any complete impressiveness, were Histories, and understood to be narratives of facts." When imagination is forced to part company with understanding, the belief and consequent enjoyment inspired is only momentary, a poor thing compared with the "perennial belief" excited by the communication of an authentic reality. Thus Carlyle arrived at the fusion of poetry and history as possessing identical attributes and serving identical ends.[34]

HISTORY THE TRUE POETRY

In every artist's work will be found, either implicit or expressed, some sort of esthetic theory resting upon the assumption of a specific relationship between form and function. The artist may start with form as more important and pass on to function; or he may elevate function to the primary position and develop from that his conception of form. Carlyle belongs in the category of those interested primarily in function. His functional point of view, indeed, and his inclusive definitions made it possible for him to identify poetry and history as similar in aim and subject matter, considerations which weighed so heavily against the minor significance of form that the syllogistic conclusion was a logical one. He did not loosely and arbitrarily identify history and poetry as one, without examining closely his own assumptions. His mind had a centripetal tendency toward unity in the sphere of esthetic thought no less than in social thought, though he never claimed validity for his esthetic theories for others than himself.

Carlyle was constantly alive to the critical values which formed the basis of his art, as his intimate writings, especially the voluminous Emerson correspondence, abundantly testify. He had a serious regard for his own ideals of workmanship and was aware how thoroughly they controlled the character of his work as it was produced. Conceding a certain measure of innate gift, he deliberately trained his endowment to an habitual response through long years of preparation and intellectual development. Like Milton, he belongs in the class of those who have "submitted the greatness of their natural talents to the corrections and restraints of art."[35]

Carlyle's esthetic theory was in harmony with the rest of his philosophy in elevating the functional aspect of the relationship between form and function to a primary position. His theory of art made no concession to "art for art's sake." It agreed, rather, with Milton's that an "art is what it is because of what it teaches."[36] Art is the higher skill possessed by those "emblematic intellects" capable of heroic endeavor, whether in poetry or politics. Carlyle distinguished often between the artist and the artisan, the poet and prosaist. The poet and artist imaginatively "body forth the form of things unseen," while the artisan and prosaist merely manufacture a duplicate of received sense impressions.[37] Goethe and Scott he contrasted as typical examples of the poet and prosaist working in verse; while Shakespeare and Voltaire were good instances of the contrast between artist and artisan in the field of history.

Carlyle's definition of the historian as both a poet and philosopher cannot be fully understood except in the light of his functional approach to art. Professor Roe emphasized Carlyle's romantic tendency to exalt the content over the form of art.[38] But the conception of function is not wholly described by this analysis. In a sense, the idea of function determines content, just as content in turn determines form. While the functional aspect is probably present in Wordsworth's attitude toward art, and Wordsworth's theories are most nearly akin to Carlyle's of any of his contemporaries, Carlyle's conception is still more closely allied to that of Milton.

In Milton we find the theory that all created things "are what in the fullest sense they do." In no other way can poets justify the beauties and ornaments of their style than by dedicating their "industry and their art" to the great ends of society. As Milton expressed it in *An Apology Against a Pamphlet:*

True eloquence I find to be none but the serious and hearty love of truth; and that whose mind soever is fully possessed with a fervent desire to know good things, and with the dearest charity to infuse the knowledge of them into others, when such a man would speak, his words . . . like so many nimble and airy servitors, trip about him at command, and in well-ordered files, as he would wish, fall aptly into their places.[39]

Milton's "true eloquence" and Carlyle's "poetry" are remarkably similar; "musical thought" spoken by one who has "penetrated into the inmost heart of the thing; detected the inmost mystery of it . . . the inward harmony of coherence which is its soul, whereby it exists, and has a right to be, here in this world."[40] The poet is he who *thinks* in that manner; and then is able, "with the dearest charity to infuse the knowledge . . . into others." At bottom, therefore, the capacity to create poetry revolves around a power of intellect, a quality of sincerity and a depth of vision. "See deep enough, and you see musically; the heart of nature being everywhere music, if you can only reach it."

Carlyle believed that poetry's great function is to reveal the truth and beauty of the reality behind the veil of appearance. His thought was suggestive of Wordsworth's when he wrote, in *Diderot:* "Poetry, it will come to be more and more understood, is nothing but higher knowledge; and the only genuine Romance (for grown persons), Reality. The Thinker is the Poet, the Seer; let him who *sees* write down according to his gift of sight; if deep and with inspired vision, then creatively, poetically; if common, and with only uninspired everyday vision, let him at least be faithful in this and write Memoirs."[41]

Carlyle's conception of the poet was a blending of Schiller's theory of the poet as the son of his time, whose mission was not to entertain but to purify it, and the Fichtean conception of a "literary priest," interpreter of the Divine Idea in such particular form as his particular age required it. With such a conception of the artist, it is apparent that all modes of creative endeavor are closely allied. The poetry of an age may be expressed in the heroic leadership of Cromwell, the dramas of Shakespeare, or the epic poetry of Dante; "all modes of representing or addressing the highest nature of man are acknowledged as younger sisters of poetry." The same glory which shines from the *Tempest* looks on us from the *Transfiguration,* from the tragedies of Sophocles, and the weather worn sculptures of the Parthenon. Though it is best seen in the "aerial embodiment of poetry, it is found spreading likewise over all the thoughts and actions of an age, and has given us Surreys, Sidneys, Raleighs, in court and camp, Cecils in policy, Hookers in divinity, Bacons in philosophy, and Shakespeares and Spensers in song."[42]

The broadly inclusive definition of poetry as the embodiment of reality in some form visible to the sense of man, and suitable to his times, illuminates Carlyle's description of his method of writing history as "poetico-historical." In *The Diamond Necklace* he experimentally determined whether he could make a "kind of poem" of the narrative, by "sticking actually to the Realities of the thing with as much tenacity and punctuality as the merest Hallam."[43] The work turned out to be even more successful that he had hoped, "truly a kind of curiosity in its way." Encouraged by his success, he wrote Emerson that it is a part of his creed "that the only Poetry is History, could we tell it right."[44] He admitted that this truth was not yet fully proved, or at least, he had not yet got to the limitations of it; "and shall in no way except by trying it in practice." Further experimentation, in the *French Revolution*, however, swiftly developed a perfected technique; and the artist-historian vindicated his theories in practice. Carlyle saw no reason later to amend his first rounded definition of history as poetry, stated in *Boswell's Life of Johnson*: "History, after all, is the true Poetry: [and] Reality, if rightly interpreted, is grander than Fiction; nay . . . in the right interpretation of Reality and History does genuine Poetry consist."[45]

Carlyle agreed with Schiller and Fichte that the possession of the superior endowment of the poet entails a responsibility to find suitable expression for the apprehension of reality and to convey it to others. He voiced this feeling to Emerson after reading the latter's Divinity address: "A man is called to let his light shine before men; but he ought to understand better and better what medium it it through, what retinas it falls on . . . a faculty is in you for a *sort* of speech which is itself *action,* an artistic sort. You *tell* us with piercing emphasis that man's soul is great; *show* us a great soul of a man, in some work symbolic of such . . . some concrete thing, some Event, Man's Life, American Forest, or piece of Creation . . . well *Emersonized,* depictured by

Emerson, and cast forth from him then to live by itself...."[46] Years later he wrote again in the same vein: "I wish you would take an American hero, one whom you really love; and give us a History of him—make an artistic bronze statue (in good *words*) of his Life and him."[47] But Emerson answered that he inclined "to write poetry, philosophy, possibility—anything but history."[48] His abstractionist tendencies were completely antithetic to Carlyle's concrete realism.

It was part of Carlyle's philosophy that the literature of an age takes on the color of the age's spiritual condition. Nineteenth century England was essentially unheroic, critical and not creative in the highest sense. Coleridge remarked that it was "living under the dynasty of the understanding."[49] The spirit of inquiry had encroached more and more on the provinces of the spiritual powers; and the "Poet of these days is he who, not indeed by mechanical but by poetical methods, can instruct us, and more and more evolve for us the mystery of our life."[50] In 1833 Carlyle wrote his brother his heterodox belief that "all Art is but a Reminiscence now, that for us in these days *Prophecy* (well understood) not *Poetry*, is the thing wanted; how can we *sing* and *paint* when we do not yet *believe* and *see* . . . ?"[51]

It is possible to observe how inevitably Carlyle came to the conclusion that his own country and generation demanded its poetry in the form of the prose historical epic. If the "struggle of man's soul against Ignorance, Sin and Suffering" is the indirect subject of most true poetry, then history is the most impressive record of that struggle. Moreover, it partakes of genuine and authentic reality. There is no denying that history is thoroughly poetic in subject, however it may fail in execution. The art of history, in Carlyle's prose era, must conspire with nature to stimulate the slumbering imagination which lives forever in man's soul so that it may once again "pour its wizard light" over the universe. The artist, whether historian or poet, "must address us on interests that *are*, not *were* ours; and in a dialect that finds a response and not a contradiction."[52]

ART OF HISTORY: THEORY 115

THE HISTORIAN'S FUNCTION

We have traced the method by which Carlyle embodied his humane interests in an esthetic theory that created a new conception of the writing of history. The process he employed represented an ingenious mixture of rationalized preferences, and sound reasoning on the basis of independent psychological assumptions. Eventually he arrived at a unique theory of impressionistic history, subjective in approach but realistic in treatment. His conception of the historian as playing the dual rôle of poet and philosopher is developed in the distinction he draws between the "sacred poet" and Dryasdust, which, in turn, has its source in his approach to the interpretation of historic evidence. We have already discussed his belief that only the things worthiest of remembrance tend to fix themselves permanently in tradition. Of all past events, those "whose fruit is still here and growing must be the greatest," the most worth remembering and writing about. The historian's task, then, is not to search out and restore, with impartial interest, all discoverable records of the past lives of people, but to interpret the value of past experience in terms of present needs. Only those phases of the past which still reach to the surface and are alive in the present satisfy Carlyle's requirements that written history must be both a credible reality and at the same time "an address out of Heaven."

The position Carlyle assumes with regard to the data of history is closely related to his conception of the purpose of history, well expressed in a letter to Mill written in 1833:

The "dignity of history" has buckramed up poor History into a dead mummy. There are a thousand purposes which History should serve beyond "teaching by experience": it is an address (literally out of Heaven) to our *whole* inner man; to every faculty of Head and Heart, from the deepest to the slightest; there is no end to its purposes; none to one's amazement and contemplation over it. Now for all such purposes, high, low, ephemeral, eternal, the first indispensable condition of conditions, is that we *see* the things transacted, and picture them out wholly as if they stood before our eyes; and this, alas, of all considerations, is the one that "dignity of history" least thinks of. You must manage this by many indirect methods for yourself in your own person.[53]

To "see the things transacted, and picture them out wholly as if they stood before our eyes" admittedly requires both a poet and a philosopher. In the introductory chapter of *Cromwell* Carlyle offers his final formula for the "art of history" conceived as the philosophic interpretation of the value of the past:

Histories are as perfect as the Historian is wise, and is gifted with an eye and a soul! For the leafy, blossoming Present Time springs from the Whole Past, remembered and unrememberable . . . and truly, the Art of History, the grand difference between a Dryasdust and a sacred Poet, is very much even this: To distinguish well what does still reach to the surface, and is alive and frondent for us; and what reaches no longer to the surface, but moulders safe underground, never to send forth leaves or fruit for mankind any more. . . . By wise memory and by wise oblivion; it lies all there![54]

The grand different between "Dryasdust and a sacred poet," therefore, lies fundamentally in their attitude toward their task. Their conception of their function controls their product; just as, in turn, their intellectual qualities of insight, sincerity, and tolerance dictate their conception of function. Carlyle accused Dryasdust of considering his task well discharged when he had compiled "torpedo Histories of the Philosophical or other sorts"; when he had collected and preserved the documents and records of the past; edited and sorted with what mixture of pedantry and intelligence was in him. Too often the voluminous efforts of Dryasdust might better have been left unprinted. "The sound of them is not a *voice*, conveying knowledge . . . but an inarticulate mumblement. Buried under them, overwhelmed with wreck and dead ashes, lie the divine heroisms. . . ."[55] Dryasdust is not wholly blamable, of course, for his limited view of his task. He is the artisan who works in the quarry of history, intent on the small area around him but with little oversight of the whole. There is need of his effort, if only to make easier the synthesizing task of the artist-historian who imaginatively resuscitates the past lives of peoples, clothes them in credible verisimilitude, and offers them to his own age as a significant and inescapable reality.

Once the philosopher has determined the value of the past, the poet's work begins. The foregoing discussion of the qualities of a poet make clear that Carlyle endeavored to fuse the reason and the understanding into a single, productive organ he called "intellect." He avoided the Kantian distinction between reason and understanding as distinct organs of knowledge with well-defined provinces; and believed, on the contrary, that a fusion was necessary to effect the highest forms of productivity. The reason and the understanding had separate tasks, however. The understanding discerned the external world in terms of relations, and governed all that was "real, practical and material" in knowledge, the palpable, visible facts and the adaptation of means to ends in the business of life.[56] The reason, on the other hand, discerned the reality behind the veil of appearance. It was at home in the invisible realm of ideas, the region of poetry, of morality, of the meaning and purpose of man's destiny.

Carlyle saw clearly the significance of the creative imagination in the writing of history. In the "field of human investigations there are objects of two sorts: First, the visible, including not only such as are material, and may be seen by the bodily eye; but all such, likewise, as may be represented in a *shape*, before the mind's eye, or in any way pictured there."[57] All the facts of history, as ordinarily understood, are included among these *visible* objects; for they can be imaged before the mind's eye and hence are really objects of sense. The mind's instruments for laying hold of the data of history are the mechanical laws of the sense perceptions and the coördinates of space and time. Possibly no historian before Carlyle saw so clearly that imagination is really an extension of reality; and that the means of seizing historic facts is not mere compilation of documentary evidence but the subjective assimilation of such evidence as exists in the terms of its existence: i.e., concrete experience.

Thus the historian's first function is essentially dramatic. He must relive the facts in his own experience before he can be said properly to possess them. As early as 1822, Carlyle defined "dramatic genius" to Jane Welsh as "a striking faculty of expressing its [human character's] peculiarities, not only by description, but imitation."[58] Years later he criticized Sterling's drama, *Strafford*, as having too little action and "far too little probability." He complained that the representation of men and things was neither credible nor conformable to the truth because the characters are not really "painted" at all, "at least, not by action; which is the only dramatic way of painting."[59] Until facts are completely realized in the concrete imagination, until they are "constructively comprehended" so that they can be taken asunder, and put together again, they are not properly the possession of the artist." Thus to the creative imagination of the artist-historian the greatest of all mysteries is revealed: "man's life as it actually is." The imaginative capacity to experience and create anew man's life as it has been lived may be called the "historic sense."

The historian of Carlyle's conception, thus, is distinguished beyond all other artists because he works solely in the sphere of reality. The material of history is no "brain-web of the poet" but a "fraction of that mystic, spirit-woven Web" from the "loom of Time." "The thing that is, what can be so wonderful; what, especially to us that are, can have such significance?" Study reality, therefore, Carlyle insisted in the introduction to the *Diamond Necklace:* "search out deeper and deeper its quite endless mystery; see it, know it. . . ."[60]

The effect he sought from written history was the effect which he acknowledged Homer had on him. "Homer's Rhapsody" he "loved better than any other Book . . . except the Bible alone." It is not the "richest intrinsically, perhaps, but the richest-oldest." It sustained and nourished him with its concrete view of how men lived and acted centuries ago. "All the Antiquity I have ever known becomes alive in my head," he wrote his brother in 1834, "there is a whole gallery of Appeleses and Phidiases that I not only look upon but make."[61] This conception of reality was not grounded on mere interpretative caprice or individual prejudice, but upon the sound psychological premise that only what can be seen and understood can be made wholly credible and believable to others. While in the midst of the Cromwell researches, Carlyle wrote to Emerson: "There is no use of writing of things past, unless they can be made in fact things present: not yesterday at all, but simply today and what it holds of fulfillment and of promises is *ours.*"[62] A few months earlier he had written of his discouragement over the impossibility of delineating Puritanism to make it comprehensible to his own generation. Unless he could discover some means of presenting his Commonwealth subject *alive* he intended to abandon it; because a "subject dead is not worth presenting."[63] It would have been more expressive of his fundamental theory of the art of history if he had said that a subject *dead* could not be presented.

HISTORY AS SOCIAL BIOGRAPHY

Reference has already been made to Carlyle's belief that history should be studied and treated in terms of massed effects; or in terms of the lives of peoples rather than the lives of men. Unquestionably this conception owed much to Schiller, whose bold use of it as a method of selecting and interpreting historical data encouraged Carlyle to make it central in his own method, although buttressing it with his anecdotico-biographical tendencies. It liberated Carlyle from the orthodox canons of history writing; and freed him from the enslavement of most historians to a mere chronological recital of doings in "court and camp." By focusing his active discontent with older methods, finally, it served as the basis for the stimulating conviction that he was breaking new paths in historical narration.

Like Schiller, Carlyle consciously assumed the rôle of rebel against old forms of writing history. Like Schiller, too, his disagreement with the established mode centered around his conception of the uses of history. Between the dates of his first acquaintance with Schiller and the writing of the *Life of Schiller*, Carlyle began preparation for his first original literary project, the plan for which he recorded in his notebook in 1822. His comments and description indicate above all else his consciousness of the fact that his theories will necessarily involve the introduction of new methods in historical writing. He proposed to do a series of essays on the Civil Wars; "not to write a history of them—but to exhibit . . . some features of the national character as it was then displayed, supporting [his] remarks by mental portraits of Cromwell, Laud . . . etc., the most distinguished actors in that great scene. I may, of course, intersperse the delineation with all the ideas which I can gather from any point of the universe."⁶⁴

When the *Life of Schiller* caused a temporary abandonment of his Commonwealth project, he expressed himself still more boldly regarding the originality of his proposed Essay, in a letter to Jane Welsh (January 1823). There he refers to his

... splendid plan of treating the history of England during the Commonwealth in a new style—not by way of regular narrative—for which I felt too well my inequality, but by grouping together the most singular manifestations of mind that occurred then under distinct heads—selecting some remarkable person as the representative of each class, and trying to explain and illustrate their excellence and defects, all that was curious in their fortunes as individuals, or in their formation as members of the human family, by *the most striking methods I could devise.*⁶⁵

This passage, written when the Schiller influence was strongest, contains the germ of all that is essential in Carlyle's later method, though it was ten years before he gave it final and practical form. The employment of the "most striking methods devisable" in resuscitating his materials; the organization of the materials into massed effects, to each of which was imparted a special quality by the dramatic exploitation of a person or event, the emphasis on the "private-biographic phasis"; the avoidance of regular narrative and the substitution of episodic and anecdotal treatment; the free interpolation of comment, not designed, like Macaulay's, to condition and determine the reader's judgment, but to contribute mood, atmosphere, a sense of immediacy, in which the reader would be invited, even overwhelmingly persuaded, to live through the events himself.

The most suggestive idea contained in the notebook entry bearing on Carlyle's biographic approach to history was the question he put to himself: why were such heroic minds engendered in those times? This idea contains the core of his entire attitude toward the writing of history. Like Schiller, he believed history should be interpretation, not mere record; but the interpreter must look for the truth or reality behind the outward fact "in the common doings and interests of men," not merely in the

ART OF HISTORY: THEORY 121

grand and spectacular event.⁶⁶ No object which throws light on these is trivial or insignificant. Indeed, the "life of the lowest mortal, if faithfully recorded, would be interesting to the highest."⁶⁷ What we want in history, Carlyle believed, is some insight into the nature of the "mighty-rolling, loud-roaring Life-current" itself, not the mere eddyings and bobbings of drift articles on its surface. The thing he wanted to see was not

> ... Redbook Lists, and Court Calendars, and Parliamentary Registers, but the *Life of Man in England:* what men did, thought, suffered, enjoyed; the form, especially the spirit, of their terrestrial existence, its outward environment, its inward principle; *how* and *what* it was; whence it proceeded, whither it was tending.⁶⁸

Carlyle put the case for his new conception of "social biography" by a vigorous polemic against orthodox history. Do we derive even the dimmest shadow of an answer to these great questions of how men lived and had their being, what wages they got and what they bought with these, in the innumerable histories of the Smolletts and Belshams and Robertsons? We learn instead that a

> ... man named George the Third was born and bred up, and a man named George the Second died; that Walpole, and the Pelhams, and Chatham, and Rockingham, and Shelburne, and North, with their Coalition and their Separation ministries all ousted one another; and vehemently scrambled for the thing they called the "Rudder of Government, but which was in reality the Spigot of Taxation." ... To the hungry and thirsty mind all this avails next to nothing.⁶⁹

Though Robertson's *Scotland* is accounted a truly great history, Carlyle continued, the author fails to answer the grand question:

> By whom, and by what means, when and how, was this fair broad Scotland, with its Arts and Manufactures, Temples, Schools, Institutions, Poetry, Spirit, National Character, created, and made arable, verdant, peculiar, great ... but this other question: How did the King keep himself alive in those old days; and restrain so many Butcher-Barons and ravenous Henchmen from utterly extirpating one another, so that killing went on in some sort of moderation?⁷⁰

This is the best that the great Robertson can show us. Then Carlyle describes how Robertson approached the "luminous age" of the Reformation, when

. . .all Scotland is awakened to a second higher life . . . is convulsed, fermenting, struggling to body itself forth anew. To the herdsman, among his cattle in remote woods; to the craftsman, in his rude . . . workship, among his rude guild-brethren; to the great and the little, a new light had arisen; in town and hamlet groups are gathered, with eloquent looks, and governed or ungovernable tongues; . . . We ask with breathless eagerness: How was it; how went it on? Let us understand it, let us see it, and know it!—In reply is handed us a really graceful and most dainty little Scandalous Chronicle . . . of two persons: Mary Stuart, a Beauty, but over light-headed; and Henry Darnley, a Booby who had fine legs. How these first courted, billed and cooed, according to nature; then pouted, fretted, grew utterly enraged, and blew one another up with gunpowder; this and not the History of Scotland is what we good-naturedly read. . . .

Thus, said Carlyle, is history written by the foremost practitioners of the art.

The time had come, in Carlyle's opinion, to attempt history on quite other principles, to relegate the "Court, the Senate and the Battlefield" to the background, and advance the "Temple, the Workshop, and Social Hearth" into the foreground. History will no longer content itself with answering the question of how men were taxed and kept quiet, but will seek an answer to the more important question: "How and what were men then?" not our government only, or "the House wherein our life was led, but the life itself we led there." Then shall history become the "essence of innumerable biographies," a true social history, and not a mere political or constitutional or military chronicle. Then we may expect it to serve as a "revocation of the Edict of Destiny . . . that Time shall not utterly . . . have dominion over us."[71]

In this timeless quality lies the source of the poetic appeal of historic facts. Critics insist, he says, that the poet "should communicate an 'infinitude' to his delineation; that by intensity of conception, by that gift of Transcendental Thought, which is

ART OF HISTORY: THEORY

fitly named genius . . . he should inform the Finite with a certain infinitude of significance; or . . . ennoble the Actual into Idealness."[72] In the case of history or historical materials, "the Poet's task is, as it were, done to his hand." Such is the "Dark grandeur of that 'Time-Element' wherein man's soul lies imprisoned . . . it invests, of its own accord, with an authentic felt 'infinitude' whatsoever it has once embraced in its mysterious folds." The one word "past" implies a meaning at once pathetic and sacred, in every sense poetic. "Rough Samuel and sleek wheedling James *were,* and *are not.* Their life and whole personal environment has melted into air, has vanished like the baseless fabric of a vision."[73] Yet only what was transitory passed away. An

> . . . immortal part remains, the significance of which is in strict speech inexhaustible,—as that of every *real* object is. Aloft, conspicuous, on his enduring basis, he [Johnson] stands there, serene, unaltering; silently addressing to every new generation a new lesson and monition. Well is his Life worth writing, worth interpreting; and ever in the dialect of new times, of re-writing and re-interpreting.

This is Carlyle's explanation of the esthetic objectivity of historical materials, to which we alluded earlier.[74] Boswell's biography not only gives us more real insight into the history of England during those days than twenty ordinary histories, it is a true heroic poem because it "turns on objects that in very truth existed" and thus in the fullest, deepest sense are wholly credible to us. The things here stated are indubitable facts; "those figures, that local habitation, are not shadow but substance. . . ."

Such a "social history" Carlyle not only demanded in theory but gave us in practice. Each of his histories may be judged from this point of view, but the most perfect is the historical vignette of twelfth century England in the second book of *Past and Present*. There Carlyle invites us to behold that

> . . . this England of the year 1200 was no chimerical vacuity or dreamland, peopled with mere vaporous Fantasms . . . but a green solid place, that grew corn and several other things. The sun shone on it; the vicissitudes of seasons and human fortunes. Cloth was woven and

worn; ditches were dug, furrowfields ploughed, and houses built. Day by day all men and cattle rose to labour, and night by night returned to their several lairs. In wondrous Dualism, then as now, lived nations of breathing men; alternating in all ways between Light and Dark; between joy and sorrow, between rest and toil,—between hope . . . and fear. . . . Not vapour Fantasms, Rymer's *Foedera* at all! Coeur-de-Lion was not a theatrical popinjay with greaves and steel-cap on it, but a man living upon victuals,—not imported by Peel's Tariff. Coeur-de-Lion came palpably athwart this Jocelin at St. Edmundsbury; and had almost peeled the sacred gold "Feretrum," or St. Edmund's Shrine itself, to ransom him out of the Danube jail.[75]

Lord Acton called Carlyle's picture of twelfth century England the "most remarkable piece of historical thinking in the language."[76] This tribute from so exacting a scientist and historian grows more significant when we reflect that in this work we have the purest instance of the subjective method in operation. Carlyle was in no sense a specialist in medieval church history or in early English history, although his voracious reading probably had not neglected any readily accessible researches on either subject. For material he relied mainly on the monastic chronicle of Jocelyn de Brakelonde, which was meager and sketchy in outline but abounded in trivial details, a gossipy, eye-witness commentary of daily happenings in the monastery. With such materials as a stimulus to his historical imagination and insight, Carlyle's capacity to think himself into the past was more thoroughly invoked than if he had possessed tons of documentary evidence in the ordinary sense. His imagination was never more intoxicated with the sense of the past as a reality that once existed, and no longer exists, and yet in a mysterious way never ceases to exist. In no other work does he convey so vivid a sense of his feeling that "Earthly Life and its riches and possessions . . . are a shadow of realities, eternal, infinite; that this Time world, as an air image, fearfully *emblematic*, plays and flickers in the grand still mirror of Eternity. . . ." This Book II of *Past and Present* is the least pretentious but the most perfect of Carlyle's historical writings in satisfying his own requirements. There is biographic interest, both individual and social; there is poetic interest of the first order; and there is over all a sense of reality which not only parts the curtains of the past but persuades the reader that he is actually experiencing life as it was lived in the twelfth century.

In the order of their importance as social biography, the *French Revolution* is next to *Past and Present* among Carlyle's histories. It is pointedly significant that he called it a "History of Sansculottism" which gives sufficient evidence of its social character. His primary interest was not that of declaring God's judgment on a rotten and spiritually dead social system, as is frequently assumed, but of *understanding* and depicting the life of the people: how they behaved when the props of civilized order were suddenly removed. God's judgment had already been delivered, in Carlyle's opinion; the world had no further need of human echoes of that. But the great lesson of the Revolution remained to be pointed out by describing the process of revolution itself; reckoning its cost in terms of human suffering and tragedy; following with almost hypnotic fascination the disintegration of the social and legal institutions of a system economically bankrupt, morally empty, and spiritually dead. At the same time he developed his theory of society as an organic growth, not to be accomplished by drafting constitutions, legislating order by laws, formulating intellectual abstractions. The vast psychic force unloosed by freeing the primitive passions of a people from habitual restraints may be expected to recognize no formula, but inevitably to advance from violence to violence until it finally exhausts itself, or meets an opposing body with sufficient moral force to tame it. In the case of the French Revolution, it was Napoleon who finally tamed it, and with his coming Carlyle's special interest in it is ended.

Carlyle's concern in *Cromwell* was the spiritual entity known as Puritanism. His original conception called for the history of the Puritan Revolution on much the same pattern he employed in the *French Revolution*. He felt that the living reality of Puritanism as a way of life needed to be "understood" and resuscitated; partly because, though buried under two centuries of calumny, it contained so vivid an instance of the fact that the fundamental laws of truth and justice do prevail; partly because buried under it was one of England's authentic great men. Until Puritanism could be delineated and the spiritual attributes of seventeenth century England made credible, Oliver Cromwell could never be "seen" as an actual "face-to-face acquaintance."

The revolutionary period, again, offered Carlyle scope for social analysis of the process of change. In this case, the problem was more difficult from the standpoint of the social biographer because the revolution had a leader of such moral force and stature that he practically dictated the course of it. Cromwell was not only a symbol of the Puritan Revolution; he *was* the Revolution and with his death it collapsed. While the process of change which he initiated by overthrowing the old system finally worked itself out in the "Bloodless Revolution" of 1688, the entire revolutionary process had to be grasped in constitutional rather than social terms. For this among other reasons Carlyle finally abandoned his original project in favor of an indirect autobiographic portrait of the Puritan leader. In his editorial elucidations, however, he gives us constant sidelights of a biographic sort on the men surrounding Cromwell, on the "inward condition" of life among the Puritans, of Cromwell's battles.

Carlyle's treatment of the Cromwell materials, as we shall see, was dictated partly by a sense of frustration at the largeness of his original intention, and partly by the impossibility of reducing the unwieldy materials to a work of art combining artistry and accuracy. Temperamentally and theoretically opposed to objective history, he accidentally achieved a thoroughly objective reconstitution of the past, conceived and executed in the most modern spirit of scientific research. Contemporary scholarship acknowledges *Cromwell* to be a great and permanent contribution to historiography, possibly Carlyle's greatest.[77] Carlyle's sense for concrete reality, his almost idolatrous regard for such human and biographic materials as letters, with the implications of factual reality they convey, guided his intuitive interpretation of events and personalities and evoked from his historical imagination a rounded portrait of Cromwell in his human and unhistorical aspects:

> How he lived at St. Ives; how he saluted men on the streets; read Bibles; sold cattle; and walked, with heavy footfall and many thoughts, through the market Green or old narrow lanes in St. Ives, by the shore of the black Ouse River. . . . Here of a certainty Oliver did walk and look about him habitually . . . a man studious of many temporal and eternal things.[78]

In a sense the history of Frederick represents the final expression of Carlyle's theories of social biography. "It is the history of a State, a Social Vitality, growing from small to great; steadily growing henceforth under guidance: and the contrast between guidance and no-guidance or misguidance in such matters is again impressively illustrated here."[79] It is not primarily the biography of a "hero," or even of a "hero" and his father, but a social history of a people struggling to establish its right of existence, symbolized in the lives of its successive leaders and even more in its army. The Prussian Army is the real hero and protagonist of the eight volumes of *Frederick*. Though we have little insight into the lives of the people themselves, we acquire a profound intimacy with the great human war machine which carved out an empire for the German people, and was the people's fit representative.

Carlyle saw in the Prussian state a model of evolutionary development, verifying his theory of the moral force residing in a well-knit, well-governed social entity. It was the constructive, positive side of the same picture he had drawn in the *French Revolution* and *Cromwell*. One reason he was attracted to it, of course, was his belief that Frederick's kingdom was able to establish itself mainly because the Holy Roman Empire was an historical anachronism and France was decadent. The rise of Prussia sounded the death knell of feudal France and the vast medieval empire of the Hapsburgs. In this sense Carlyle's chief historical writings fit into one great design intended to illuminate for his own generation how the "leafy blossoming Present has sprung out of the whole Past," and how the entire process of growth reveals a purposeful plan cognizant of the fundamental human ideals of truth and justice.

INDIVIDUAL VS. SOCIAL BIOGRAPHY

The emphasis we have placed on Carlyle's belief that history should offer us a splendid vision of the inward life and spiritual condition of a people cuts athwart the impression so generally held that Carlyle's theory of history had room only for heroes. It, in turn, is related to another equally erroneous notion that Carlyle believed that the course of history has been dictated, has been guided and controlled by the great men who have worked here. Modern refinements of this misconception have gone so far as to claim that, since Carlyle's only motive in writing was ego aggrandizement, the only men he admired were the successfully heroic; and that for these his admiration was so idolatrous as to obscure his understanding.[80]

Passages like the following, taken from *Heroes and Hero Worship*, are summoned before the bar to prove the hero theory:

> For, as I take it, Universal History, the history of what man has accomplished in this world, is at bottom the History of the Great Men who have worked here. They were the leaders of men, these great ones; the modellers, patterns, and in a wide sense creators, of whatsoever the general mass of men contrived to do or to attain; all things that we see standing accomplished in this world are properly the outer material result, the practical realisation and embodiment of Thoughts that dwelt in the Great Men sent into the world: the soul of the whole world's history, it may justly be considered, were the history of these.[81]

When we examine this characteristic passage, however, we discover it to be wholly consonant, indeed confirmatory, of the larger view we have taken to express Carlyle's underlying purpose. To the biographic historian, nothing could be more axiomatic than the statement that universal history is the history of the great men who have lived and worked in the world. Thucydides conveyed the same thought, when he remarked that the earth is the sepulchre of the great men who have lived on it. Both Carlyle and his Greek predecessor thought of history in terms of dramatic action; both believed that apart from the lives of men, or unrelated to those lives, there is no history.

Carlyle's positive theory of creative forces as the primary determinant in history also rests upon the human quotient. The man whom Carlyle designates "great" is "an original man; he comes to us first hand. A messenger he, sent from the Infinite Unknown with tidings to us. . . . Direct from the Inner Fact of things. . . . It is from the heart of the world that he comes; he is a portion of the primal reality of things."[82] Such a great man may be a poet, a prophet, a warrior, a king. He may lead political revolutions like a Cromwell, or spiritual revolutions like a Goethe. Or he may be one of the countless thousands of "nameless innovators" whose inventions and spiritual legacies have made them the intangible "modellers and patterns" of our civilized order.[83] Carlyle's optimistic faith in the opulence of Nature has been alluded to already. He was sensitive to the invisible influences on history represented by the slow deposit of wisdom and experience accumulated through ages of unrecorded heroisms, the work of those nameless great ones whose exercise of spiritual force resulted in work honestly done and lives well lived, an imperishable deposit in universal history, even if wholly unrecorded.

Viewed in the light of his broad definition of great men, and with the knowledge that Carlyle always used the term "universal history" to include everything thought and done by men, of which the merest fraction is recorded, it is apparent that we have only another confirmation of our belief that Carlyle's profoundest interest was in social biography: the lives of people, not of individuals except as the parts are indispensable in making up the whole. So far from being absorbed in the doings of the successfully great, he is almost too insistent on the importance of the silent great ones. The conquerors and political revolutionists, and quite generally those who make the loudest noise in the world are significant in inverse proportion to the loudness of the uproar they have caused. Johannes Faust was a greater hero than twenty Tamerlanes; Goethe will be legislating destiny when the noise made by Napoleon has become a faint whisper. Shakespeare is a more potent and enduring force in preserving a spiritual unity among the far-flung English-speaking peoples than the acts of kings and presidents. A dozen similar instances could be cited to support the hypothesis that Carlyle's interpretation of the "successfully heroic" was as far as possible from being a mere glorification of physical and moral force.

Further evidence of his interest in social entities being greater than his interest in individuals lies in his choice of themes. His first great history is altogether without a hero. Mirabeau, Danton, Napoleon, all had heroic qualities, intellectual sincerity, a realistic sense of reality, moral force; yet Carlyle's portraits of them are not done with a degree more of art and tolerant insight than the opposing portraits of Robespierre, the King, the Queen, Madame Roland. While it is certainly true that no event in modern history is richer in the dramatic clash and interplay of human personalities than the French revolution, making it admirably adaptable to social biographic treatment, Carlyle's gift for portraiture he lavished on all alike. Wherever the materials offered, the portrait was forthcoming.

In the case of Cromwell, again, it will be recalled that Carlyle's original interest in that theme was psychological: "Why were such heroic minds engendered in those times?" Cromwell, "the wily fanatic," was far, indeed, from being a hero to Carlyle in 1822; his interest in Cromwell was subsidiary to an interest in the age and the "heroic minds" it produced. The same construction may be placed on his interest in Frederick. If, from the standpoint of what is "still alive and frondent for us," the French Revolution was the theme of themes for his generation, and if the age of Cromwell was the last "believing" age in English history, the mid-eighteenth century had a part in the same broad design as the breeding ground of the French Revolution. The Prussian nation and the Prussian king were the most vital realities in eighteenth century Europe; and from the standpoint of Carlyle's interpretative method, the history of Prussia, therefore, most truly deserved treatment. But he enlarged his canvas to include a panoramic view of the entire sphere of eighteenth century continental history.

A final bit of illumination on Carlyle's attitude toward the heroic is contained in the biographies of John Sterling and Abbot Samson. Professor Saintsbury considered *Sterling* in many respects the greatest of Carlyle's writings, and also "in a certain way" the greatest of nineteenth century biographies.[84] Yet Sterling was neither an heroic character nor a successful man. His biography demonstrates Teufelsdröckh's opinion that the "life of the lowest mortal, if well presented, will be interesting to the greatest." If, as Professor Saintsbury believed, Carlyle accomplished this telling effect by creating a romance of "Carlyle's Sterling" rather than a biography of the real Sterling, the same charge may be brought against all of the greatest biographies, where a complete unity of artistic effect creates a reality which maye be "truer than the truth itself because voiced in more expressive symbols."

Carlyle unquestionably held a high opinion of formal biography as the sublimest representation of poetic reality. The biography of a hero, in particular, had a unity of artistic effect and purpose which inevitably made it the most artistic form of historical writing. But Carlyle believed that as great a hero was required to write a true biography as to live the life of a hero. Therefore the world has witnessed few really great biographies; in the whole world, perhaps a baker's dozen; in England, only one.[85] Yet there is no heroic poem that is not at bottom, a biography, the life of a man; and on the other hand, no life of a man, faithfully recorded, but is a heroic poem of its sort.

THE THEORY OF EVIDENCE

A critical study of Carlyle's treatment of historical evidence is outside the scope of the present inquiry, but no discussion of Carlyle as a historian is complete without presenting his expressed attitude toward his materials as a phase of his belief that he was opening up fresh fields of historical inquiry in which the scholar's accuracy would be fused with the philosopher's insight and the poet's effective expression of discovered truths. Carlyle's method of writing history sought to accomplish these aims, and even succeeded magnificently, which has been more a matter for admiration than for imitation. He founded no school of historical writing; the tools he forged for himself were not suitable for the hands of others. The fact that Carlyle's histories stand alone as unique things of their kind, however, has led to confusion regarding his principles of composition and scholarship. And while his principles of composition have attained a degree of irrefutability because of their obvious success in application, all the more of a hue and cry has been raised regarding his principles of scholarship. The ancient saw that histories which read too well are suspect is as true today as it was in Polybius' day.

Carlyle's early scientific prepossessions and exceptional scholarship trained and disciplined a mind already capable of rigor and precision of thought and of independent judgment. What there was of scientific method, as we understand it today, in the early nineteenth century, Carlyle's training and aptitudes had tended to give him. Possessing a practical, concrete mind, diligent and methodical, Carlyle probably would have made an admirable scientist. The mathematician, de Morgan, never ceased regretting that in Carlyle the world had lost a great mathematician, even though it had gained an artist.

The period of his research into the sources for his work on the French Revolution offers particularly clear evidence of Carlyle's attitude toward historical data, and his belief that absolute accuracy must accompany his subjective treatment. "The two pinions of History," he declared in *Cagliostro*, "are stern accuracy in inquiring, bold imagination in expounding and filling up." He was still feeling his way toward an effective method which would combine accuracy with artistry. His letters throughout 1834, 1835, and 1836 contain many references revealing the interaction of his temperament and the materials with which he is working. In a letter to Emerson, in 1835, he complained that the books he has available are "inaccurate, superficial, vague," and contradict one another hopelessly; and "without accuracy, at least, what other good is possible?"[86] In the same vein he wrote to his mother: "I am very anxious to be perfectly accurate (which I find to have been exceedingly neglected by my forerunners); the consequence of that is great searching and trouble."[87] He finally reached the point of saturation where additional reading added nothing to his impression: "More books on it," he wrote to his brother, "are but a repetition of those before read; I learn nothing further by Books; yet I am as far as possible from understanding it."[88] About the same time he recorded in his *Journal:*

> I have again been *resolute* about the writing of a book. . . . Subject, the French Revolution. Whole boxes of books about me. Gloomy, huge, of almost boundless meaning, but obscure, dubious, all too deep for me . . . gleams, too, of a work of Art hover past me; as if this should be a work of art. . . . I feel at every sentence the work will be strange: that it must be so or be nothing but another of the thousand-and-one "Histories" which are so many "dead thistles for pedant chaffinches to peck at and fill their crops with"; a kind of thing I for one wish to have no hand in.[89]

Carlyle's conviction that his "History of Sansculottism" was destined to proceed on radical principles guided his choice of materials (so far as he had any real choice. Some of the most important materials were not accessible to him).[90] He had already experimented with his "poetico-historical" method of biography in the *Diamond Necklace* and *Cagliostro,* but his new project was to be a truly social biography. The facts he wanted were those describing how a revolting people behaved, how social life went on when suddenly stripped of the "thin rind of habit." In 1833 he wrote to Mill: "*Understand* me all those sectionary tumults, convention harangues, guillotine-holocausts, Brunswick discomfitures; *exhaust* me the meaning of it! You cannot, for it is a flaming reality."[91] Again he deplored the fact that the information he most particularly desired is not to be found:

> For instance, any book about the state of the prisons, the behavior of the prisoners under Fouquier-Tinville's reign? I have heard of a work expressly composed of Bon Mots uttered on the scaffold then. Those queues formed at the Bakers' shops, and generally that whole business of the Assignats, how it worked and was endured. . . . I do not so much as understand sufficiently what an assignat was; and wished

often I had been there to buy one when they were so cheap, that I might see how it was worded.[92]

Carlyle's constant search for graphic details led him to acquire pianoforte scores of *Ça Ira* and the *Marseillaise* that he might both see and hear the music which had inflamed the Parisian mobs. He had stored away many impressions of Paris collected during his brief visit in 1824. To these he added whatever graphic details Mill's knowledge of Paris could give him, and precise descriptive details which he commissioned John Carlyle to secure in 1835. Among the latter, significantly, was a request for a description of the famous Lanterne, in the Hotel de Ville, and the elm "Tree of Liberty" planted in the Faubourg St. Antoine in 1790.

Carlyle always surrounded himself with maps, portraits, caricatures, any real or vivid thing which assisted him to seize the details in concrete form. In 1833 he wrote Mill that he has finally "dug out a series of Revolution engravings," and got great good out of them. The men and women of the Revolution drama gradually came to life under his gaze. Even Mirabeau's "ugliness became a kind of truth" to him. Still more valuable was Vernet's "Collection of Caricatures" which contained vivid illustrations of the costume and dress of the revolutionary time. "I find the whole Revolution *new* to me in a manner," he wrote his brother, "when I bring it actually *home*. The thing *happened*, was visible in one form or the other; he who paints a Fact and Truth paints *Something*."[93] Carlyle had the gift of translating the trifling detail of costume, speech, manner into the corporeal object it represented. The true facts which he coveted, no matter how trivial or insignificant, he interpreted to be the outer garment of human emotions, motives, thoughts; "the state and structure of the soul" of those whom he was portraying. Yet Carlyle was no dealer in conjectural or hypothetical history. When he is forced to hypothecate, he does so with sound common sense and good judgment, and he candidly offers his conjecture for what it is worth.

Such facts as these that Carlyle sought—the bon mots of condemned men, the queues of breadless Parisians, details about manners and costumes, hints about life within the prisons, are biographic and at the same time relate solely to social history. He believed that such evidence would give him the insight he desired into the "inward life and spiritual condition" of a revolutionary people. The importance of such materials for his purposes dwarfed into insignificance the constitutional debatings, the governmental problems of taxation, currency, international relations, although all of these are glanced at as subsidiary and contributing to the central problem of how people lived and behaved. He professedly did not desire to describe the "House wherein the Life was led, but the Life itself," of the French people. Furthermore, he was not directly concerned with primary causes, or proximate issues of the conflict, but with the revolutionary crisis itself; first as a sociological phenomenon, second as a drama of unexampled power and effectiveness in which human passions and interests, deprived of their habitual restraints, contended in all their primary strength and force.

The necessity for concrete visualization led Carlyle to visit, whenever possible, the scenes about which he intended to write. He drew on his store of impressions of Paris for the *French Revolution*. While writing *Cromwell* and *Frederick* he searched out the actual scenes of all the notable events, particularly the battles. Cromwell's battlefields were visited and the most detailed information gathered relative to topography, vegetation, water courses, buildings. Two trips were made to Germany in order that Carlyle might see all of Frederick's important battlefields. The resulting descriptions of battles are among the most vivid in military annals. Carlyle had the graphic mind of a born strategist. Once he had noted the details of a battlefield, the number and position of the natural defenses, the roads leading to and from, the nature of the terrain, he was able to reconstruct a lively account of the battle on the basis of the barest statistical details. Frederick's victory at Rossbach, or Cromwell's victories at Naseby and Dunbar are described with the most vivid and detailed exactitude. The description of Dunbar, indeed, is sometimes alluded to as the most graphic piece of military description in English literature.

Interesting instances of the opposite, the want of concrete knowledge about places, are Carlyle's treatment of Cromwell's Irish Campaigns and Frederick's Battle of Kunersdorf. In 1844 he noted in a letter: "I have never yet been in Ireland with Cromwell, and will not go . . . if I can help it. . . . Besides I never *saw* a square inch of Ireland [except] with my mind's eyes, and do not know it at all."[94] The battlefield of Kunersdorf "has had the peculiar fate of being blown away by the winds. The then scene of things exists no longer; the descriptions in the old Books are gone hopelessly irrecognizable."[95] The fact is, the scene of Kunersdorf had become a tract of tumbled sand. The vegetation had been killed; the wind had set it dancing and the scene of Frederick's battle had become a heaped barrenness; "the features of the battle quite blown away, and undecipherable in our time." With the features of the battlefield obliterated, Carlyle found it practically impossible to construct a plausible account of the battle.

While Carlyle seems to have examined every bit of evidence available in the preparation of his histories, he preferred what we may term primary sources: letters, newspapers, official documents, memoirs, pamphlets, anything which had not been subjected to interpretation by a third person. In the "History of the French Revolution" he described what was in his opinion one of the "most interesting English biographies . . . a long, thin Folio on Oliver Cromwell . . . where the editor has merely clipt out from the contemporary newspapers whatsoever article, paragraph, or sentence he found to contain the name of Old Noll, and printed them in the order of their dates. It is surprising that the like has not been attempted in other cases."[96] The *Histoire Parlementaire* was a source book constructed on such a principle, containing pamphlets, books, newspapers, ephemeral printings and paintings, even sheets and handbills, but unfortunately was not wholly completed while Carlyle was writing the *French Revolution*. His most valued sources, the hundred volumes of Memoirs, and the picturesque history by the anonymous *Deux Amis de la Liberté*, seem inadequate to the modern scholar. In defense of Carlyle's scholarly thoroughness, however, M. Aulard maintains that he had found not only nearly everything that was available at the time, but had applied critical judgment of the most discriminating sort in weighing his evidence. In this respect, M. Aulard considers him superior to Thiers, and quite on a par with Michelet and Taine.[97]

A recent study of Carlyle's treatment of his Revolution sources, with particular regard to the accuracy of his translations and general method of dealing with the materials, concludes that he treated his sources with a "really singular exactness and fidelity to the original."[98] The translations show occasional rearrangement of sentences and phrases to heighten the tone, without effecting a definite change of meaning. Carlyle had the habit of taking his materials from the memoirs pretty much as he found them; making his work a "prodigious canto of fragments from the memoirs and histories which made up the bulk of his sources." Rather than endeavoring to blend the various details into a smooth-running narrative, he took paraphrased bits or actual translations of the details themselves and displayed them with a running commentary of Carlylean interpretation. This was done freely with the materials on Frederick too.

The episodic nature of the *French Revolution* arises thus, in Professor Harrold's opinion, from the episodic character of the sources: memoirs, letters, reminiscences, pamphlets, diaries, materials naturally deficient in coherence but charged with the evocative power of picturesque reality. Carlyle's work, compared with that of his contemporaries, is carefully documented and extraordinarily trustworthy. In speaking of Thier's ten volumes on the Revolution, Carlyle criticized the absence of documentation. Thiers has only one footnote in the entire ten volumes, and that is to a book, without notation of chapter or page.[99] Carlyle himself cited eighty-three different sources, and the three volumes contain eight hundred and fifty footnotes, representing a really prodigious degree of scholarship.[100] It is probable that a student of Carlyle's treatment of his *Cromwell* and *Frederick* would come to the same general conclusions. Carlyle's principles of scholarship rested fundamentally on the soundest of all foundations: honesty, intelligence and common sense. Possibly no great historian of the impressionistic sort, intent on dramatically recreating the past in terms of art, built his structures on so solid a foundation.

V

THE ART OF HISTORY IN PRACTICE

THE CREATIVE CONSCIOUSNESS

IN THE preceding chapter Carlyle's attitude toward the historian's craft was considered, with emphasis upon the vital importance of his conception of the function of history in any adequate evaluation of his esthetic and scientific theories. The present chapter will deal with the more practical problem of what methods Carlyle actually used in recapturing an image of the past for his readers: "where lies his peculiar sleight of hand in this craft." It will be sufficiently clear by now that Carlyle's attitude toward the craft of history writing was both original and daring in its fundamental premises. He deliberately followed the example of Schiller in elevating the artist above the antiquarian; but he went much further than Schiller in justifying the license he exercised by enlarging the artist's function to include the true business of the antiquarian. How far he succeeded in verifying his own principles of historical composition is our primary concern.

The problem of human productivity, in one or another of its many aspects, was central in most of Carlyle's speculative thinking. We have already pointed out that he sought to avoid the dualism inherent in the denomination of the reason and the imagination as separate organs, either one of which might be disparaged to the advantage of the other, by considering productivity to lie within the province of a single faculty he called "intellect," which represented a composite of all the faculties of mind and will comprising human consciousness. He decried the procedure common in his day of assigning separate spheres to the faculties of imagination, fancy, understanding, and reason as a "capital error," partly due to the necessities of language, he admitted, but dangerous when we permitted the words "to harden into things for us. . . . We ought to know withal, and to keep forever in mind, that these divisions are at bottom but *names;* that man's spiritual nature, the vital *Force* which dwells in him, is essentially one and indivisible; that what we call imagination, fancy, understanding, and so forth, are but different figures of the same Power of Insight . . . that if we knew one of them, we might know all of them. . . . You may see how a man would fight, by the way in which he sings. . . He is *one;* and preaches the same Self abroad in all these ways."[1]

Carlyle's conception of the human consciousness as a dynamic, mysterious force, only the surface of which is understood, governed his reflections on the process of literary creation. While the "Debater and Demonstrator," whom he ranked as the lowest of true thinkers, "knows what he has done and how he did it, the Artist, whom we rank as the highest, knows not; must speak of Inspiration, and in one or the other dialect, call his work the gift of a divinity." The truest force, and the healthiest, is that of which the possessor is unconscious; or, expressed in modern terminology, the artist has a dual consciousness, two planes of consciousness in partial communication, the lower and livelier plane feeding the upper, articulate plane. Carlyle voiced his belief in such a theory of artistic creation in "Characteristics":

In our inward, as in our outward world, what is mechanical lies open to us: not what is dynamical and has vitality. Of our Thinking . . . it is but the mere upper surface we shape into articulate Thoughts; —underneath the region of argument and conscious discourse, lies the region of meditation; here, in its quiet mysterious depths, dwells what vital force is in us; here, if aught is to be created, and not merely manufactured and communicated, must the work go on. Manufacture in intelligible, but trivial; Creation is great, and cannot be understood.[2]

The belief that many of the most vital and significant scenes in the drama of man's life are played off the boards in the realm of the unconscious was an outgrowth of Carlyle's revolt from the mechanistic association psychology current in his day and earlier. Whereas the associationalists explained the continuity of mental life by means of innate ideas, static entities lying in wait below the threshold of consciousness for their cues before appearing on the level of consciousness, Carlyle shifted the emphasis from a static to a dynamic subconsciousness and anticipated the findings of modern psychology.[3] As one present-day writer has expressed it, in terms very like Carlyle's, "daylight consciousness only flickers over an obscure and voluminous mystery."[4] The source of the most ordinary man's ideas are as inexplicable as those of the artist. Some place in the twilight region on the edges of consciousness or under it we must look for the explanation of the content of mental processes, including the poet's inspiration or the historian's conception as well as the commonplace thoughts of lesser beings.

THE PROCESS OF HISTORICAL COMPOSITION

Carlyle has left us plenty of evidence illuminative of his general method of composition. Always extremely articulate regarding his own state of mind, he recorded on many occasions, in letters and private writings, the semi-hypnotic state, "the half-asleep, half lotos-eating mood," which eventually overpowered him when he reached a point of complete saturation with his subject matter. It was his custom to steep himself in the materials relative to each successive history, a process consuming a considerable length of time, two years or more on the *French Revolution*, four years on *Cromwell*, and nearly twelve years on *Frederick*. He did not depend upon notes or other aids but rather upon a highly assimilative memory. When he finally reached the point of saturation and additional research seemed to add nothing to his store of impressions, he had formed chains of associations in the "living memory" capable of unraveling themselves once a discharge had been set off.

He made an interesting avowal of this, in reply to a query from Alexander Scott (1845).

I would very gladly tell you all my methods if I had any, but really I have as it were *none*. . . . I find that every business requires . . . a new scheme of operations, which amid infinite bungling and plunging unfolds itself at intervals . . . as I get along. The great thing is, not to stop and break down . . . as to the special point of taking excerpts, I think I universally, whether from habit or otherwise, rather avoid writing beyond the very minimum: mark in pencil the very smallest indication that will direct me to the thing again; and on the whole try to keep the whole matter simmering in the *living mind* and memory rather than laid up in paper bundles or otherwise laid up in an inert way. For this certainly turns out to be a truth; only what you at last *have living* in your own memory and heart is worth putting down to be printed; this alone has much chance to get into the living heart and memory of other men.[5]

Carlyle's confession of the necessity of keeping "the whole matter simmering in the living mind" suggests the dual consciousness familiar to the experience of the poet.[6] The passages leading downward to the subconscious are thrown open during the act of composition, and the communication between the upper and lower planes is full and free. Carlyle's letters offer an interesting series of revelations describing the nature of this experience. His earliest comment on the act of composition occurred in 1823, while he was still engaged on *The Life of Schiller*. He wrote Miss Welsh that original composition "is an agitating, fiery, consuming business when your heart is in it: I can easily conceive a man writing the soul out of him . . . when the matter engages him properly!"[7] Significantly, Carlyle's letters contain few comments suggestive of the creative mood during the period of the essays and of *Sartor*, and even of *Cagliostro* and the *Diamond Necklace*. This is explainable when we reflect that Carlyle would have called them (with the exception of *Sartor*) merely "manufactured," a product of the upper, articulate level of consciousness. While the *Diamond Necklace* and *Calgiostro* were frankly experiments with the "poetico-historical" narrative technique he had fashioned for the "story of the Time-Hat" in which his "mind would so fain deliver itself of that 'Divine Idea of the World'," the critical and experimental spirit dominated their production. *Sartor*, on the other hand, differed in the method by which it came into existence by being composed of material that was wholly subjective. Carlyle, in a state Professor Cazamian describes as "semi-conscious automatism," merely projected the content of his own consciousness, without the preliminary necessity of saturating himself in his subject matter as in the case of the later histories.

By the time Carlyle undertook the *French Revolution* his method was fairly well developed, and from that period onward his letters reveal his state of mind before and during composition. He began to assume the dual rôle of creator and spectator which became more pronounced with each work. In 1834 he acknowledged to his brother that his researches had progressed to the point where he seemed to learn nothing further from books. More books were just a repetition of those already read.[8] Later he wrote his wife in a similar vein: ". . . it all stands pretty fair in my head; nor do I mean to investigate much more about it, but to splash down what I know, in large masses of colour; that it may look like a smoke and flame conflagration in the distance,—which it is."[9]

The tragic loss of the first volume of the *French Revolution* gave Carlyle an opportunity to test the practical value of his "poetico-historic" method of writing only what he held "simmering in the living memory."[10] Probably few historians could duplicate his feat of reproducing the lost volume from memory. The loss was a severe shock to him, however. He confessed feeling like a schoolboy whose master has torn his copy. "The thing was *lost*, and perhaps worse," he wrote his brother, "for I had not only forgotten all the structure of it, but the spirit it was written with was past; only the general impression seemed to remain, and the recollection that I was on the whole well satisfied with that, and could now hardly hope to equal it."[11] Yet when the burnt volume was finally replaced he admitted that the "work does not seem . . . very much worse than it was; it is worse in the style of expression, but better compacted in the thought."[12] This is interesting evidence of what we would normally expect to have ocurred: a certain loss of spontaneity resulting from the necessity of rekindling the fires of imaginative enthusiasm. The ordinary reader can detect little difference in tone in the first as compared with the two suceeding volumes; and this fact is testimony to the fiery heat engendered by the entire conception of the *French Revolution*. The book was, indeed, what he declared it to be to Sterling: "a wild, savage Book . . . hot out of my own soul; born in blackness, whirlwind and sorrow."[13]

Before the *French Revolution* was completed Carlyle began to liken the creative mood to a spell of enchantment, a figure of speech which occurred more and more frequently. In 1836 he wrote Sterling that he is "floundering along, hoping that the heavy hand of this Enchantment shall be got loosened from me (for it is really like a spell) and I be free." He often recorded a mixture of fascination and horror as he felt the spell take hold of him. Another letter to Sterling contains characteristic expression of this: "If you mean to write a book," he wrote, "see that you have been right despondent, as near hanging yourself as might be, for some months before . . . this is true . . . and known to me by older experience than yours." The mood of creation was a "descent into primeval Night." "I have again got down into primeval Night, and live alone with the Manes," he wrote Emerson, ". . . uncertain whether I shall ever more see day. I am partly ashamed of myself; but I cannot help it."[14] Again, while working on *Cromwell*, he wrote Sterling that his work looked fruitless: "a mole's work, boring and digging blindly underground; my own inner man is sometimes very busy (too busy) but the rest is all silence."[15] He described his mood similarly to Emerson: "Partly I was busy; partly, too, as my wont is, I was half-asleep:—perhaps you do not know the *combination* of these two predictables in one and the same unfortunate human subject."[16]

With the researches on Frederick the process was the same and the sense of dual consciousness was even more pronounced. In 1852 Carlyle wrote Emerson: "I am sunk deep here, in effete manuscripts, in abstruse meditations, in confusions old and new; sinking . . . through stratum after stratum of the Inane,—down to one knows not what depth!"[17] Two years later he was still struggling stubbornly through the materials relative to Frederick's epoch. "I bore and dig toilsomely through the unutterablest mass of dead rubbish, which is not even English, which is German and inhuman. . . . And on the whole Fritz himself is not sufficiently divine to me . . . in short, it oftenest seems to me I shall never write any word about that matter; and have again fairly got into the element of the Impossible."[18] In 1855 he was still "wriggling and wrestling on the worst possible terms with a Task . . . that generally seems not worth doing and yet must be done."[19]

Carlyle frequently likened the process of composition to that of gestation. In 1831 he requested the publishers to return his essay, *Thoughts on Clothes,* because he realized it was not finished: "the thing still lives and produces with me," he reported to his brother.[20] More than once he alluded to experiencing the "birth-throes of a Book."[21] After the completion of the *French Revolution* and *Chartism* he complained to Sterling that he was in a state of complete idleness: "A Book, I suppose, will grow in me if I live some years," he wrote, "but as yet it lies swimming over Infinitude; sunk beyond sounding in Chaos and Night. Really, I find it a dreadful piece of work to write anything that is worth writing."[22] To Emerson he wrote in similar vein: "I do feel sometimes as if another Book were growing in me,— although I almost tremble to think of it. . . ."[23] Fifteen years later he told Emerson again: "I even think there is yet another Book in me . . . and if it were a right one, *rest* after that."[24]

The assembled evidence is probably more than sufficient to demonstrate Carlyle's extreme subjectivism; the state of "semi-conscious automatism" in which he wrote his histories; the sense of dual planes of consciousness which overpowered him when he had read himself into his subject matter deeply enough to become possessed by it. It was part of his esthetic theory that the artist must attain a state of complete surrender to his conception before he can render it in terms vivid enough to reach the "living mind" of others. For the historian, working in the sphere of reality, the necessity of completely assimilating his materials imposes an even greater obligation upon the fusing power of the imagination because the material is so generally "dead," a veritable prison house of reality.

It was at this point that Carlyle blended the methods of the scientist and the artist. His methods of research were the recognized methods of the scientific inquirer. He collected all the evidence available; sifted it with patience and scholarly accuracy; and applied to it intellectual standards in which sound

ART OF HISTORY: PRACTICE 145

intuitive judgment was fortified by scrupulous honesty. In his assimilation of the materials, however, his method became that of the artist. He did not take notes, or otherwise lay by materials "in an inert way," but absorbed them until they became part of the subjective content of consciousness. It was a process of "emotionalized thinking," which a contemporary philosopher believes is a characteristic of both the artist and the scientist so far as they are of comparable rank.[25] The creative imagination, especially in its highest exercise, cannot work in a vacuum. Its material is fact, somehow experienced.[26] The only significant distinction between the artist and the scientist lies in the kind of material to which the emotionalized imagination applies itself. Artists usually choose for their subject matter the qualities of things of direct experience; while scientists deal with these same qualities at one remove, through the medium of symbols.[27] Carlyle's fundamental interest in the mystery of the human personality led him to consider the materials of history an inexhaustible fountain head, uniting the qualities of things of direct experience with the objective scientific reality of proved facts. It belongs to the very nature of the creative mind, whether artistic or scientific, to seize the particular sort of material that stirs it; and to press out the value of that material to become the basis of a new experience.

Two requirements were indispensable before Carlyle could proceed with a projected undertaking. The first was to get a "blazing, radiant insight into the fact itself"; the second was the "kindling of the heart round the object." Without these two essential qualities, Carlyle could make nothing of his conceptions. In 1842 he wrote Sterling that the

. . . first and last secret of *Kunst*, is to get a thorough *intelligence* of the *fact* to be painted, represented, or in whatever way set forth;— the *fact*, deep as Hades, high as Heaven, and written *so*, as to the visual face of it, on our poor Earth! This once *blazing* within one, if it will ever get to blaze, and bursting to be out, one has to take the whole dexterity of adaptation one is master of . . . and contrive to exhibit it one way or other.[28]

The process by which Carlyle's enthusiasm was slowly kindled on the Cromwell and Frederick projects is fully revealed in his letters. He sought to get a "credible face-to-face acquaintance" with the periods and the men who lived in them, in terms of contemporary experience, which was difficult because they seemed so generally unintelligible to his own century. Mainly for this reason he found the resurrection of Puritanism to be not a "tenth-part such a subject as the French Revolution, nor can Art of man make such a book out of it." Carlyle gradually came to "see," however, that "this Cromwell was one of the greatest souls ever born of English kin."[29] He became convinced that a "Great Man does lie buried under this waste continent of cinders, and a Great Action," could he but "unbury them, present them visible, and so help, as it were, in the creation of them."[30]

The same genetic process took place in connection with *Frederick*. He wrote to Emerson: "Being in a reading mood . . . and not being capable of reading except in a train and about some object of interest" he had taken to reading about Frederick (having approached it twice before).[31] In a year or two he had "tumbled up, in a loose way, an immense amount of shot rubbish on that field . . . not with much decisive approach to Frederick's *self*. . . . The man looked brilliant and noble . . . but how love him, or the sad wreck he lived and worked in?" He did not "even yet see him clearly; and to try making others see him?" Frederick attracted Carlyle at first sight still less than Cromwell because he had even less subjective sympathy for eighteenth century Europe than he had possessed for Puritan England. Frederick was "not half or tenth-part such a man as Cromwell, that one should dive and swim for him in that manner."[32] Yet the "vague shoreless nature" of the subject and the "want of sufficient love for lean Frederick" gradually yielded to continued research, and Frederick eventually became a "pretty little man," veracious, courageous, invincible in his small sphere, even if he never rose into the empyrean regions.[33]

By no "art or aid of Clio" could Carlyle ever make a history of a man or of an historical epoch as long as it remained inaccessible to his concrete imagination. The fullness of emotion and spontaneity of utterance which characterized his work were

ART OF HISTORY: PRACTICE 147

the result of a long period of incubation in which he steeped himself in the recorded materials. He underwent the subjective process of feeling himself into the objective situations; observing the related events; reconstructing what he saw and heard. After a prolonged period of assimilation, expression became an acute necessity, and its form more or less inevitable. Once he had gained a "credible face-to-face acquaintance" with the fact to be represented, it began to "blaze" within him, "bursting to be out"; and the act of composition resolved itself into the effort to "exhibit it one way or another," with the "whole dexterity of adaptation" at his command.

THE SECRET OF BEING GRAPHIC

We have observed Carlyle's own documentation of the mental state out of which his histories took their being, yet we are possibly no nearer an understanding of the fundamental mystery that lies implicit in the relationship between the raw materials and the finished product. Of what does the artist's "inspiration" consist? Modern psychology is not much closer to a clue than were the romanticists of Carlyle's generation who considered genius an underived force out of God's own hand, mysterious and inexplicable. Carlyle advanced beyond most of his contemporaries, and anticipated the modern attitude, in insisting that all so-called inspiration occurs only within the limits of the individual's capacity. The artist's revelation may be a flash-up from the unconscious; but it never occurs to men who are weak either intellectually or morally. Carlyle had no more patience than have contemporary students of the problem with the Platonic conception of divine inspiration as a power outside the artist which moves the hand that writes the poem.[34] He believed that the poet's power is only the sight that sees more clearly, the ability to embody the revelation more truly in act or word than do other men.

Artists as a class have a more lively subconscious than other men, in Carlyle's opinion. They possess what he called "lively minds," wherein lie the "foundation of every sort of talent, poetical and intellectual." Such a mind expresses itself in a "perpetual, never-failing tendency to transform into shape, into life, the opinion or feeling of the poet. Carlyle did not mean "mere metaphor or rhetorical trope," which he rightly regarded as the "scaffolding of the edifice which is to be built up (within our thoughts) by means of them." The poet's conceptions take form, possess visual existence; the "poet's imagination bodies forth the forms of things unseen, his pen turns them to shape."[35] Homer surpassed all men in possessing such an emblematic intellect, though not far behind him were Shakespeare, and Goethe, Burns, Defoe, Richardson.

Carlyle gives us further insight into his conception of the secret of being graphic in the essay on Burns. He believed that Burns was distinguished no less "for the clearness than for the impetuous force of his conceptions." Who ever uttered "words more memorable," or found a single phrase sufficient to depict a whole scene? he asked. Burns had a "resonance in his bosom for every note of human feeling," a "lightly moved and all conceiving spirit" which was wedded to a "fierce prompt force" in grasping the subject, "fixing the full image of the matter in his eye ... amid a thousand accidents and superficial circumstances, none of which misleads him."[36] No poet ever excelled Burns in this graphic power of description; "three lines from his hand and we have a likeness."

It is no accident that Carlyle brought such subtlety and insight to the analysis of the workings of the plastic or concrete imagination; it was the sort he himself possessed. His type was so strongly marked, moreover, that he had little real sympathy for or understanding of the opposite emotional or "diffluent" imagination, with its abstractionist tendencies, such as Emerson possessed. The plastic imagination tends always to construct images in "subservience to the dictates of objective reality."[37] The opposite or diffluent imagination tends to transform reality to become a "carrier of the strange ecstacies and despairs of the inner life." The plastic imagination, when so strongly accented as Carlyle's, becomes "intoxicated with the aspects of sharply individualized things"; it belongs, therefore, most frequently to those who are sensitive to spatial measures, linear representa-

ART OF HISTORY: PRACTICE   149

tions; and tend to represent the world in vivid and concrete images with definite space-time relationships and definite sensory values.[38]

The demand of Carlyle's strongly plastic imagination for the concrete, the visual in art, led him to decide that the artist's aim "is, above all things, to be memorable."[39] This thought holds the secret of Carlyle's technical method of historical narration. The writing of history, in his opinion, was not mere chronological narration, or analysis, but the resurrection of the past by means of such facts as he possesses in such a way as to be "memorable."[40] These facts may be mean, or trivial or even ugly, but if real and well presented, they will force a lodgment in the mind of the reader and evoke images in the "susceptive memory as indelibly bright as to seem more real than reality itself." Emerson acknowledged Carlyle's own power to achieve this effect when he told him his words were "barbed and feathered [so] the memory of men cannot choose but to carry them whithersoever men go."[41]

Carlyle evidently gave much serious thought to the origin and effect of this "genius for description" which he believed to contain the secret of the artist's power, before he attempted to exploit his own possession of it. Particularly in the essays on Burns, Goethe, and the speculative essay "Biography," he specifically discussed the secret of being graphic. Half its effect, he believed, depended on the *quality* of the artist's vision of the thing, as we have already pointed out. The object must have been *real*, and it must have been *seen*, from the artist's point of view. The other half, however, depended upon the observer, and the question then becomes:

How are real objects to be *so* seen; on what quality of observing or style of describing, does this so intense pictorial power depend? Often a slight circumstance contributes to the result; some little, and to appearance, accidental feature is presented; a light gleam, which instantaneously *excites* the mind, and urges it to complete the picture, and evolve the meaning thereof for itself.[42]

In the course of these essays, Carlyle cited two interesting examples of what he considered an effective resuscitation of a "reality" by means of this so-called "genius for description." The first is from Clarendon, and when we recall his careful study of Clarendon as early as 1822, his remarks take on added significance.

We ourselves can remember reading, in Lord Clarendon, *with feelings perhaps somehow accidentally opened to it,*—certainly with a depth of impression strange to us then and now, that insignificant looking passage, where Charles, after the battle of Worcester, glides down, with Squire Careless, from the Royal Oak, at nightfall, being hungry: how, "making a shift to get over hedges and ditches, after walking at least eight or nine miles, which were the more grievous to the King by the weight of his boots (for he could not put *them* off when he cut off his hair, for want of shoes), before morning they came to a poor cottage, the owner whereof, being a Roman Catholic, was known to Careless.

The rustic hides the king in his haymow; brings him bread and buttermilk; finally exchanges clothes with him. What was there in this anecdote that "somehow accidentally awakened" Carlyle to the profound effectiveness of the graphic portrayal of facts in the re-creation of the past? It is not Charles or Careless who tears asunder the "blanket of the Night" and stands there for a moment visible to us. It is the sudden vision of the nameless rustic who opens a vista into that dead age and vanished manner of existence.

This, then, was a genuine flesh and blood rustic of the year 1651; he did actually swallow bread and buttermilk (not having ale and bacon), and do field labor: with these hob-nailed "shoes" has sprawled through mud roads in winter, and, jocund or not, has driven his team afield in summer: he made bargains; had chafferings, and higglings, now a sore heart, now a glad one . . . toiled in many ways, being forced to it, till the strength was all worn out of him. . . . How comes it, that he alone of all the British rustics who tilled and lived along with him, on whom the blessed sun on that same "fifth day of September" was shining, should have chanced to rise on us. . . . We see him but for a moment; for one moment, the blanket of the Night is rent asunder, so that we behold and see, and then closes over him—forever.[43]

Another "indelible and magically bright . . . little Reality" is cited from Boswell's *Johnson*. It is the familiar anecdote in which Boswell tells of Johnson being accosted by a prostitute, "in itself the smallest and poorest of occurrences," but conveyed with a compelling sense of reality because Boswell convinces us of its truth by making us see it with our mind's eye, making us hear Johnson's voice as he dismissed the girl "without harshness." "Johnson said, 'No, no, my girl; it won't do'; and then 'we talked'—and herewith the wretched one, seen but for the twinkling of an eye, passes on into utter Darkness."[44]

These passages which Carlyle employed to demonstrate his conception of how the historian may resurrect the past in terms of a graphic image have two striking features in common. One is the extremely concrete character of the image itself, possessing a blend of motor, visual and auditory qualities. The second and more striking feature is the particularization of the anonymous figures of the seventeenth century rustic and the eighteenth century prostitute. The individuation of these anonymous figures is accomplished in so subtle and effective a way that the "blanket" of the past is torn agape and the reader not only catches an authentic glimpse of the social pattern of existence but has a sense of immediacy, of participation in it. The nameless rustic becomes no less a flesh-and-blood reality than King Charles himself. Emerson hinted at the secret of this when he declared that before history could become "fluid and true," "all public facts are to be individualized, all private facts are to be generalized."[45] In anecdotes such as these we have the dual quality of the individuation of the "public fact" and the generalization of the "private fact." History cannot be comprehended except by relating the "public facts" to the individualized human equation; and simultaneously lifting the "private fact" to the generalized sphere of the universal attributes of the human personality.

In *Past and Present* Carlyle gives us a better instance of the effect obtainable from the individuation of a particular fact than the examples he cited from Boswell and Clarendon. Jocelin de Brakelonde made the briefest mention of a visit John Lackland once paid St. Edmundsbury; of how he boarded there with his retinue for a fortnight; of how he left as payment "thirteen pence." Carlyle took this meager anecdote and did not merely retell it; he *relived* it in terms of Jocelin's own experience. Lackland had been

> ... daily in the very eyesight, palpable to the very fingers of our Jocelin: O Jocelin, what did he say, what did he do; how looked he, lived he;—at the very lowest, what coat or breeches had he on? Jocelin is obstinately silent.... With Jocelin's eyes we discern almost nothing of John Lackland ... with our own eyes and appliances, intensely looking, discern ... a blustering, dissipated human figure, with a kind of blackguard quality air, in cramoisy velvet ... with much plumage and fringing; amid numerous other human figures of the like; riding abroad with hawks; talking noisy nonsense,—tearing out the bowels of St. Edmundsbury Convent (its larders namely and cellars) in the most ruinous way, by living at rack and manger there. Jocelin notes only, with a slight subacidity of manner, that the King's Majesty ... did leave, as gift for our St. Edmund Shrine, a handsome enough silk cloak,—or rather pretended to leave, for one of his retinue borrowed it of us, and *we* never got sight of it again; and, on the whole, that the *Dominus Rex*, at departing, gave us "thirteen sterlingii," one shilling and one penny, to say a mass for him; and so departed,—like a shabby Lackland as he was.... How much in Jocelin, as in all History, and indeed in all Nature, is at once inscrutable and certain; so dim and yet so indubitable; exciting us to endless considerations. For King Lackland *was* there, verily he; and did leave these *tredecim sterlingii*... and did live and look in one way or the other, and the whole world was living and looking along with him! There, we say, is the grand peculiarity; the immeasurable one; distinguishing, to a really infinite degree, the poorest historical fact from all Fiction whatsoever.[46]

M. Henri Poincaré, the French mathematician, cited Carlyle's use of this small historical fact as a means of illustrating the difference between an artist and a scientist. To Carlyle, the fact that John Lackland passed by here *once* is a reality surpassing all the theories in the world. M. Poincaré suggests that the scientist's attitude would be just the opposite: "John Lackland passed by here; that makes no difference to me, for he will never pass this way again."[47] A fact, M. Poincaré maintained, is not a fact except in relation to other facts, and unless it permits us to infer further facts.

M. Poincaré is assuming the point of view of the typical man of science who looks at the individual as a link in an endless chain. The individual is interesting only as one of a series of like individuals. The supreme fact to which Carlyle called our attention —the mystery of the origin of the individual life and personality —M. Poincaré does not pretend to solve. Carlyle studied history from the standpoint of the individual considered, not only as one in a geneological series extending back through remote time, but as a world in himself. The individual is both a microcosm and a macrocosm. It was by the process of particularizing the individual, making him like all others and at the same time like no other, that Carlyle endeavored to resurrect the past for his readers.

Carlyle's thinking upon the problem of particularization led him to realize that the fundamental secret of being graphic lay in the artist's selection of details. The image he uses must not be merely a material copy of the thing seen if it is to possess the desired evocative power. The image must be only a highly suggestive part of the whole; "some slight detail, some little, and to appearance, accidental feature" must be presented. The reader's imagination is drawn to supply the representative meaning or content value of the image while his attention is centered on the sensory detail. The latter acts as the "light gleam" which "instantaneously excites the mind" and urges it to complete the picture, and evolve the meaning thereof for itself.

Carlyle's thought bears a remarkable resemblance to that of his great French contemporary, Gustave Flaubert. With the latter's realistic method, Carlyle's has many points in common. Flaubert believed that the means to the degree of individuation which would give a complete illusion of reality was to find the unknown or unremarked quality in each object we contemplate.[48] Even the smallest and most trivial object has about it some feature or quality distinguishing it from all others of its kind. The problem is to find it; and when found, to discover the one noun that will express it; the one verb capable of giving it life; the one adjective properly qualifying it. The artist must know how to eliminate the ordinary details which everyone perceives, and to throw into strong and distinct light all those which have remained unperceived by the ordinary observer. It is from these latter that the evocative power of his image is derived.

Emerson also testified to the power to fix the "momentary eminency of an object," which he found so remarkable in Carlyle, as a power residing in "the detachment or sequestration of one object from an embarrassing variety."[49] Some minds, he wrote, have the capacity to give an "all-excluding fullness to the object, the thought, the word they alight upon, and to make that for the time the deputy of the world." The problem of accomplishing adequate individuation so as to effect a union between the sense of immediacy and the consciousness of a content value derived from the deposit of experience embedded in the self from the past is highly complex. Each artist has his own method, and does not exactly repeat himself in individual instances. A brief consideration of Carlyle's use of imagery may throw a little light on the numerous technical devices he carried in his full quiver of artistic resources.

CARLYLE'S USE OF IMAGERY

We have already pointed out that Carlyle's entire theory of esthetic response rests upon the spontaneous act of psychic participation on the part of the one contemplating the work of art. This process of "feeling in," of assuming attitudes and emotions in obedience to the demands of the artist, imparts, to the one contemplating, a response intensified by the intimate realization of the artist's meaning through actual subjective experience. In this experience, imitation probably plays the most subtle part, particularly in the understanding of human personalities, which it was Carlyle's chief concern to portray. Through inner imitation, "psychic posturings, and organic echoes," we assume a foreign personality; we become aware of how it feels to behave in such and such a way; then we read back into the other person our consciousness of how his behavior feels.[50] In the subjective realization of the motor and emotional attitudes of the person portrayed resides the unique esthetic experience. The image lodged in the "susceptive memory" has become "so indelibly bright" as to be "more real than reality itself."

ART OF HISTORY: PRACTICE   155

What are the characteristics of the image as Carlyle used it? It is evident that the requirements of biographic word-painting should rest upon images which most effectually stimulated the reader to the act of inner imitation: i.e., kinetic, auditory, visual, and tactile images. These indeed are the kinds used most freely by Carlyle. Adequate treatment of the richness of Carlyle's imagery and its effectiveness in graphically portraying biographic facts would more than fill a volume devoted to it alone; and the present limited space permits little more than mention of the several qualities of his pictorial power. A few illustrative instances will be cited, each one of which could be multiplied many times, if space permitted.

The most remarkable characteristics of Carlyle's imagery are those by means of which he creates a sense of substantiality in the thing represented. His pictorial images always convey the impression of occupying a position in the visible, concrete world of space and time. He accomplished this primarily by means of spacing; by introducing the element of time (mention of the date or hour of day, of the seasons, of the weather); by imparting a feeling of the energy and rhythm of life through the medium of a phrase with a motor value. His pictorial images have a three-dimensional quality: a sense of depth as well as length and breadth. Thus he succeeded admirably in verifying his belief that the most effective representation of historical action must be "solid," as contrasted with the mere "linear" character of conventional historical narrative. All action, he wrote in the essay "On History," is extended in depth as well as in length and breadth; "that is to say, is based on Passion and Mystery, if we investigate its origin."[51] But passion and mystery are subtle, affective qualities, to be evoked through a stimulus to the emotions. This Carlyle sought to do by means of his "historico-biographic" details. Like Homer, Tacitus, and Shakespeare (no one of whom distinguished between history and poetry), Carlyle was not interested in presenting a "nomenclature of things done, or a dusty herbarium of events," but in exhibiting to view those springs of action in which events, great and small, take their rise.

While the sensory appeal of Carlyle's imagery is so immediate that the reader feels his senses as well as his imagination engaged, Carlyle seems to have had little conscious regard for the purely sensorial values. At least they were dwarfed by the meaning or content value of his images. His prose has an impressively marked rhythm and a richness of auditory imagery, yet he seems to have been uninterested in music. His visual imagery is still more vivid than the auditory, though it seems to have been divorced from an interest in other forms of representative art. He had a keen eye for color, for line and design, but his interest was fixed not on the quality but on the spatial representation. In short, his images furnish us with the material for esthetic judgments rather than esthetic pleasures. The latter are usually regarded as a matter of immediate apprehension; while esthetic judgments are the fruit of reflection. It is by means of esthetic judgments that we share the interpretative process of the artist and become, not a spectator only, but an actual creator of the experience transmuted into art.

Emerson commented, rather ruefully, on Carlyle's constant tendency to form a graphic image: "those thirsty eyes, those portrait eating, portrait painting eyes of thine, those fatal perceptions have fallen full on the great forehead which I followed about all my young days."[52] The pictorial portrait which elicited this comment is a good instance of Carlyle's success with a purely auditory effect. His impression of Webster had been of a "sufficient effectual man. . . . The sound of him is nowise poetic-rhythmic; it is clear, one-toned, you might say metallic, yet distinct, significant, not without melody."[53]

The use of auditory imagery is particularly frequent in the *French Revolution*. The surging roar of inflamed mobs, the "grim-silent seas" of people, the bellowing of the "mad, mad-making voice of rumor," the "Thunder-peals of Fury stirred on by Fear" admirably convey the impression of confusion, of violence and terror. "The Cry, *To Arms,* roars ten-fold; steeples with their metal storm-voice boom out, as the sun sinks . . . the streets are a living foam-sea, chafed by all the winds," as "seven hundred thousand individuals, on the sudden, find all their old paths, old ways of acting and deciding, vanish from under their

ART OF HISTORY: PRACTICE

feet. And so there they go, with clangour and terror ... headlong into the new Era."[54]

The mixture of auditory and kinetic effects is responsible for some of the most effective scenes in the book: the taking of the Bastille, for example, is as audible to the reader's imagination as it is lively and exciting. The effect is subtly heightened by interrupting the account of the roaring mob with a brief description of how the

> ... Bastille Clock ticks (inaudible) in its Inner Court there, at its ease, hour after hour, as if nothing special ... were passing! It tolled One when the firing began; and is now pointing toward five, and still the firing slakes not,—Far down in their vaults, the seven Prisoners hear muffled din as of earthquakes; their Turnkeys answer vaguely."[55]

Still more effective is the description of Mirabeau declaring the Third Estate to be the National Assembly. The King, retinue, Noblesse, most of the Clergy filed out of the States General, "through grim-silent seas" of people.

> Only the Commons Deputies file not out; but stand there in gloomy silence, uncertain what they shall do. One man of them is certain; one man of them discerns and dares! It is now that King Mirabeau starts to the Tribune, and lifts up his lion-voice. Verily a word in season; for, in such scenes, the moment is the mother of ages!! ... List to the brool of that royal forest-voice; sorrowful, low; fast swelling to a roar! Eyes kindle at the glance of his eye:—National Deputies were missioned by a Nation; they have sworn an Oath; they— but lo! While the lion's voice roars loudest, what Apparition is this? Apparition of Mercurius de Brézé, muttering somewhat! "Speak out," cry several,—"Messieurs," shrills de Brézé, ... "you have heard the King's orders!"—Mirabeau glares on him with fire-flashing face; shakes the black lion's mane: "Yes, Monsieur, we have heard what the King was advised to say; and *you* ... are not the man to remind us of it. Go ... tell those who sent you that we are here by the will of the People, and that nothing but the force of bayonets shall send us hence!" And poor de Brézé—shivers forth from the National Assembly; and also ... finally from the page of history.[56]

The invitation to psychic participation in such passages is not to be resisted. The use of direct conversation, whether documentary or conjectural, is highly effective in stimulating the reader to the process of "inner imitation" or psychic participation. Two instances from *Cromwell*, one wholly conjectural, the other documentary, are further illustrative of this. Carlyle found the name of "Oliver Cromwell, Cornet" in the Army Lists; took him to be the great Oliver's eldest son, "now a stout young man of twenty. 'Thou too, Boy Oliver, thou art fit to swing a sword. If there ever was a battle worth fighting, and to be called God's battle, it is this; thou too wilt come!' "[57] The other instance is the familiar anecdote which describes Cromwell's dismissal of Mr. Hitch, the "scandalous minister," and the choir-service in Ely Cathedral. The Governor of Ely, with a

... rabble at his heels, with his hat on, ... walks up to the Choir, says audibly: "I am a man under Authority; and am commanded to dismiss this Assembly,"—then draws back a little, that the Assembly may dismiss with decency. Mr. Hitch has paused for a moment; but seeing Oliver draw back, he starts again: "As it was in the beginning"—!—"Leave off your fooling, and come down, Sir!" said Oliver, in a voice still audible to this Editor; which Mr. Hitch did now instantaneously give ear to. And so, "with his whole congregation," files out, and vanishes from the field of History.[58]

Carlyle's visual imagery, like the auditory and motor, was always concerned with creating a sense of viability and an affective judgment; almost never with creating a purely pictorial effect. Very often the reader is made to see notable scenes through the eyes of one whose emotions are already involved, as when Cromwell witnessed the beheading of Sir Walter Raleigh and the trial of King Charles; or one of the glimpses we get of Robespierre, through the eyes of Mirabeau, or of Marie Antoinette's trial through the eyes of Robespierre. Carlyle's portraits are usually of the predominantly sensual sort, using spatial or color attributes, with auxiliary kinetic qualities introduced to give a sense of movement. The extremely vivid picture of Monk Samson may be cited.

The Reader is desired to mark this Monk. [Carlyle frequently fixes our attention in this manner.] A personable man of seven-and-forty;

ART OF HISTORY: PRACTICE

stout-made, stands erect as a pillar; with bushy eyebrows, the eyes of him beaming into you in a really strange way; the face massive, grave, with "a very eminent nose"; his head almost bald, its auburn remnants of hair and the copious ruddy beard getting slightly streaked with gray. This is Brother Samson; a man worth looking at.[59]

One other, too, of a very different sort: Marat, singled out by the historian from among the six hundred deputies to the States-General.

Surely, also, in some place not of honour, stands or sprawls up querulous, that he too, though short, may see,—one squalidest bleared mortal, redolent of soot and horse-drugs; Jean Paul Marat of Neuchâtel! O Marat, Renovator of Human Science, Lecturer on Optics; O thou remarkablest horse-leech, once in D'artois Stables;—as thy bleared soul looks forth, through thy bleared, dull-acrid, woe-stricken face, what sees it in all this?[60]

This portrait is a good instance of Carlyle's employment of dissonant, unpleasant details to convey the emotional tone he desired. One other deputy's portrait might be added—one who commanded a different tone from the historian:

There is one there who, by character, faculty, position, it fittest of all [to rule].... He with the thick black locks, will it be? With the ... black *boar's head*, fit to be "shaken" as a senatorial portent? Through whose shaggy beetle brows, and rough-hewn, seamed carbuncled face, there look natural ugliness, small-pox, incontinence, bankruptcy,—and burning fire of genius.... It is Gabriel Honoré Riquetti de Mirabeau, the world-compeller; man-ruling Deputy of Aix.[61]

Carlyle's gallery of historical portraits is conceded to be the largest, the most varied, and the most effective in the annals of historical literature.[62] Many figures that passed under his "stereoscopic" eye are still much as he left them; Mirabeau, Marie Antoinette and Louis XVI, Marat and Robespierre, Lafayette, Cromwell, Friedrich Wilhelm I, the "Great Drill Sergeant." He had a sure, quick insight into character and motive, and an unfailing sense for the qualities that would "ticket" his characters in an unforgettable way. Emerson called his method a "wonderful new system of mnemonics, whereby great and insignificant men are ineffaceably ticketed and marked and modelled in memory by what they were, had and did."[63] Carlyle verified beyond cavil that "biographic" history is the most "memorable" kind of history because it is the most vivid, the most dramatic, the most stimulating to the esthetic judgment. From his own point of view he also verified his further conviction that the ultimate value of history is its social value expressed in terms of the work it does in the world.

Related to Carlyle's use of imagery as a fundamental feature of his style is his use of figurative language; his apt comparisons; his employment of hyperbole and metonymy; his irresistible weakness for nicknames. Robespierre, "the sea-green incorruptible," has never shaken off Carlyle's descriptive epithet. Neither has "horse-leech Marat"; nor "Cromwell-Grandison" Lafayette, the "thin constitutional pedant"; nor "the Prince of Quacks"; nor "the Great Persifleur"; nor "perpetual President" Maupertuis; nor August "the Physically Strong," nor "the little corporal"; to name only a few out of Carlyle's gallery who have remained fixed in the public memory by the apt nicknames he coined for them. This cartooning device, in which the part is substituted for the whole, or a simple attribute is allowed to represent a concrete object, is a short-circuiting procedure which has the specific psychological effect of narrowing the consciousness with a subsequent emphasis on whatever is at the point of focus. It gives rise to striking, frequently grotesque, but nearly always unforgettable effects. Carlyle's thought stuff was highly emotionalized, woven largely of motor and organic threads. His tendency to exaggeration was the inevitable result of his desire to create in the reader as vivid an emotion as he himself felt.

Carlyle's imagination was of the metaphorical kind, furthermore, which delighted in the process of substitution and identification of ideas; in the union of quite heterogeneous things to create a new mental content. His use of metaphors fused in the fire of an intense emotional mood is prevalent in his writing from *Sartor* to *Frederick;* reaches a kind of climax of intensity in the *French Revolution;* diminishes in emotional intensity but increases in humor and variety in *Past and Present* and *Frederick.*

One recalls Emerson's description of the latter as "infinitely the wittiest book that was ever written."[64]

After reading the *Diamond Necklace*, first fruit of Carlyle's method, Emerson wrote its author that the "eye" of his readers would be bewildered by the "multitude of brilliantly colored hieroglyphics" which characterized his "stereoscopic style"; a style "so vast, enormous, related to all the world, and so endless in details."[65] Sterling, too, in his criticism of *Sartor*, complained of the "heightened and plethoric fulness" of Carlyle's style; its "accumulation and contrast of imagery; its occasional jerking and almost spasmodic violence; and above all, the painful subjective excitement, which seems the element and groundwork even of every description of Nature."[66]

Carlyle received the criticism of his friends on his "Gothic efflorescence" as part of the appointed order, and persisted in his own way. Current tendencies encouraged him in his experiments in expression; his friends learned to tolerate and then to admire; and the reading public grew increasingly responsive as Carlyle's successive histories made plainer his artistic purpose. He desired above all else to appeal to the affective judgment of his readers; and he adhered to the romantic principle that "mood-toning" by means of the sensuously unpleasant as well as the pleasant, the sad and melancholy, the dissonant and misshapen, the ugly and grotesque, was a surer means of securing the desired effect than the harmonious and symmetrical. "Incompleteness always hints at Infinitude."

OTHER TECHNICAL DEVICES

While imagery and metaphor were the fundamental elements of Carlyle's biographic method of writing history, he had a variety of other artistic devices. Some of these contributed to the sense of spatial reality; others to temporal reality. The reader is constantly made to feel, not how unlike his own day were those "dim old times" but how like it. There are constant references to such stable and fixed realities as the rising and setting of the sun, the march of the seasons, the sowing and harvesting of crops. The emotional overtones which surround such universal happenings as birth, death, marriage, parenthood, are freely invoked. He believed that men are not interested in history for the sake of the events and personalities themselves; but because these things happened and these men lived in God's world, which has changed little since Homer's day.

This capacity to make time seem like a transparent veil and the past and future seem a part of the "contemporaneous present" Carlyle demonstrated most vividly in *Past and Present*. "Bozzy" Jocelin opens to mankind the floodgates of authentic Convent gossip. We listen, because "even gossip, seven centuries off, has significance." "List," says Carlyle, "how like men are to one another in all centuries." While we listen Carlyle artfully exploits every item of biographic fact, every morsel of gossip, every concrete detail relating to how men managed life in the twelfth century. We watch the government of the Convent, the collection of tithes and revenues, the acquisition of food, even the repairing of houses. We accompany Monk Samson on a journey to Rome; we observe the disciplining of recalcitrant monks. What we see is how, "in its undeniable but dim manner," old St. Edmundsbury spins and tills, and laboriously keeps its pot boiling, and St. Edmund's Shrine lighted, "under such conditions and averages as it can."[67]

The use of dates, frequently the day of the week or the month, a phrase relative to the weather or the diurnal routine, conveys a sense of homely realism and authenticity. The pouring rain which wetted the Commons Deputies as they waited "under mean porches and at back doors" while the King and nobles filed into the assembly of the States-General added a final affliction to the already sore trials of the outraged Third Estate.[68] The effect of this vivid detail in rendering the scene both significant and memorable to the reader is greater than pages of analysis of sovereign rights, legal issues, constitutional questions. If the reader is interested in the constitutional aspects of the question, he will find this inadequate, but if he is interested, as the vast majority of readers are, in understanding the motives and complex emotional attitudes which nerved the Third Estate to take the law into its own hands and declare itself the National

ART OF HISTORY: PRACTICE 163

Assembly, arbiter of France's destiny, he will find in Carlyle's account a credible reality.

Details about the weather frequently add a heightening effect of violence and terror to battle scenes. The battle of Dunbar, for example, had a dramatic setting against wild storms. Cromwell's soldiers stand to their arms all night; "being upon an engagement very difficult indeed. The night is wild and wet—second of September. . . . The Harvest Moon wades deep among clouds of sleet and hail. . . . We English have some tents; the Scots have none. The hoarse sea moans bodeful, swinging low and heavy against these whinstone bays; the sea and the tempests are abroad, all else asleep but we. . . ."[69]

There is occasional use of anecdotes of a grotesque or ludicrous nature, yet vivid and concrete, which shake the reader into an instant perception of a visible reality. This is one of Carlyle's most striking means of individuation. Describing Naseby Hill, scene of the battle of Naseby, he mentions "hollow spots, of a rank vegetation" still to be seen on that broad moor, and understood to be burial mounds. He tells of the discovery of "two ancient grinder teeth, dug lately from that ground. . . . Sound effectual grinders, one of them very large; which ate their breakfast on the fourteenth morning of June two hundred years ago, and except to be clenched once in grim battle, had never work to do more in this world."[70]

A similarly vivid resurrection of an obscure but indubitable fact is the description in *Past and Present* of the "glorious victory over the Flemings at Fornham" in 1173:

The river Lark, though not very discoverably, still runs or stagnates in that country; and the battle ground is there; serving at present as a pleasure ground to his Grace of Northumberland. Copper pennies of Henry II are still found there;—rotted out from the pouches of poor slain soldiers, who had not had *time* to buy liquor with them. In the river Lark itself was fished up . . . an antique gold ring; which fond Dilettantism can almost believe may have been the very ring Countess Leicester threw away, in her flight, into that same Lark river. Nay, few years ago, in tearing out an enormous superannuated ash-tree . . . long a fixture in the soil . . . there was laid bare, under its roots, "a circular mound of skeletons wonderfully complete" all radiating from a centre, face upwards, feet inwards . . . evidently the fruit of battle; for "many of the heads were cleft, or had arrow holes in them." The Battle of Fornham, therefore, is a fact, though a forgotten one; no less obscure than undeniable,—like so many other facts.[71]

Another effective means of making the reader realize the solid tissue of happenings which constitute the pattern of history at any one moment, is the use of contemporaneous occurrences. Oliver Cromwell, for instance, registered for his first term at Cambridge the day that Shakespeare died.

Oliver's Father saw Oliver write in the Album at Cambridge; at Stratford, Shakespeare's Ann Hathaway was weeping over his bed. The first world-great thing that remains of English history, the Literature of Shakespeare was ending; the second world-great thing that remains of English History, the armed Appeal of Puritanism to the Invisible God of Heaven . . . was beginning.[72]

Again, an extensive world-transaction, the death of Gustavus Adolphus, occurred while Oliver Cromwell "walked peacefully intent on cattle husbandry, that winter day, on the grassy banks of the Ouse at St. Ives." Far away on the battlefield of Lützen, Gustavus Adolphus, shot through the back, sank from his horse with the words: *"Ich habe genug, Bruder; rette Dich."*[73] This kaleidoscopic device, particularly effective with readers whose knowledge of history is extensive, is used more freely in *Frederick* than elsewhere. It is the primary means by which Carlyle keeps the crowded canvas of continental Europe distinctly before the reader. He even carries us beyond the seas, to Braddock and Wolfe's campaigns in America, giving brief, vivid glimpses of Washington's expedition to Fort Duquesne, the rough trip through the forest and over mountain. He lavished his descriptive powers on even the most ancillary and remote incidents; so that they stand in the mind of the reader as vividly as the most significant.

A final technical device may be noted here, and that is Carlyle's tendency to heighten our sympathy or engage our interest in a person by hinting at his future, when it would be useful, or recalling illustrative incidents out of his past, thus impressing the reader with a constant sense that he is in possession of the entire history centrally seen. Sometimes he compresses a whole biography into a paragraph or two, particularly in *Frederick,* where the stage is crowded with figures. The effect resembles that of the Greek chorus, recalling the past, hinting at the future, especially if bodeful. Carlyle seemed under the necessity of following all of the personalities who come under his eye to the end of their careers. Possibly no phrase recurs more than this ultimate one: "and thus he vanishes from History." Frequently he uses the moment of greatest triumph to acquaint the reader with the ultimate destiny of a character, as in his narration of the bright rôle "Dogleech" Marat played in the storming of the Bastille. Carlyle reminds him of a different rôle he will soon play: "Great, truly, O thou remarkable Dogleech, is this thy day of emergence and new-birth: and yet this same day come four years—!— But let the curtains of the Future hang."[74] This epic tendency became more pronounced as Carlyle grew older. In *Frederick* it is the chief factor accounting for the work's length and rather unwieldy proportions. To readers with whom subjective interest in personality is paramount, however, possibly no other of Carlyle's devices is more pleasing.

CARLYLE'S THOUGHTS ON STYLE

"There are always two parties to a good style," Carlyle wrote his brother in 1836, "the contented Writer and the contented Reader."[75] The language in which Carlyle's thought clothed itself was necessarily abrupt, vivid, ejaculating, because he intended it as a heightened rendering of dramatic speech. If the subject suffered frequent divorce from the verb, or sharply cut phrases did without the subject-object relationship altogether, the effect desired was that of direct speech, the nervous, broken rhythms which have become a commonplace in English prose of the present generation. Carlyle declared his principle of style in the introductory essay on Goethe prefacing *Wilhelm Meister* in 1824, a principle from which he never departed. "Language, in the hands of a master, is the express image of thought . . . it is the body of which thought is the soul."[76] He quoted Lessing's phrase—"'Every man has his own style, like his own nose"; and agreed with Lessing that "the outward style is only to be judged of by the inward qualities of the spirit which it is employed to body forth ... the former may vary into many shapes as the latter varies.... The grand point is to be genuine, vigorous, alive." If Carlyle incited a perennial "quarrel between the nominative and the verb"; disdained the science of grammar in a "certain latitudinarian spirit; dealt liberally in "parentheses, dashes, and subsidiary clauses"; invented new words and altered old ones; used "figures without limit"; it was because the meaning his words subserved seemed to require it.[77] "These poor people seem to think a style can be put off or put on, not like a skin but like a coat," he wrote Sterling, but is not a "skin verily a product and close kinsfellow of all that lies under it; exact type of the nature of the beast; not to be plucked off without flaying and death?"[78]

THE SENSE OF ARTISTIC FINALITY

A word remains to be said about the principle upon which Carlyle constructed the architectural design of his histories. In general, he followed Schiller's plan of proceeding from "eminence to eminence, and thence surveying the surrounding scene." His histories are not built around the strict chronological principle; but the materials are gathered up into masses which are successively exhibited, minor facts being grouped around some leading one to which our attention is chiefly directed. Yet few historians give a more effective impression of the stream of events flowing through time, borne along by an inner momentum which does not depend upon the narrator. This Carlyle attained, partly by the sagacious choice of details, partly by copious use of "time, occasion, circumstance, and name of some eye witness," which serves both a realistic and a scholarly purpose.[79]

Professional historians complain that Carlyle emphasized events, particularly in his treatment of the French Revolution, which they regard as less important than other events which he neglected altogether. Yet Carlyle's choice needs no defense if we judge his history as Carlyle believed one should judge any work of art: i.e., in the light of the artist's express intention. His selection of details from among the materials at his disposal precisely suited his purpose, which was not to write a constitutional history, nor a political history, nor a party history of the French Revolution, but a sociological history. The "history of a mind," Emerson called it; possibly no phrase describes it more aptly. Carlyle organized the confused emotional pattern of the French people during the revolutionary years around striking and symbolic events. Hence it is that the insurrection of women, and the fête of the Champ de Mars (the importance of which has sadly diminished among professional historians) take their places along with the storming of the Bastille and the formation of the National Assembly. Professor Cazamian likened the structure of the *French Revolution* to a perfectly organized drama in three acts.[80] Actually Carlyle found the structure ordained in the logic of the events themselves. He deliberately took the French people to be the collective hero of his book; and he followed the action of the collective causes throughout. The events are always presented to us from the standpoint of the folk hero; and only those events in which the collective group plays a part are exhibited.

Carlyle apparently intended to do a history of the Puritan Revolution on much the same principles. He soon found, however, that "poor Oliver" was buried under such a "scandalous accumulation of Human Stupidity" that no real historical work of art could be composed of such a "waste continent of cinders." "I have come at last to the conclusion" he wrote Emerson, "that I *must* write a Book on Cromwell; that there is no rest for me till I do it. This point fixed, another is not less fixed . . . that a Book on Cromwell is *impossible*. Literally so. . . ."[81] He at length discerned that one thing alone was possible, and that was the gathering of Oliver's letters and speeches, stringing them together according to their order in time; "a series of fixed rock-summits, in an infinite ocean of froth." Carlyle edited the letters and speeches on this principle, and the result achieved was, after all, a biography of Cromwell as artistic and complete as he could have wished. The Cromwell volumes are about "half letters, half comment"; very dull, said Carlyle, but legible enough as a "kind of life of Oliver."

Carlyle's ingenious elucidations of Cromwell's letters and speeches convey so vivid an impression of reality as to be a true reflection of real life. His interpretations of Oliver's motives, of the working of his mind in speech and action, of his relations with his family, his friends, his enemies, imparts a unified and artistic impression of a complete human personality. Modern discoveries have altered details, have thrown new light on his motives and hesitancies, and even have altered the details of the magnificent picture of the battle of Dunbar. But adding and subtracting details in any of Carlyle's histories tends to effect conscientious accuracy, at the cost of destroying the illusion of reality. Until Dryasdust can demonstrate that even the most just and accurate documentation of historic events represents more than a "more or less plausible account of the transaction," the sacrifice of the illusion of reality effected by the greatest historians of the past is uncalled for.

Carlyle's effort to synthesize the history of eighteenth-century Europe proved too vast in design to be made wholly subject to the rules of art. *Frederick* alone of Carlyle's histories falls short of the artistic unity which characterizes the *French Revolution, Cromwell, The Life of Sterling, Past and Present*. Yet few histories carry the reader's interest as steadily forward through eight long volumes as does this; nor is it wanting in harmony of design. Its episodic and somewhat fragmentary method exercise the reader's patience; but interest is never lacking. Carlyle seemed fatigued by the vastness of his own synthetic vision in the later volumes of *Frederick;* he relied more and more on notes scattered through the text in small print, interpolations obviously of material he had prepared and introduced without the final effort of assimilation into the body of the text. In these notes, which Carlyle sometimes attributes to Dryasdust, sometimes to a "learned Professor," sometimes to an "Able Editor" without deceiving the most casual reader, we may see the raw materials of Carlyle's histories in the first form in which his imagination has cast them.

Carlyle sensed strongly the inviolable character of his histories once they were a complete and artistically unified whole. In the introductions to the second and third editions of *Cromwell*, he confessed his reluctance to take apart his book and insert the flood of letters and documents relating to Cromwell which had been brought from hiding by the first edition of Carlyle's history. "To unhoop your cask again," he wrote, "and try to insert new staves, when the old staves, better or worse, do already hang together, is what no cooper will recommend."[82] The necessity of admitting new evidence which materially altered or corrected any features already assigned to Cromwell, he freely admitted; "limited only by this consideration: not to damage by it to a still greater degree the already extant, and so by one's effort accomplish only loss." For all such letters as neither added to nor subtracted from his portrait, he created an appendix, "a loose back-room . . . not bound to be organic or habitable," into which such might be swept.

In the preface to the Third Edition Carlyle proclaimed the inviolability of the artistic unity with still more confidence. The influx of new Cromwell material had revealed nothing of real importance affecting the outlines of the portrait as Carlyle had drawn it. The problem had been

> . . . not to improve the Book as a practical Representation of Cromwell's Existence in this world, but in hindering it from being injured as such,—from being swollen out of shape by superfluous details, defaced by dilettante antiquarianism, nugatory tag-rags; and in short turned away from its real uses, instead of furthered toward them.[83]

Carlyle's conception of the "real uses" of history is the irreconcilable point of difference between his point of view and that of the contemporary scientific historian. Sir Alfred Lyall warns us that the nature of the times compels the acceptance of the change from the artistic to the scientific conception, though we may regret it as unavoidable.[84] The significant tendencies of the twentieth century all point to the writing of history based upon exhaustive research, the accumulation and minute sifting of available details, the relentless verification of every statement, the intensive cultivation of a contracted area—tendencies which Carlyle acknowledged to be the limitations of Dryasdust. There are those among the professional historians themselves, however, who believe that the scientific history is merely an accumulation of the materials for an imaginative historical synthesis such as Carlyle gave us; and that the day of the great literary historians is not past, but merely eclipsed for the moment.

VI

CARLYLE'S POSITION AS A HISTORIAN

THE FOREGOING analysis has been limited, deliberately, to an expository account of Carlyle's fundamental attitude as a historian. A proper appraisal of his attainments in historical literature can be made only in the light of a full understanding of his conception of the art of history, which included both philosophic interpretation of the historic processes themselves, and the method of handling the materials of history. Without interpretation, in Carlyle's opinion, there could be no selection; and without method there could be no organization, synthesis, or, ultimately, effective presentation. Few historians have applied more effectively a rigorous and well-disciplined mind to a critical understanding of their own intellectual operations than Carlyle. Few have adhered more consistently to their own standards of scholarly accuracy and scrupulous integrity.

A grasp of Carlyle's fundamental attitude requires more than a fleeting knowledge of his historical writings. It demands primarily a careful study of his letters, his notebooks, his essays and other early writings. Without a genetic study of these, the evidence offered by the histories is inconclusive. Above all, the student of Carlyle as a historian must pursue his own way and disregard the dubious and untrustworthy opinions of those whom we would naturally expect to have the most impartial judgment. Even a cursory review of the stock criticisms which possess wide currency among the professional historians reveals how inadequately Carlyle's theories have been understood, and how readily succeeding generations of critics have been willing to accept the judgments of their predecessors, without question and without review of the evidence. It is readily admitted, of course, that Carlyle might have expected some retaliation from Dryasdust for a lifetime of abuse. But the modern historian should ask himself if Carlyle's charges were not true, and whether he himself does not bring precisely the same charges against the pedantic antiquarian whom Carlyle dubbed Dryasdust. Lord Morley remarked that Carlyle's genius gave him a right to mock at the ineffectiveness of Dryasdust, but his "genius was also too true to prevent him from adding that always needful supplement of a painstaking industry that rivalled Dryasdust's own most strenuous toil."[1]

Undoubtedly the most serious charge brought against Carlyle by his professional critics was that he arbitrarily defined the limits of his own task. The methods he employed could not be recognized as legitimate and sound because they were applicable only by one with his undeniable genius. No matter how rigorously scrupulous Carlyle may be shown to have been in his approach to his materials, or how careful and accurate in his use of authorities, the fact remains that he was not subject to generally recognized rules. When the charges brought against him are seriously examined, this appears to be the first and most grievous. The imaginative reconstruction of the past which he effected could not be added to nor subtracted from, without spoiling it altogether. One might inquire whether the results he obtained could not have been accepted at their face value, but the ideals dominating historical scholarship, particularly in the late nineteenth century, made no allowances for acknowledged works of art. No one could deny that Carlyle's imaginative reconstructions of vanished events and characters had immense power as art, but it could be denied that they were history.

This point of view toward literary history has been voiced recently by Professor Shotwell. Admitting that history "should be preserved, not as detached specimens, but as living organisms" if it is to recover successfully "the living past," the scientific historian has reason to be "eternally distrustful" of the literary historian.[2] History, a poor enough mirror of reality in any case, "is readily warped by art," and rhetoric is art of the most formal kind. The historian's "method of investigation often seems to weaken as his rhetoric improves." Art, according to Professor Shotwell, "distorts into ordered arrangement the haphazard, unformed materials which chance produces or preserves. It sets its pieces like an impresario and completes with convincing elegance the abrupt and incomplete dramas of reality. All history writing does this to some degree, since it is art. But rhetoric passes easily over into the sphere of conscious distortion. A phrase is worth a fact; and a fact must fit the liking of the audience, or serve to point a moral."[3] A strictly scientific definition of terms would condemn Professor Shotwell's identification of rhetoric with art. In fact, it is not clear precisely what Professor Shotwell does mean by his use of "rhetoric" and "art." Certainly the truth attained by a poetic representation of reality is not to be confused with the spurious copy of the truth to be found in rhetoric.

A similar view has been expressed by Professor Cheyney. Literary history is open to suspicion because of its deliberate choice of theme, and "the accompanying vices of a weak hold on reality and incautious use of materials."[4] The literary historian thinks first of his reader, only secondarily of his facts. He is striving to produce an esthetic effect, not to elucidate the past. He does not look narrowly at what he finds in the sources; he carelessly misinterprets, and he neglects what he does not find suitable. His "creative imagination" even tends to find things which are not there. Professor Cheyney acknowledges that the use of the imagination is an absolute necessity in all intellectual production; but it is also a dangerous foe to clear and exact knowledge. The same snares reside in "literary devices," toward which the scientific historian must maintain an attitude of wary caution. He must keep in mind the facts, and not be too much concerned with the method of presentation. If he is scientific, and at the same time vivid, it must not be by deliberate planning, but as if by accident.[5]

These expressions of opinion tend to indicate a want of introspective inquiry into the exact nature of the intellectual operations the historian must undertake, in contrast with Carlyle's self-knowledge. The function of the imagination in modern scientific historiography is precisely what it was understood to be by Carlyle: a process of subjective assimilation of the materials, and a fusion of them into an organic unity. The overt process of articulation by which the fused product is turned into written history is the point at which the expressive skill or narrative excellence of the historian enters. The process by which rhetoric is manufactured, on the other hand, is objective, calculated, and artificial. Such opinions, moreover, impugn the motives of the literary historian. They imply that his aims are necessarily less disinterested than those of the scientific historian. They imply that he is bent on creating art, and therefore is not primarily interested in resuscitating the past and would willingly distort it to secure the esthetic effect or point a moral. Most of the specific criticisms of Carlyle are shot through with inferences based on such assumptions. Whether we have demonstrated sufficiently that such charges are unsubstantiated or irrelevant, it is important to understand the thought patterns out of which they have arisen in considering Carlyle's eclipse as a historian.

A second important reason for Carlyle's eclipse lies in the fact that he represents the apotheosis of the romantic movement in historiography. Just as the romantic historians of the early nineteenth century disparaged and sought to invalidate the theories of the historians of the Enlightenment, so the scientific school of the late nineteenth century disparaged the romanticists. Their points of view had nothing in common; their ideals were not compatible; and yet they shared, with Carlyle for example, the same intimate relationship that Carlyle had shared with his eighteenth-century predecessors. The scientific historians had received their initial impetus toward historical research in an environment colored by the great prestige of romantic literary history. Their attitude shows emphatic evidence of the same negative conditioning toward romantic theories that Carlyle had held toward rationalist theories. Judged thus, it is possible to understand and even forgive the emotional bias of their criticism; but it is difficult to forgive a later generation, which has largely turned away from the narrowly scientific hypothesis, for continuing to compound the errors of their elders.

It is possible to understand, too, the "university tabu" against Carlyle in the late phases of his career. The critical methodology imported from Germany was naturalized in England largely through the patient and scholarly efforts of Professor Stubbs of

Oxford (later Bishop of Oxford). Stubbs was an admirable scholar and philologist who devoted a long and arduous life to more or less unrewarded efforts in editing and publishing the documentary sources of early English history. His *Constitutional History of England*, published in 1874, was a wise, impartial, scholarly, and not very readable contribution to historical scholarship. His *Essays in Medieval and Modern History*, on the other hand, display a philosophic conception of his task, and a subjective grasp of his materials, with a corresponding effectiveness of presentation, which raise them to the level of fine historical writing. The theories he advances in the half dozen speculative essays contained in this volume challenge comparison with Carlyle's.

It seems singularly unfortunate, therefore, that Stubbs and the group of which he was the center (including E. A. Freeman and J. R. Green), whose methods were different but whose ideals of interpretation and scholarship differed little from Carlyle's, should have held both Carlyle and Macaulay in suspicion, mainly because of their prestige with the reading public.

Carlyle suffered further obloquy from his position as master of J. A. Froude, and the consequent necessity of shouldering responsibility for Froude's limitations. Historiographers generally agree that Froude was a great historian in many respects. He was one of the first students of medieval and renaissance history to work almost altogether from unpublished documents. He possessed a narrative style practically without rival for brilliancy, sustained excellence and perspective. Essentially honest and scientific in general method, he had nevertheless a chronic tendency toward trivial inaccuracies and carelessness in his use of sources. His culpabilities subjected him to severe attacks from his professional colleagues, particularly the Oxford group.[6] More than any other historian he dramatized the weaknesses of the literary historians and gave the *coup de grâce* to literary history. The "nemesis of Froude" did more than damage Carlyle's reputation as a man; it also helped greatly to eclipse his reputation as a historian.

Carlyle's modern position as a historian receives added illumination when we contrast it with Macaulay's. The emotional bias and generally negative attitude so dominant in the criticism of Carlyle is lacking in the criticism of Macaulay. Macaulay was Carlyle's only contemporary rival among serious historical writers. Both men attained great fame among their contemporaries although Macaulay's arrived sooner and was of a more popular nature than Carlyle's. They knew each other casually and mingled in the same society. Carlyle read Macaulay's histories "with interest and astonishment," but Macaulay never glanced at Carlyle's, according to his nephew and biographer. With regard to their essential points of view a more complete antithesis could scarcely be found than that between Carlyle and Macaulay.

Macaulay owed nothing to the romantic tradition in historiography. He perpetuated the nationalistic, partisan tradition descending from Hume through Hallam. Like Hallam, he substituted Whig ideals for the Tory principles of Hume. In addition to the historical essays which appeared at regular intervals beginning in 1825 in the *Edinburg Review*, his output of historical writing is confined to the *History of England from 1660 to 1688*, the first volumes of which appeared in 1848. He interpreted the "Glorious Revolution" in terms of bourgeois values, and became the great apostle of middle class philosophy. He had a genius for narration and story-telling of the energetic, swift and voluble sort. His style runs to action and movement; and is devoted to the display of objective details. It has the hardness of wrought metal and none of the "liquid continuity" of an author possessed by his subject instead of merely possessing it. Lord Morley remarked that he could not imagine Macaulay "as meditating, as modestly pondering and wondering, and possessed for as much as ten minutes by that spirit of inwardness, which has never been wholly wanting in any of those kings and princes of literature with whom it is good for men to sit in counsel."[7] Macaulay was not capable of the spirit of analysis, or the "divine spirit of meditation." One can allow for his partisan bias, but even so his judgments are superficial, wanting in penetrative insight, and frequently untrustworthy.

Carlyle referred to him as "an emphatic, tersely forcible person, but unhappily without divine idea."[8] His philosophy represented "the sublime of the commonplace." Lord Morley remarked that Macaulay's entire success and reputation depended upon the fact that his work "abounded in the commonplace."[9] He came on the world just as the middle classes were expanding into enormous prosperity, and were becoming alive to the existence of literary interests. Macaulay threw a "golden halo round the secularity of the hour ... the narrowest limitations of the passing day."[10] He was silent on the deep and universal problems of humanity; he contributed no philosophic ideas or social truths to the speculative stock; he never paused to brood over the complex intricacies of motives and causes, impulses, calculations, and incentives. His favorite historian and model among the ancients was Thucydides, and when we recall that Carlyle's was Tacitus we have the best possible contrast between the men.

Yet H. E. Barnes calls Macaulay's *History of England* "the most brilliant of English contributions to historical literature, as well as a valuable, though partisan, body of historical knowledge."[11] Professor Gooch is more moderate in his judgment, although no less tolerant of Macaulay's limitations. He calls Macaulay the first historian to produce a work which could be read by every literate person. He acknowledges that Macaulay never grasped the notion that there has been a history of the human mind paralleling that of events, that he was partial, unfair in his judgment, unsound in his scholarship, and deficient in the lighting and shading necessary to set forth facts accurately. He admits that Macaulay honestly believed that the Whig manifesto represented the ultimate in political wisdom, but, says Professor Gooch, it is unfair to apply to his works the same standards as those we apply to professional scholars! He is the "most brilliant of English historians," even if he is "one of those who possess the least weight."[12]

We referred briefly in the introductory chapter to Carlyle's immense prestige as a historian in his own day. His *French Revolution*, although it encountered much unfavorable criticism from the more conventional critics, was well received by his most discerning contemporaries. John Stuart Mill, in reviewing it, declared it

... not so much a history, as an epic poem, and notwithstanding this, the truest of histories. His [Carlyle's] characters are realities, like those of Shakespeare's plays. An ordinary historian sets before us mainly his *opinions*. Mr. Carlyle brings the thing before us in the concrete; and in short, brings us *acquainted* with persons, things, and events, before he suggests to us what to think of them. *This is the very process by which he arrives at his own thoughts.*[13]

John Sterling's essay on Carlyle, written in 1839, likewise judged his history of the French Revolution as a "genuine, breathing epic. Complete and fixed in its design, it thrills with life blood through and through."[14] It is a "book that makes the heart ache more than Tacitus, though somewhat in the same way." Carlyle's theory of the social organism and of individual psychology was entirely too advanced for the Coleridgean Sterling, but he does not miss the most important thing: that Carlyle's great power is in the historic delineation of men and events, to which he gives extraordinary vividness and boldness; and this, "not by knack or system, or a draughtsman's eye for the outwardly picturesque, but by intense feeling of the effectual and expressive everywhere, and of the relation in which all objects stand to the natural hearts of men."[15] Sterling perceived, too, the truth which became a stumbling-block for so many; that to Carlyle the objects of chief interest are the memorable persons— "men who have fought strongly the good fight"—but the objects chiefly exciting his passionate sympathy are the

... dusky millions of human shapes that flit around us and in history stream away ... their hunger and nakedness, their mistakes, terrors, pangs and ignorances, press upon his soul like personal calamities. Of him more than of all other English writers, perhaps writers of any country, it is true that ... man, however distant and rude a shadow, is to him affecting, venerable, full of a divine strength, which, for the most part, is rather cramped and tortured than ripened to freedom in this fleshly life and world.

Emerson's opinion of the *French Revolution* is a blend of the best of the other verdicts. Like Sterling, he was particularly impressed by Carlyle's interest in the social group as a whole, and not just the outstanding figures. More deeply than any other of the contemporary critics, he perceived Carlyle's sociologico-psychological interest which possibly was the most advanced and least understood of his fundamental attitudes. "I think you have written a wonderful book, which will last a very long time," Emerson wrote Carlyle.

> I see that you have created a history, which the world will own to be such. You have recognized the existence of other persons than officers, and of other relations than civism. You have broken away from all books and written a mind. It is a brave experiment, and the success is great. We have men in your story and not names merely; always men, though I may doubt sometimes whether I have historic men. We have great facts,—and selected facts,—truly set down. We have always the co-presence of Humanity along with the imperfect damaged individuals.[16]

Thackeray's criticism of the *French Revolution* reveals the force of the impression Carlyle made on the cultivated but somewhat worldly readers of his time. Neither so wise nor so profound as Emerson, Thackeray yet realized that the "strange storm of applause and discontent" raised among the critics and the reading public had its origin in the undoubted genius of the author of the *French Revolution*. Too many of Carlyle's early critics, said Thackeray, damned him because they were too lazy to expend the energy his books required or they had not yet "passed the veil of Kantian philosophy." The book

> ... betrays most extraordinary powers—learning, observation and humor. Above all, it has no Cant. It teems with sound, hearty philosophy (besides certain Transcendentalisms which we do not pretend to understand). It is the product of genius, if any book ever was. It wanted no more for keen critics to cry fie upon it. Clever critics who have such an eye for genius, that when Mr. Bulwer published his forgotten book concerning Athens, they discovered that no historian was like to him; that he on his Athenian hobby, had quite out-trotted stately Mr. Gibbon; and with the same creditable unanimity they cried down Mr. Carlyle's history, opening upon it a hundred little piddling sluices of small wit, destined to wash the book sheer away; and lo! the book remains, it is only the poor wit which has run dry.[17]

Carlyle's contemporary reputation as a historian was established by the *French Revolution*. Each succeeding history added to his influence and scholarly prestige. But paralleling his growing fame was an under-the-surface development of several currents of thought which eventually converged to form the stream which has dominated historiography for the past half century. First was the critical methodology imported from Germany. Leopold von Ranke believed that history should be objective, scientifically impartial. The historian's duty is to collect his sources, present a neutral mind like a highly polished mirror and permit the past to reproduce itself, *"wie es eigentlich gewesen est."*[18] Another stream of influence was that emanating from Comte and exemplified in English thought in the *History of Civilization* (1857) of Thomas Buckle. Comte, Gūizot, Buckle, and their followers believed that the process of history could be reduced to fixed laws based on the influence of man's physical environment in determining the course of his history.

Greater than Buckle in the amplitude of his intellectual reach and influence was Karl Marx. A more instructive parallel cannot be found in nineteenth century thought than that between Marx and Carlyle. Contemporary residents of London, their actual orbits probably never crossed. Marx's collaborator, Engels, acknowledged the influence of Carlyle in the powerful *Condition of the Working Classes in 1844*, which was partly inspired by *Past and Present*. If Carlyle had known Marx, he would have found little to admire in his historical materialism. They waged battle over the opposite phases of their eighteenth century inheritance. Carlyle's profoundest stimulus came from the negative quality of the rationalization of historical traditions, the denial of soul to the world. Karl Marx, on the other hand, carried that rationalization to its ultimate consequences by logically analyzing and discrediting historical mysteries and traditions. Professor Berdyaev observed that

> the impugnment of the mystery of the "historical" in the sphere of religion initiated at the Reformation, became more general in the age of the Enlightenment and reached its full development as a fundamental principle of historical science in the nineteenth century. Marxian materialism pursued this process of the de-animation of history and

the annihilation of its inner mysteries by the reduction of the historical process to terms of production, and the development of mankind's productive resources.[19]

All forces other than economic are secondary, contingent. The historical process, in the Marxian dialetic, is devoid of soul, of spiritual reality, of mystery. Culture, religion, art, society itself, are represented as "mere accidents of matter in movement and devoid of substantial reality."[20]

The economic determinism of Marx developed a type of evolutionary doctrine which, coinciding with the Darwinian discoveries in the biological field and the scientific methodology imported from Germany, established the most vital current in late nineteenth-century historiography. The scientific advances during the period deepened the emphasis on the material and economic forces, hugely expanded the sphere of historical research, and opened up the allied fields of philology, archaeology, anthropology, sociology, and economics. The writing of history became more and more secondary to the study of sources, the collection and criticism of documents, as the scientific school gradually achieved preëminence. The impulse initiated by Voltaire and the eighteenth-century rationalists was fed by the speculations of Comte, Marx, Buckle, Niebuhr, von Ranke, and Savigny, and culminated in the mighty tide of scientific historiography which reached its crest near the turn of the twentieth century.

Criticisms of the assumptions underlying the theories of the scientific school were not wanting even in its heyday. Lord Morley admitted:

... It may perhaps be contended that the conception of history has on the whole gone back rather than advanced within the last hundred years. There have been signs in our own day of its becoming narrow, pedantic, and trivial. It threatens to degenerate from a broad survey of great periods and movements of human societies into vast and countless accumulations of insignificant facts, sterile knowledge and frivolous antiquarianism, in which the spirit of epochs is lost, and the direction, meaning and summary of the various courses of human history, all disappear.[21]

Such an admission becomes more significant when we recall Lord

Morley's position as a leader in the positivist movement of late nineteenth century rationalism.

Frederic Harrison, writing a little later, deplored the fact that the modern school of historians, under the influence of Ranke, Guizot, and Sir Henry Ellis, devoted themselves to "original research rather than eloquent narrative."[22] The scientific study of limited periods, special institutions and minute details, has displaced the old conception of history as literature and caused it to be looked upon as scientific research. Harrison believed that there is more to be said for literary distinction in historical composition than the world is wont to allow. All calculations of historical research not fused into the form of art remain merely the textbooks of special students and are closed to the general public. However profound their learning or brilliant their discovery, as in the case of Savigny, Pertz, and Migne, they have a purely esoteric value for the few.

Harrison agreed with Carlyle that history must reach, modify, and instruct the public if it is to rise to the level of a humane science and be more than pedantic antiquarianism. "And nothing can reach the public as history, unless it be organic and proportioned in structure, impressive by its epical form, and instinct with the magic of life." Since the totality of history never can be ascertained, the best approximation is a "reduced miniature of the vast area of actual events, in such just proportions as to leave on the mind a true and memorable picture."[23] In Tacitus, in Gibbon, in Carlyle, truth of proportion is to be found, and this is a more essential quality than accuracy of details. Falsity of proportion, growing out of a wilderness of unassimilated details, ruled only by antiquarian curiosity, is both confusing and deceiving.

The excesses of the scientific school brought an inevitable reaction, and the tide has swung back toward a more liberal and humane attitude within the last two decades. Typical of the most advanced point of view are the opinions expressed by Professor Carl Becker in his Presidential Address before the American Historical Association in 1931. History is still in essence what it has always been, said Professor Becker, "however camouflaged by the disfiguring jargon of science"; a story, in aim always a true story, employing all the devices of literary art to present the succession of events in the life of man, and from the succession to derive a satisfactory meaning.[24] "The history written by historians is thus a convenient blend of truth and fancy, or what we commonly distinguish as 'fact' and 'interpretation.'" Historians of the preceding generations turned away from interpretation to a pure examination of factual materials, as they thought. They perfected critical techniques of investigating and testing documentary materials under the impression that the facts once uncovered would speak for themselves. They rejected the theological and metaphysical theories of causation, only to submit to a fixed idea that they possessed no philosophy of history. They believed that by not taking thought, a philosophy would emerge from the facts; and the final and irrefutable meaning of life and human experience would be revealed. Professor Becker called this naïve hope of finding something by not looking for it a "romantic species of realism." Those who accepted the Marxian materialism on the other hand, adopted a vast rationalization as rigid and uncompromising as the Augustinian philosophy of history. In place of God, they put economic laws; substituted for the conflict between God and Satan for the possession of the human soul the conflict between social classes for productive wealth. The Marxian dogma of the chain of inevitable causation is theological rather than scientific.[25]

The same may be said of other theories of interpretation. History cannot be written without interpretation. Left to themselves the facts mean nothing. The historian's most fundamental task is to select and present the facts, and thus give them a certain place in a pattern of ideas from which they derive their meaning.[26] However accurately they are determined, the facts themselves, and our interpretation of them, and our interpretation of our interpretation, will be seen differently by succeeding generations. An illusory impression also exists from generation to generation that the present version alone is valid because the facts presented are true, whereas preceding versions are correspondingly invalid because based upon inaccurate or inadequate facts."[27] Actually, the historian works the malleable facts into a pattern consistent with his own experience and idea of the world. History from this point of view is an imaginative creation, fashioned out of the materials of the present, adapted to its practical and emotional needs, and adorned to suit its esthetic taste.

Increasing recognition has been accorded the fact that the ideal of history which made it subservient to science, concerned only with the establishment of facts, was "blind of an eye and lame of gait."[28] It was based upon a specious theory that facts are objective entities, valid for all time once they are established. Today the form and substance of historical facts are seen to be subjective with a "negotiable existence only in literary discourse, and varying with the words employed to convey them."[29] The simple historical fact, which is the cornerstone of scientific historiography, has proved to be the "illusion of the simple-minded and inadequately informed."[30] With the return of the subjective approach and the recognition that form and substance are inseparable attributes of successful history, and the belief that the historian's product belongs to the present no less than it is conditioned by the present, it appears that very little real difference separates the attitude of Carlyle from that of the more humane, modern historians.

The object of the present study has been less to rehabilitate Carlyle as a historian than to reëxamine his theories from the point of view of present-day tendencies in historiography. What his theories were we have attempted to show; and why they were disliked by his immediate successors. From this distance, however, one finds in them much that accords with prevailing views; much that is constructive and valuable. G. M. Trevelyan warned his contemporaries in 1895 that the growing tendency among historians to deny Carlyle a proper place among them "might succeed in persuading students to regard his historical writings as works of fiction where truth cannot even be gleaned."[31] The historians succeeded in putting Carlyle out of court and proceeded to enforce a monopoly in their profession with privileges only for licensed practitioners. The evil outcome of the establishment of such a principle of course involves not only Carlyle's reputation but that of historical writers in general. Trevelyan holds that they have ostracized him "really because they do not understand him . . . but nominally on account of his inaccuracies." It is to be hoped that a more liberal generation of students will acknowledge Carlyle's unique position as a historian.

The point of view maintained throughout this inquiry has been based on the assumption that the recovery of the past requires the intimate blending of art, philosophy, and science; and that history, so considered, takes a preëminent position among humane studies. Historical research, on the other hand, which is not transmuted into readily accessible knowledge can never hold so lofty a position. "The history that lies inert in unread books does no work in the world."[32] Posterity will be the ultimate judge of Carlyle as a historian. If men continue to read him, and his undoubted literary genius will assure that, his histories will continue to exercise an influence on the world. Macaulay, nettled by Emerson's caustic criticism of his *History*, confided to his diary that by the year 2850, Emerson would be in the limbo of forgotten authors, whereas he and Herodotus would still be read.[33] Macaulay's confidence seems a trifle overweaning, but we feel certain that Carlyle's name will be among the great names circa 2850. Lord Morley observed that Carlyle's qualities of style tended to conceal from his contemporary readers the "intensely practical turn of his whole mind." His constant awareness of "the Eternities, the Immensities and the like . . . veiled his almost narrow adherence to plain record without moral comment. The highest souls are held to be deeply conscious of these vast unspeakable presences, yet even with them they are only inspiring accessories; the true interest lies in the practical attitude of such men towards the actual and palpable circumstances that surround them."[34] Our belief in Carlyle's claim to be ranked among the great historians is based fundamentally, not on his transcendentalism, nor his poetic style, but on his remarkable capacity to present a "plain record" of "actual and palpable circumstances" rescued from the past. His literary excellence will contribute in large measure to his permanent fame, but great as his service was to literature, his service to history was still greater. His insight into the motives of men, his extraordinary power of revivifying the past in terms of human experience, his sociological analysis of the nature of the historic process and his philosophic interpretations of the ultimate meaning of history offer a broad basis for the assumption that his historical writings will be among those works of art which will endure.

NOTES

CHAPTER I. INTRODUCTORY

1. Gooch, George Peabody, *History & Historians of the Nineteenth Century*, London, 1913, 2nd ed., p. 324.
2. *Ibid.*, p. 327.
3. Typical of a large portion of current Carlyle criticism among professional historians are the remarks of Dr. Harry Elmer Barnes, which can hardly be excelled for critical blindness, but unfortunately can be matched in many quarters. Dr. Barnes says that the "least attractive personality of the group (of romantic historians) and the least worthy as a historian was Thomas Carlyle. In radical contrast with Michelet, he was possessed of a sour contempt for the masses and an equally exaggerated interest in the picturesque figures of history. To him history was but the collective biography of the conspicuous figures through the ages, and he was responsible more than any other historian for the conventional disdain of the modern historian for those commonplace things of daily life which have had incomparably greater influence upon social development than the picturesque personalities. Carlyle indulged his prejudices in his *Letters and Speeches of Cromwell*, his *History of Frederick the Great*, and his *French Revolution*. While possessing only moderate value as sources of information on account of the writer's uncontrolled prejudices and his utter lack of critical method, they earned him the undisputed position as 'the greatest of English portrait painters.'" See "History, Its Rise and Development," *The Americana*, Vol. 14, p. 234. The same criticism, virtually unchanged, appeared in Dr. Barnes' recent *History of Historical Writing*, University of Oklahoma Press, Norman, Okla., 1937.
4. Gooch, *op. cit.*, p. 326.
5. Fueter, Eduard, *Histoire de l'Histoire Moderne*, Paris, 1912, p. 589.

6. Fletcher, C. R. L., ed., *French Revolution*, 3 vols., New York, 1902. See Intro.
7. Gooch, *op. cit.*, p. 232.
8. Buckle, Thomas, *History of Civilization in England*, London, 1857, I, p. 289.
9. Quoted by André Maurois, *Poets and Prophets*, New York, 1935, p. 226.
10. Beard, Charles A., *The Discussion of Human Affairs*, New York, 1936, p. 101.
11. Saintsbury, George, *A History of Nineteenth Century Literature*, New York, 1896, p. 251.
12. Wordsworth, William, *Lyrical Ballads*, 2nd edition, 1800. Preface. Quoted by George Saintsbury, *Loci Critici*, Boston, 1903, p. 273.
13. Saintsbury, *op. cit.*, p. 251.
14. *Ibid.*, p. 251.
15. Lowell, J. R., *Literary Essays*, Cambridge, 1890, II, p. 118.
16. James, Henry, *The Sense of the Past*, New York, 1917, p. 48.
17. *Sartor* (Modern Students' Library Edition, New York, 1921), p. 84.
18. David Masson's compilation of Carlyle's borrowings from the Edinburgh University Library during his first two sessions includes: Robertson's *Scotland*, Vol. II; *Cook's Voyages*; Byron's *Narrative of the Great Distresses Suffered by Himself and his Companions on the Coast of Patagonia*; Gibbon's *Decline and Fall of the Roman Empire*, Vol. I; two volumes of Shakespeare; a volume of the *Arabian Nights*; Congreve's *Works*; two volumes of Hume's *England*; *Gil Blas*; a third volume of Shakespeare; and a volume of the *Spectator*; a collected series of *Voyages and Travels*; a volume of Fielding; a volume of Smollett; Reid's *Inquiry into the Human Mind*; *Scotland Described*; two more volumes of Fielding; Locke's *Essay on the Human Understanding*; another volume of Fielding; Abbé Barthélemy's *Travels of Anarcharsis*; a volume of *Don Quixote*. See Masson, David, *Edinburgh Sketches and Memories*, London, 1892, pp. 229-33. Additional titles, particularly in historical and speculative writings of the eighteenth century, can be added from the letters.
19. *Sartor*, p. 90.

CHAPTER II. BACKGROUNDS

1. *Misc.*, I, p. 398.
2. Wilson, David Alec, *Carlyle Till Marriage*, New York, 1925, p. 74.
3. *Misc.*, IV, p. 456.
4. Gibbon, Edward, *History of the Decline and Fall of the Roman Empire*, ed. with intro. by J. B. Bury, 2nd ed., London, 1929. See intro.
5. Hume, David, *An Inquiry Concerning Human Understanding*, Oxford, 1894, Sec. VIII, pt. I, p. 83.
6. Black, John B., *The Art of History, A Study of Four Great Historians of the Eighteenth Century*, New York, 1926, p. 128. The ancient historians quite generally held this view.
7. Voltaire's *Essais sur les Moeurs et l'Esprit des Nations*, 1756, is the first of the so-called histories of civilization, objective records of the cultural manifestations of social groups; and represents an important landmark in historiography, from the standpoint both of art and science. See Flint, Robert, *Philosophy of History in Europe*, Edinburgh, 1874, pp. 119-23.
8. From Voltaire to the materialist historians of our day is a continuous stream of thought which regards history as a rational process characterized by the interplay of ideas (Voltaire); the interplay of human wills (Hume); or the interplay of economic forces (Buckle and Marx).
9. Black, *op. cit.*, p. 75.
10. Peardon, Thomas P., *The Transition in English Historical Writing, 1760-1830*, Columbia University Press, New York, 1933, pp. 210-1.
11. Peardon, *op. cit.* Professor Peardon traces not only the vigorous dissent against the prevailing rationalist school among minor writers in the late eighteenth century but follows through the main positive contributions of the rationalists to the romantic, nationalistic and scientific schools of the next century.
12. Wilson, *op. cit.*, p. 67.
13. Masson, *op. cit.*, p. 231.
14. *Early Letters*, I, pp. 143-4.
15. *Early Letters*, II, p. 268.
16. Windelband, W., *A History of Philosophy*, New York, 1898, p. 476.

17. Gooch, G. P., *Germany and the French Revolution*, London, 1920. Herder was probably influenced by Hume, in Professor Gooch's opinion. See pp. 160-1.
18. *Early Letters*, I, p. 42.
19. *Reminiscences*, II, p. 28.
20. *Early Letters*, II, p. 180.
21. *Early Letters*, I, p. 144.
22. *Early Letters*, II, pp. 180-1.
23. *Reminiscences*, II, p. 28.
24. *Early Letters*, I, p. 143.
25. *Ibid.*
26. *Reminiscences*, II, p. 28.
27. *Notebooks*, p. 85.
28. *Misc.*, I, pp. 414 *passim*.
29. *Misc.*, I, p. 416.
30. *Misc.*, I, p. 399. The same idea appears in the *Notebooks*, p. 124. "An historian must write . . . in lines; but every event is a superficies; nay, if we search out its *causes*, a *solid*; hence a primary and almost incurable defect in the art of narration; which only the very best can approximately remedy. . . . I understand this myself. I have known it for years; and written it now with the purpose perhaps of writing it at large elsewhere." Carlyle carried out his purpose in the essay *On History*, published in *Fraser's* in 1830.
31. *Misc.*, I, pp. 447-9.
32. *Misc.*, I, p. 450.
33. Gooch, *op. cit.*, p. 160.
34. Gooch, *op. cit.*, pp. 35-8.
35. *Cambridge Modern History*, Vol. X, p. 386.
36. *Ibid.*, p. 386.
37. Robertson, J. S., *The Genesis of Romantic Theory*, Cambridge, 1923, pp. 288-9. Professor Robertson contends that Vico's influence on Herder has been underrated, while Rousseau's has been correspondingly overrated. He believes that many of the ideas which make Herder a pioneer of modern intellectual development are essentially Vichian; the fundamental *Sturm und Drang* concept of the totality of human effort, the whole man working toward a common end. The general scheme of the *Ideen* might well have been patterned after the *Scienza Nuova*.

38. Despite Lessing's pioneering efforts, it was Herder who first made clear to German readers the real nature and genius of Shakespeare. It was he who inspired the youthful Goethe with such enthusiasm for Shakespeare that the latter felt, as he put it, "like a blind man upon whom the power of sight had suddenly been conferred."
39. Quoted by Ergang, Reinhold R., *Herder and the Foundations of German Nationalism*, New York, 1931, p. 82.
40. It is scarcely possible to emphasize too strongly the importance of Herder's idea regarding the "national soul." Ranke's "Zeitgeist" originated here and became a controlling conception in German historiography. Likewise the modern consciousness of nationality, with its fateful consequences in contemporary history stems from this theory of the social group to which Herder first gave clear expression. It became one of the cardinal principles of Carlyle's critical approach to history.
41. Ergang, *op. cit.*, pp. 86 ff.
42. Flint, *op. cit.*, pp. 172 ff.
43. *Notebooks*, pp. 33-5.
44. *Ibid.*, p. 42.
45. *Ibid.*, p. 72.
46. *Ibid.*, p. 73.
47. Colvin, Thomas, *Life and Writings of Friedrich Schiller*, New York, 1902, p. 231.
48. Fueter, *op. cit.*, p. 499. Also Gooch, *op. cit.*, p. 210.
49. Friedrich Schiller, *Complete Works*, ed. by C. J. Hempel, Philadelphia, 1870, Vol. II, p. 10. In the introduction to the *Revolt of the Netherlands* he voices the hope of convincing the reading public of "the possibility of writing a history with historic truth without making a trial of patience to the reader" and of proving that "history can borrow from a cognate art, without thereby of necessity becoming a romance."
50. Quoted by Colvin, *op. cit.*, p. 232.
51. Gooch, *op. cit.*, p. 209.
52. Fueter, *op. cit.*, p. 501.
53. Carlyle's debt to German thought has been made the subject of several critical studies. There is general agreement that the debt is more truly one of affinities than of direct borrowings. He approached metaphysical ideas as an amateur, seizing the heart of abstract principles when they pleased him and sel-

dom acknowledged a direct indebtedness. His primary purpose in reading himself into German thought was to reassure himself regarding the reality of the spirit; in other words, to secure a theoretical basis for convictions already held. By temperament and situation he was predisposed to the German revolt from the Enlightenment; to the elevation of the creative, shaping imagination in Kant, Schiller, and Fichte; to the distinction between reason and understanding in the epistemology of Kant; to the resifting of moral values and the stimulating power of great personalities in Goethe and Schiller; to the illuminating new concepts of history in Herder, Kant, Schiller, Fichte, and Schelling; and to the general moral seriousness of tone and purpose characterizing most of the participants in the German Renascence.

The most recent and also most complete examination of Carlyle's ideas in relation to German sources is that of Charles Frederick Harrold, *Carlyle and German Thought*, Yale University Press, New Haven, 1934.

Other studies concerned with this phase of Carlyle research are C. E. Vaughan, *Carlyle and His German Masters*, Essays and Studies of the English Association, I, 1910; Susanne Howe, *Wilhelm Meister and His English Kinsmen*, Columbia University Press, New York, 1930; Margaret Storrs, *The Relation of Carlyle to Kant and Fichte*, Bryn Mawr, 1929.

There has been no attempt in the present study to duplicate the efforts of previous investigators in this field, except in the special cases of Schiller and Herder.

54. *Early Letters*, I, p. 213.
55. Ewen, *op. cit.*, p. 135.
56. Quoted by Moncure Conway, *Carlyle*, London, 1881, p. 202.
57. The impulse to master the German language grew out of Carlyle's scientific pursuits and not his curiosity about German literature. Mineralogy had occupied him during the winter of 1817-18. Since a German mineralogist, Werner, had written the most complete treatise extant on the secrets of rocks, Carlyle determined to learn German to read him. He mentioned learning German in the letter to Robert Mitchell cited above. *Early Letters*, I, p. 209.

58. Quoted by Wilson, p. 212, from a letter to Irving. See "Unpublished Letters of Carlyle," *Scribner's Magazine*, 1893, p. 417.
59. Wilson, *op. cit.*, p. 212.
60. *Ibid.*, p. 212.
61. Ewen, *op. cit.*, p. 145.
62. Ewen supports this position. See p. 136.
63. See Max Batt's "Carlyle's *Life of Schiller*," *Modern Philology*, I, pp. 391-2, for a detailed comparison of the serialized and book forms. He found a considerable number of minor changes, no important alterations.
64. *Notebooks*, p. 54.
65. *Ibid.*, p. 51.
66. *Ibid.*, p. 54.
67. *Ibid.*, p. 59.
68. *Life of Schiller*, p. 18.
69. Miss Storrs and Professors Ewen and Harrold agree that Carlyle's knowledge of Kant was extremely meager and superficial. Apparent Kantian borrowings were really derived second hand through Schiller and Fichte especially.
70. *Notebooks*, p. 170.
71. *Life of Schiller*, p. 41.
72. *The Autobiography of Edward Gibbon*, ed. by John Murray, London, 1896, p. 193.
73. David Brewster, editor of the *Edinburgh Encyclopedia*, commissioned Carlyle in 1820 to do sixteen biographical sketches for the fourteenth, fifteenth, and sixteenth volumes, then in preparation. The articles cover an assortment of historical personages and places, including Montaigne, Lady Mary Wortley Montagu, Montesquieu, The Netherlands, William Pitt, Earl of Chatham, William Pitt the younger, Bernard de Montfaucon, Sir John More, Nelson, Mungo Park and others. Carlyle was poorly paid and apparently took little interest in the writing of these sketches, working at them off and on during 1820-22.
74. *Notebooks*, pp. 21 and 25.
75. *Ibid.*, pp. 78-9. This project, probably suggested by Burke's *Annual Register*, would have undertaken to record the "actual progress of the mind" throughout the year. One part was to comprise biographical sketches of persons who had died

within the year, from a "flowing, popular and anecdotal aspect." "Dead details" were to be suppressed in favor of an "honest likeness" of the person concerned. Three parts were to be devoted to reviewing the year's achievements in literature, art, science and "manners." The final and most important division is of particular interest. Restricting himself to what is "intellectual and moral," he would undertake to "collect, sift and preserve" any incidents, misfortunes, delusions, crimes, heroic actions, which seemed to illustrate the spiritual condition of the time, because he considered these the most valuable primary materials of history.

76. *Life of Schiller*, pp. 84 ff.
77. *Notebooks*, p. 28.
78. Schiller, *Complete Works*, II, *op. cit.*, p. 9.
79. *Life of Schiller*, pp. 95-6.
80. *Ibid.*, p. 100.
81. Gooch, *op. cit.*, p. 210.
82. Schiller sets forth his philosophic formula in the Inaugural Address delivered at Jena in 1789, entitled *What Is Universal History and with what Views Should it be Studied?* In theoretic originality this ranks far below Kant's brief essay on the *Idea of a Universal History from a Cosmopolitan Point of View*, from which it is mainly derived. Kant advanced nine propositions: history is the realization of a hidden plan of nature to create a perfect constitution through which our aptitudes can be developed. Nature's instrument for developing the capacities of men is the friction and conflict arising from life in social groups. This conflict eventually becomes the cause of social order regulated by law. Man desires peace, but nature desires progress, and progress is only possible through conflict. (See Flint, *op. cit.*, pp. 390-1.)
83. Schiller, *Complete Works*, II, p. 270.
84. *Ibid.*, p. 346.
85. *Life of Schiller*, pp. 102-3.
86. *Misc.*, II, p. 198.
87. *Life of Schiller*, pp. 77-8.
88. Coleridge, S. T., *Works*, ed., T. Ashe, London, 1884, IV, pp. 255-6.
89. *Notebooks*, p. 41.

NOTES: CHAPTER II

90. Peardon, *op. cit.*, p. 160.
91. Taine, H. A., *History of English Literature*, II, pp. 254-5.
92. *Misc.*, IV, pp. 77-8.
93. *Ibid.*, p. 75.
94. Fueter, *op. cit.*, p. 497.
95. *Coleridge's Miscellaneous Criticism*, ed., T. M. Raysor, London, 1935, p. 341.
96. *Ibid.*, pp. 323, 329, 341.
97. Taine, *op. cit.*, p. 258.
98. Brown, Philip Anthony, *The French Revolution in English Literature*, New York, 1924, p. 213.
99. *Reminiscences*, II, p. 289.
100. Wordsworth, William, *Complete Poetical Works*, III, New York, 1919, *Prelude*, X, p. 253.
101. Cazamian, Louis, *Carlyle*, New York, 1932, p. 154.
102. Brown, *op. cit.*, p. 25.
103. Hearnshaw, F. J. C., *Social and Political Ideas of the Revolutionary Era*, London, 1931, Chapter IV.
104. *Cambridge Modern History*, Vol. VIII, p. 757.
105. Hearnshaw, p. 96.
106. Burke, Edmund, *Works*, III, Boston, 1881. "Reflections on the Revolution in France," pp. 359 *passim*.
107. *Ibid.*, p. 350.
108. Burke, *Works*, IV, pp. 165-6.
109. Coleridge, S. T., *Essays on His Own Times*, ed. by Sara Coleridge, London, 1850, pp. 363 *passim*.
110. *Life of Sterling*, p. 57.
111. Coleridge, S. T., *Works*, I, pp. 33-4.
112. Mill, J. S., *Dissertations and Discussions*, Boston, 1865, Vol. I, p. 14, "Coleridge."
113. *Life of Sterling*, p. 53.
114. Coleridge, *Works*, IV, p. 242.
115. Coleridge, "Idea of Church and State," *Works*, Vol. VI, p. 44.
116. Coleridge, *Works*, IV, p. 146.
117. *Ibid.*, p. 76.
118. *Ibid.*, p. 245.
119. *Ibid.*, p. 109.
120. *Ibid.*, p. 245.
121. Ewen, *op. cit.*, p. 145.

CHAPTER III. CARLYLE'S PHILOSOPHY OF HISTORY

1. Mazzini, Guiseppe, *Essays*, London, 1887, p. 161.
2. Nordau, Max, *The Interpretation of History*, tr. by M. A. Hamilton, New York, 1910, pp. 5-6.
3. Langlois and Seignobos, *Introduction to the Study of History*, tr. by S. S. Berry, New York, 1909, p. 56.
4. M. Alphonse Aulard, noted historiographer of the French Revolution, states in his essay on Carlyle's *French Revolution*, that Carlyle "s'est commenté et expliqué lui-même, avec bien plus d'autorité et d'éloquence [than his critics] dans çe livre." See Aulard, A., *Études et Leçons sur la Révolution Française*, septième série, Paris, 1913, p. 196.
5. The breadth of Carlyle's conception is not only of revolutionary importance but has been overlooked by his critics. It is interesting to observe that now, a century later, the idea of bringing into one focus the historical study of events and the scientific investigation of processes operative in time, such as Carlyle attempted in the *French Revolution*, is advanced by an eminent scholar in the field of historiography, Professor Frederick J. Teggart. See his *Theory of History*, Yale University Press, New Haven, 1925.
6. Maccunn, John, *The Political Philosophy of Burke*, London, 1913, pp. 1-3.
7. *Literary Remains of Henry James*, ed., Wm. James, Boston, 1885, p. 426.
8. *Misc.*, III, p. 25.
9. *Sartor*, p. 235.
10. *Notebooks*, p. 36.
11. *Misc.*, II, p. 28.
12. *Sartor*, p. 47.
13. It should be noted here that with Hegel the interest lay less in the individual conceptions than in the systematic combinations which he brought about between them. By this means he succeeded in portraying the meaning and significance of individual details in a masterly way. He often violated actual matters of fact; but he atoned for that by the new and surprising light he threw on long-standing structures of thought. To him, however, and in this he differs most from Carlyle, fact is usually subordinate to theory. See

NOTES: CHAPTER III

      Flint, *Philosophy of History in France and Germany*, *op. cit.*, p. 140.
14. *Misc.*, I, p. 389.
15. For the best discussion of this, see J. B. Bury, *The Idea of Progress*, New York, 1912.
16. The evolutionary concept was common property among the natural sciences by the turn of the nineteenth century. As a matter of fact, the German geologist, Werner (to read whom it is recalled Carlyle learned German), employed the evolutionary hypothesis in his analysis of rock structure and classification, and helped to revolutionize the science of geology. See F. J. Teggart, *The Theory of History*, *op. cit.*, pp. 125-6.

      Carlyle is frequently criticized for speaking contemptuously of Darwin and his theory of biological evolution. His hostility was directed less at Darwin, however, than at the tendencies which the latter's work let loose in English thought, particularly the mechanists' assumption of the theory as the scaffolding on which to erect a materialist conception of society and history.
17. *Misc.*, II, p. 80.
18. *Sartor*, p. 220.
19. *Ibid.*, pp. 228-9.
20. Quoted by Flint, *op. cit.*, p. 440.
21. *Misc.*, II, pp. 342-4.
22. *Sartor*, p. 153.
23. *Misc.*, II, p. 29.
24. *Sartor*, pp. 58-9.
25. See Cazamian, Louis, *Carlyle*, New York, 1932, pp. 95-7.
26. Flint, *op. cit.*, p. 387.
27. *Sartor*, p. 60.
28. *Misc.*, II, p. 68.
29. Windelband, *op. cit.*, p. 489.
30. *Misc.*, II, p. 73.
31. *Troilus and Cressida*, Act III, Scene III.
32. Windelband, *op. cit.*, p. 464.
33. *Sartor*, pp. 193-4.
34. *Notebooks*, p. 164.
35. *Ibid.*, p. 165.
36. *Sartor*, p. 52.

37. *Ibid.*, p. 192.
38. See *Notebooks*, p. 158 and Flint, *op. cit.*, pp. 164-5. St. Simon's doctrine divided historic periods into organic and critical eras. In the former the minds of men are busy investigating the principles of government, etc., in an effort to amend old institutions and invent new ones, and no creed commands the assent of all. Hence society is in a state approaching anarchy. Organic periods are ages of faith, in which accepted doctrines cement society through the synthesis of a common faith, and in which existing institutions give men satisfaction and their minds are at rest.

    St. Simon's period of productive activity was from 1807 to 1825. Carlyle's correspondence with him was in 1830. Long before this Carlyle had accepted a theory of periodicity, but the close parallels between his expression of the idea and that of the St. Simonians suggests that he used their elaboration in detail.
39. *Sartor*, p. 205.
40. *Notebooks*, p. 141.
41. *Sartor*, p. 211.
42. M. Aulard supports this view. See *op. cit.*, pp. 202-8.
43. *French Revolution*, I, p. 38.
44. *Heroes*, p. 210.
45. Tacitus, *Histories*, Loeb Classical Library, London, 1925, I, p. 6.
46. *French Revolution*, III, p. 138.
47. *Ibid.*, I, pp. 211-2.
48. Gooch, *op. cit.*, p. 3.
49. *French Revolution*, I, p. 175.
50. See especially Gooch, G. P., *History and Historians of the 19th Century*, London, 1913, pp. 324 *passim*.
51. *French Revolution*, I, p. 28.
52. *Ibid.*, pp. 61 *passim*.
53. *Ibid.*, p. 96.
54. *French Revolution*, II, p. 249.
55. *French Revolution*, I, pp. 250-1.
56. *French Revolution*, II, pp. 14-5.
57. *Ibid.*, p. 121.
58. Quoted by Gooch, *Germany and the French Revolution*, p. 206. Only Goethe among the Germans held a philosophy of revo-

lution similar to Carlyle's. Goethe's was derived mainly from Herder, while Schiller and the Kantians held to the abstract principles of Rousseau. Herder held the method of institutional rejuvenescence by revolution the most barbaric, least effective, because furthest removed from nature's evolutionary method. Yet he believed firmly that only the wisest and best should be rulers; that hereditary rule was an abomination; that leaders are ordained by God and nature. Such a theory, naturally, constitutes the very charter of revolt under certain conditions. Goethe's opinions closely follow Herder's, and whether Carlyle was more influenced by them in their original or their Goethean version matters little. See Gooch, *op. cit.*, pp. 163-6.

59. James, Lewis G., "Carlyle's Philosophy of History," *Westminster Review*, Vol. 132, 1889, p. 420.
60. Carlyle, R. W. and A. J., *Medieval Political Theory in the West*, Edinburgh, 1936, Vol. VI, pp. 334 *passim*.
61. *Ibid.*, pp. 268-9.
62. Goethe likewise held this view.
63. *Heroes*, pp. 2-3.
64. *Ibid.*, pp. 156-7.
65. *Heroes*, p. 43.
66. *Notebooks*, p. 188. See also essay on Burns.
67. *Latter Day Pamphlets*, p. 185.
68. *Heroes*, p. 21.
69. Cazamian, *op. cit.*, p. 172.
70. *Ibid.*, pp. 275-7.
71. *Heroes*, p. 160.
72. *Misc.*, I, p. 399.
73. *Heroes*, p. 13.
74. M. Aulard emphasizes this point in his analysis of Carlyle's attitude toward his material. See *op. cit.*, p. 206.
75. Teggart, *op. cit.*, p. 16.
76. *Misc.*, II, p. 369.
77. *Ibid.*, p. 400.
78. Vaughan, C. E., *Studies in the History of Political Philosophy*, Manchester University Press, 1925, Vol. I, pp. 66-7.
79. Burke, *Works*, I, p. 192.
80. Vaughan, *op. cit.*, p. 124.

81. Quoted by Vaughan, II, p. 126. Fichte's *Werke*, IV, p. 436.
82. Cazamian, *op. cit.*, p. 178.
83. *French Revolution*, III, pp. 121-2.
84. *Life of Sterling*, p. 130.
85. *French Revolution*, I, p. 10.
86. *Literary Remains of Henry James*, p. 426.
87. Windelband, *op. cit.*, p. 640.
88. *Ibid.*, p. 640.

CHAPTER IV. THE ART OF HISTORY IN THEORY

1. *Sartor*, p. 232.
2. *Letters*, II, p. 3.
3. See *supra*, p. 116.
4. *Correspondence of Thomas Carlyle and Ralph Waldo Emerson, 1834-1872*, ed., C. E. Norton, Boston, 1888, II, pp. 10-1.
5. *Misc.*, I, p. 399.
6. Downey, June E., *Creative Imagination*, London, 1929, p. 195.
7. *Carlyle's Letters to Mill, Sterling, Browning*, ed., A. Carlyle, New York, 1923, p. 57.
8. Wilson, David Alec, *Carlyle to the French Revolution*, see pp. 15-9.
9. *Letters*, II, p. 105.
10. Conway, Moncure, *Thomas Carlyle*, London, p. 235.
11. Thrall, Miriam, *Rebellious Fraser's*, Columbia University Press, New York, 1934, p. 27.
12. James Mill, father of John Stuart Mill, is remembered today for a *History of British India*, published in London in 1817.
13. *Letters to Mill, etc.*, p. 33.
14. *Misc.*, III, pp. 44 *passim*.
15. *Wilhelm Meister*, I, p. 29.
16. Emerson, R. W., "On History," *Essays*, 2nd series, etc., pp. 8 *passim*.
17. *Life of Schiller*, p. 2.
18. *Misc.*, III, p. 195.
19. *Life of Schiller*, p. 51.
20. *Misc.*, I, p. 199.
21. *Misc.*, I, p. 51.
22. *Misc.*, I, p. 261.

NOTES: CHAPTER IV

23. Professor Saintsbury discusses the dwindling of the literary interest from a somewhat different angle. See Saintsbury, George, *History of Criticism*, Vol. III (2nd ed., New York, 1906), pp. 495-500.
24. *Misc.*, II, pp. 83 passim.
25. *Misc.*, II, p. 85.
26. *Letters to Mill, etc., op. cit.*, pp. 263-4.
27. *Misc.*, II, p. 88.
28. *Misc.*, III, p. 53.
29. *Misc.*, III, p. 167.
30. *Misc.*, III, p. 175.
31. *Misc.*, III, pp. 173 *passim*.
32. *Misc.*, III, p. 174.
33. *Misc.*, III, pp. 49-50.
34. For a recent, comprehensive study of Carlyle's efforts to achieve a unity in his theories of poetry, history and religion, see Professor Hill Shine, *Carlyle's Fusion of Poetry, History and Religion by 1834* (University of North Carolina Press, 1938). While the findings of the present inquiry into Carlyle's fusion of poetry and history were arrived at independently, they are substantially in accord with those of Professor Shine.
35. Addison's *Spectator*, No. 160, Sept. 3, 1711 (ed., Henry Moreley, London, n.d.), p. 234.
36. Langdon, Ida, *Milton's Theory of Poetry and Fine Art* (Yale University Press, 1924), p. 2.
37. *Misc.*, I, pp. 244, 255.
38. Roe, *op. cit.*, pp. 27-30.
39. Quoted by Langdon, *op. cit.*, p. 9.
40. *Heroes*, pp. 83-4.
41. *Misc.*, III, p. 356.
42. Cf. Emerson's "The true poem is the poet's mind. The true ship is the ship-builder." "On History," *Essays*, 2nd series, p. 17.
43. *Letters to Mill, etc.*, p. 87.
44. *Carlyle-Emerson Corres.*, I, p. 25.
45. *Misc.*, III, p. 247.
46. *Carlyle-Emerson Corres.*, I, pp. 216, 217.
47. *Carlyle-Emerson Corres.*, II, p. 99.
48. *Carlyle-Emerson Corres.*, I, p. 325.

49. Coleridge, S. T., *Complete Works*, "Literary Remains" (ed. Shedd, New York, 1884), p. 90.
50. *Misc.*, II, p. 284.
51. *Letters*, II, p. 123.
52. *Wilhelm Meister*, intro., pp. 28, 29.
53. *Letters to Mill, etc.*, pp. 82-3.
54. *Cromwell*, I, pp. 7, 8.
55. *Cromwell*, I, p. 3.
56. *Misc.*, I, p. 82.
57. *Misc.*, I, p. 71.
58. *Early Letters*, II, p. 62.
59. *New Letters*, I, pp. 251, 252.
60. *Misc.*, III, p. 357.
61. *Letters*, II, pp. 118n, 142.
62. *Carlyle-Emerson Corres.*, II, p. 6.
63. *Carlyle-Emerson Corres.*, I, p. 293.
64. *Notebooks*, pp. 20-1 and *Early Letters*, II, p. 57.
65. *Early Letters*, II, p. 170. Italics mine.
66. *Misc.*, II, p. 198.
67. *Misc.*, III, p. 86.
68. *Ibid.*, p. 81.
69. *Ibid.*, pp. 80-1.
70. *Ibid.*, pp. 82 *passim*.
71. *Ibid.*, p. 80.
72. *Ibid.*, p. 78.
73. *Ibid.*, p. 79.
74. See *supra*, p. 120.
75. *Past and Present*, pp. 44-5 (Chapman & Hall ed. of 1870).
76. Acton, John E. Dahlberg, *Lectures in the French Revolution*, London, 1910, p. 358.
77. Acton, *op. cit.*, p. 358 and Abbott, W. C., *A Bibliography of Oliver Cromwell*, Cambridge, 1929, XXIV.
78. *Cromwell*, I, p. 92.
79. *Frederick II*, Vol. I, p. 17. Carlyle wrote Emerson, confessing a "real love for Frederick's dumb followers, the Prussian soldiers. I often say to myself, 'Were not here the real priests and virtuous martyrs of that loud-babbling, rotten generation.'" (*Carlyle-Emerson Corres.*, II, pp. 247-8.)
80. See Brinton, Crane, "Thomas Carlyle," *Encyclopedia of the Social Sciences*, Vol. III, pp. 229-30.

81. *Heroes*, p. 1.
82. *Heroes*, pp. 45-6.
83. *Misc.*, III, p. 278.
84. Saintsbury, *op. cit.*, p. 253.
85. *Misc.*, III, p. 60.
86. *Carlyle-Emerson Corres.*, I, p. 42.
87. *Letters*, II, p. 268.
88. *Letters*, II, p. 210.
89. *Letters*, II, pp. 237-8.
90. See *infra*, p. 174.
91. *Letters to Mill, etc.*, pp. 70-2.
92. *Ibid.*, p. 33.
93. *Letters*, II, p. 352.
94. *New Letters*, I, p. 306.
95. *Frederick*, V, p. 260.
96. *Misc.*, IV, p. 8.
97. Aulard, *op. cit.*, pp. 196-208.
98. Harrold, Charles Frederick, "Carlyle's General Method in the French Revolution," *P.M.L.A.*, XLIII, 1928, p. 1168.
99. *Misc.*, IV, p. 3.
100. Harrold, Charles Frederick, *op. cit.*, p. 1165.

CHAPTER V. THE ART OF HISTORY IN PRACTICE

1. *Heroes*, pp. 106-7.
2. *Misc.*, III, p. 5.
3. See Downey, June E., *Creative Imagination*, London, 1929, p. 158.
4. *Ibid.*, p. 155.
5. *New Letters*, II, p. 50.
6. Cf. Amy Lowell's definition of a poet: "a man of extraordinarily sensitive and active subconscious personality, fed by and feeding, a non-resistant consciousness." Quoted by Downey, *op. cit.*, p. 166.
7. *Love Letters*, I, p. 358.
8. *Letters*, II, p. 210.
9. *New Letters*, I, p. 17.
10. The manuscript of the first volume of the *French Revolution* was loaned to Mill, who in turn loaned it to his friend, Mrs. Taylor. While in the latter's possession, it was inadvertently de-

stroyed by a careless housemaid who, according to the legend, used it to start a fire.
11. *Letters*, II, pp. 288-9.
12. *Letters*, II, p. 355.
13. *New Letters*, I, p. 50.
14. *Ibid.*, p. 37.
15. *New Letters*, I, p. 244.
16. *Carlyle-Emerson Corres.*, I, p. 327.
17. *Ibid.*, II, p. 183.
18. *Ibid.*, II, pp. 270-1.
19. *Ibid.*, II, p. 278.
20. *Letters*, I, p. 262.
21. *New Letters*, I, 258.
22. *Letters to Mill, etc.*, pp. 215-6.
23. *Carlyle-Emerson Corres.*, I, p. 197.
24. *Ibid.*, II, p. 170.
25. Dewey, John, *Art as Experience*, New York, 1929, p. 73.
26. See Lowes, J. L., *The Road to Xanadu*, Cambridge, 1927, p. 426. Professor Lowes emphasizes the fact that many of the works belonging to the army of "imaginative masterpieces" have been built upon masses of raw fact, particularly the *Odyssey*, the *Aeneid*, *Paradise Lost*, the *Divine Comedy*, the *Ancient Mariner*. He might have added the *French Revolution*. Facts may swamp the imagination and remain untransformed; or they may be transmuted into a work of art. "The instincts of the scholar and of the artist lie side by side in geniuses."
27. Dewey, *op. cit.*, p. 189.
28. *New Letters*, I, p. 254.
29. *Ibid.*, p. 220.
30. *Ibid.*, p. 220.
31. *Carlyle-Emerson Corres.*, II, pp. 247-8.
32. *New Letters*, II, p. 142.
33. *Carlyle-Emerson Corres.*, II, p. 278.
34. Welch, Livingston, *Imagination and Human Nature*, London, 1937, p. 64.
35. *Misc.*, I, p. 244.
36. *Misc.*, I, pp. 274-5.
37. Downey, *op. cit.*, p. 2.

NOTES: CHAPTER V

38. *Ibid.*, pp. 2-3.
39. *Misc.*, III, p. 55.
40. Cf. Michelet's comment: "Augustin Thierry saw in history a narrative, Guizot an analysis. I call mine a resurrection." Quoted by Barnes, *op. cit.*, p. 188.
41. *Carlyle-Emerson Corres.*, II, p. 307.
42. *Misc.*, III, p. 57.
43. *Misc.*, III, pp. 54-5. Italics are Carlyle's.
44. *Ibid.*, p. 56.
45. Emerson, *Essays*, Second Series, Boston, 1903, p. 21.
46. *Past and Present*, pp. 45-6.
47. Poincaré, Henri, *Foundations of Science*, tr. by G. B. Halsted, New York, 1929, p. 128.
48. Flaubert's thoughts on the problem of particularization are quoted by his disciple, Guy de Maupassant, in the intro. to *Jean and Pierre*, trans. by Hugh Craig, New York, 1910.
49. Emerson, R. W., *Essays*, First Series, Boston, 1904, p. 355.
50. Downey, *op. cit.*, pp. 175-8.
51. *Misc.*, II, p. 88.
52. *Carlyle-Emerson Corres.*, I, p. 268.
53. *Ibid.*, p. 19.
54. *French Revolution*, I, p. 178.
55. *Ibid.*, p. 193.
56. *Ibid.*, pp. 164-5.
57. *Cromwell*, I, p. 127.
58. *Ibid.*, p. 179.
59. *Past and Present*, p. 69.
60. *French Revolution*, I, p. 136.
61. *Ibid.*, I, p. 137.
62. By acclamation among professional historians. See Barnes, *op. cit.*, p. 359; Gooch, George P., *History and Historians in the 19th Century*, London, 1913, p. 324.
63. *Carlyle-Emerson Corres.*, II, p. 306.
64. *Ibid.*, II, p. 305.
65. *Ibid.*, I, pp. 118-9.
66. *Life of Sterling*, p. 112.
67. *Past and Present*, p. 65.
68. *French Revolution*, I, p. 164.
69. *Cromwell*, II, p. 205.

70. *Cromwell*, I, p. 212.
71. *Past and Present*, p. 66.
72. *Cromwell*, I, pp. 40-1.
73. *Ibid.*, I, pp. 71-2.
74. *French Revolution*, I, p. 194.
75. *New Letters*, I, p. 33.
76. *Intro. Wilhelm Meister*, I, p. 26.
77. *Misc.*, I, p. 19.
78. *Letters to Mill, etc.*, p. 203.
79. *Frederick*, II, pp. 252-3. Curiously enough, Carlyle is criticizing Leopold von Ranke, father of so-called scientific history.
80. Cazamian, *op. cit.*, pp. 157-8.
81. *Carlyle-Emerson Corres.*, II, p. 44.
82. *Cromwell*, I, preface to second edition.
83. *Ibid.*, preface to third edition.
84. Lyall, Sir Alfred, *Studies in Literature and History*, London, 1915, p. 385.

CHAPTER VI. CARLYLE'S POSITION AS A HISTORIAN

1. Morley, John, *Critical Miscellanies*, London, 1898, I, pp. 140-1.
2. Shotwell, James T., *An Introduction to the History of History*, New York, 1923, p. 7 *passim*.
3. *Ibid.*, p. 184.
4. Cheyney, E. P., *Law in History and Other Essays*, New York, 1927, pp. 139 *passim*.
5. *Ibid.*, p. 165. Other interesting expressions of the imagination's function in historical research include A. F. Pollard's admission (*Factors in Modern History*, London, 1907, p. 1): "I make no apology for placing imagination in the forefront of all qualifications indispensable for the student and teacher of history. . . . Probably it includes fact as well as fiction, and signifies the power of realizing things unseen." Or Theodor Mommsen's remark (*Roman History*, Berlin, 1885, p. 5) that "fancy is the mother of history, as of all poetry."
6. See especially *Letters of William Stubbs*, ed., W. H. Hutton, London, 1904, and Gooch, *op. cit.*, pp. 334-7.
7. Morley, John, *Critical Miscellanies, II*, London, 1877, p. 387.
8. *New Letters*, II, p. 120.
9. Morley, *op. cit.*, p. 380.

10. *Ibid.*, p. 401.
11. Barnes, *op. cit.*, p. 219.
12. Gooch, pp. 297 *passim.*
13. Quoted by Wilson in *Carlyle till the French Revolution* from Mill's review in *The London and Westminster*, p. 416. Italics mine.
14. Sterling, John, *Essays and Tales*, ed., Julius Hare, Vol. I, London, 1848, p. 366.
15. *Ibid.*, p. 372.
16. *Carlyle-Emerson Corres.*, I, p. 129.
17. Thackeray, W. M., *Sultan Stork and Other Stories and Sketches*, ed. by R. H. Shepherd, London, 1887, pp. 99-113.
18. Gooch, pp. 346 *passim.*
19. Berdyaev, *op. cit.*, p. 9.
20. Space forbids more than a cursory survey of historical materialism, but its fundamental contradiction has a bearing on our theme. If human consciousness is a mere adjunct of man's economic activities, how are we to explain the origin of such an intellect as that possessed by Marx himself, which certainly towers over mere passive reflection of economic relations. As one critic observed: "The Marxian dialectic explains everything but Marx himself." See Sée, Henri, *Economic Interpretation of History*, trans. by M. M. Knight, New York, 1929; and Croce, Benedetto, *Historical Materialism and the Economics of Karl Marx*, trans. by C. M. Meredith, London, 1922.
21. Morley, John, *Diderot and the Encyclopedists*, new ed. in 1 vol., New York, 1878, p. 378.
22. Harrison, Frederic, *Tennyson, Ruskin and Mill and Other Literary Estimates*, New York, 1900, pp. 221 *passim.*
23. *Ibid.*, p. 223.
24. Becker, Carl, "Presidential Address," *Am. Hist. Assoc.*, Dec. 1931, repr. in *Am. Hist. Review*, Vol. 37, Jan. 1932, p. 231.
25. Sée, *op. cit.*, p. 24.
26. Becker, *op. cit.*, p. 233.
27. *Ibid.*, p. 231.
28. Black, *op. cit.*, p. VII.
29. Becker, p. 232.
30. See Barnes, *op. cit.*, pp. 267-70. Possibly the best discussion of

the "simple historical fact" is to be found in Professor Becker's paper, "What Are Historical Facts?" delivered before the Am. Hist. Association December, 1926, and reprinted in the *Am. Hist. Review,* January, 1927.
31. Trevelyan, G. M., "Carlyle as an Historian," *Living Age,* Vol. 223, pp. 366-75.
32. Becker, *op. cit.,* p. 234.
33. Trevelyan, G. O., *Life and Letters of Lord Macaulay,* 2 vols., New York, 1875, II, p. 234.
34. Morley, Lord, *Critical Misc.,* I, p. 219.

BIBLIOGRAPHY

Carlyle, Thomas, *WORKS, Centenary edition,* 30 Vols, London, 1895.
Carlyle, Vol. I, Sartor Resartus, the Life and Opinions of Herr Teufelsdröckh.
Carlyle, Vols. II-IV, The French Revolution: a History.
Carlyle, Vol. V, Heroes and Hero Worship.
Carlyle, Vols. VI-IX, Oliver Cromwell's Letters and Speeches.
Carlyle, Vol. X, Past and Present.
Carlyle, Vol. XI, The Life of Sterling.
Carlyle, Vols. XII-XIX, History of Frederick II of Prussia.
Carlyle, Vol. XX, Latterday Pamphlets.
Carlyle, Vol. XXI-XXII, German Romance.
Carlyle, Vols. XXIII-XXIV, Wilhelm Meister's Apprenticeship and Travels.
Carlyle, Vol. XV, Life of Friedrich Schiller, Comprehending an Examination of His Works.
Carlyle, Vols. XXVI-XXX, Critical and Miscellaneous Essays.
Carlyle, Vol. XXXI, Historical Sketches of Notable Persons and Events in the Reigns of James I and Charles I (ed. A. Carlyle).
Carlyle, Collectiana (ed. S. A. Jones, Canton, Pa., 1903).
Carlyle-Emerson Correspondence (ed. C. E. Norton, 2 vols., Boston, 1888).
Carlyle-Goethe Correspondence (ed. C. E. Norton, London, 1887).
Carlyle, Early Letters of (ed. C. E. Norton, London, 1886).
Carlyle, *Letters,* 1826-1836 (2 vols. ed. C. E. Norton, London, 1888).
Carlyle, *Letters to John Stuart Mill, John Sterling and Robert Browning* (ed. A. Carlyle, New York, 1923).
Letters to His Younger Sister (ed. C. T. Copeland, Cambridge, 1899).
Love Letters (Thomas Carlyle and Jane Welsh Carlyle), 2 vols., ed. A. Carlyle, London, 1909.
Carlyle, New Letters of (ed. A. Carlyle, 2 vols., London, 1904).
Carlyle, *Reminiscences* (ed. J. A. Froude, 2 vols., New York, 1881).

Carlyle, *Two Notebooks* (ed. C. E. Norton, Grolier Club, New York, 1898).
Carlyle, *Unpublished Letters* (Scribner's Magazine, 1893).
Carlyle, Jane Welsh, *Letters and Memorials* (ed. J. A. Froude, 2 vols., New York, 1883).
Carlyle, Jane Welsh, *New Letters and Memorials* (ed. A. Carlyle, 2 vols., New York, 1903).

CRITICISMS OF CARLYLE

Abbott, W. C., *A Bibliography of Oliver Cromwell*, Cambridge, 1929.
Addison, Joseph, *Spectator*, No. 160, ed. Henry Moreley, London, n.d.
Aulard, A., *Études et Leçons sur la Révolution Française*, Paris, 1913, Septième Série.
Batt, Max, Carlyle's *"Life of Schiller," Modern Philology*, I, pp. 391-2.
Brownell, W. C., *Victorian Prose Masters*, "Carlyle," pp. 47-96, London, 1901.
Caird, Edward, *Essays on Literature*, Glasgow, 1909.
Cambridge History of English Literature, Vols. X and XIII.
Cambridge Modern History, Vols. VIII and X.
Canning, Albert S. G., *Lord Macaulay: Essayist and Historian*, London, 1882.
Carlyle, R. W. and A. J., *Medieval Political Theory in the West*, Vol. VI, Edinburgh, 1936.
Cazamian, Louis, *Carlyle*, tr. E. K. Brown, New York, 1932.
Conway, Moncure, *Carlyle*, 1881.
Craig, R. S., *The Making of Carlyle*, New York, 1909.
Dowden, Edward, *Transcripts and Studies*, "Carlyle's Lectures on the Periods of European Culture" (a transcript), London, 1897, 2nd ed. These transcripts taken from a copious stenographic transcript of all but the ninth lecture. Dowden was given the shorthand notes, did not make them.
Duffy, Sir Charles Gavan, *Conversations with Carlyle*, New York, 1892.
Ewen, Frederick, *The Prestige of Schiller in England*, Columbia Univ. Press, New York, 1932.

BIBLIOGRAPHY

Flügel, Ewald, *Thomas Carlyle's Moral and Religious Development*, tr. J. S. Tyler, New York, 1891.
Froude, J. A., *Thomas Carlyle*, 4 vols., New York, 1882-4.
Garnet, Richard, *Life of Thomas Carlyle* (Great Writers Series), London, 1887.
Greg, W. R., *Literary and Social Judgments: Kingsley and Carlyle*, London, 1877.
Grierson, H. J. C., "Scott and Carlyle," *English Association Essays and Studies*, Vol. 13, pp. 88-111.
Hamilton, Mary Agnes, *Thomas Carlyle*, London, 1926.
Harrison, Frederic, *Tennyson, Ruskin, Mill and Other Literary Estimates*, New York, 1900.
Harrold, C. F., "Carlyle's General Method in the French Revolution," *P.M.L.A.*, XLIII, 1928, pp. 1150-69.
Harrold, C. F., "Carlyle's Interpretation of Kant," *Philological Quarterly*, Vol. VII, 1928, pp. 345-57.
Harrold, C. F., "Translated Passages in Carlyle's French Revolution," *Journal of English and Germanic Philology*, 1928, pp. 51-66.
Harrold, C. F., *Carlyle and German Thought* (Yale Studies in English), New Haven, 1934.
Hensel, Paul, *Thomas Carlyle*, Stuttgart, 1901.
Howe, Susanna, *Wilhelm Meister and His English Kinsmen*, Columbia Univ. Press, 1930.
James, L. S., "Carlyle's Philosophy of History," *Westminster Review*, 1889, pp. 414-28.
Küchler, Frohwalt, *Carlyle und Schiller*, Halle, 1902.
Larkin, Henry, *Carlyle*, 1886.
Lehman, Benjamin H., *Carlyle's Theory of the Hero: Its Sources, Development, History and Influences on Carlyle's Work*, Duke University Press, Durham, N.C., 1928.
Lewes, G. H., "Carlyle's Frederick the Great," *Fraser's Magazine*, Dec. 1858, Vol. LVIII, pp. 631-49.
Lowell, James R., *Literary Essays*, Vol. II, Cambridge, 1890, "Carlyle," pp. 77-119.
Masson, David, *Edinburgh Sketches and Memories*, London, 1892.
Mazzini, Joseph, *Essays: Camelot Series*, London, 1887.
Mead, Edwin D., *The Philosophy of Carlyle*, Boston, 1881.
Mill, J. S., "The French Revolution," *London & Westminster Review*, July, 1837, Vol. XXVII.

Montégut, Emile, "Thomas Carlyle, Sa Vie et Ses Ecrits," *Revue des Deux Mondes*, avril 15, 1849, vol. II, pp. 278-314.
Morley, John, *Critical Miscellanies*, London, 1898, I and II.
Neff, Emery E., *Carlyle*, New York, 1932.
Neff, Emery E., *Carlyle and Mill: An Introduction to Victorian Thought*, second edition revised. New York, 1926.
Nichol, John, "Carlyle," *English Men of Letters*, New York, 1892.
Robertson, J. M., *Modern Humanists*, London, 1895.
Roe, Frederick W., *The Social Philosophy of Carlyle and Ruskin*, New York, 1921.
Roe, F. W., *Thomas Carlyle as a Critic of Literature*, New York, 1910.
Rose, Henry, *New Political Economy: Social Teaching of Carlyle, Ruskin and Henry George*, London, 1891.
Saintsbury, Geo., *History of Criticism*, Vol. III (2nd ed.), New York, 1906.
Saintsbury, Geo., *A History of Nineteenth Century Literature*, New York, 1896.
Saintsbury, George, *Corrected Impressions*, New York, 1895.
Shine, Hill, *Carlyle's Fusion of Poetry, History and Religion by 1834*, University of North Carolina Press, Chapel Hill, N.C., 1938.
Shepherd, R. H., *A Bibliography and Ana of Carlyle*, London, 1881.
Stephen, Leslie, *Hours in a Library*, Vol. III, New York, 1894.
Stewart, Herbert L., "Carlyle's Place in Philosophy," *The Monist*, 1919, Vol. 29, pp. 161-89.
Storrs, Margaret, *The Relation of Carlyle to Kant and Fichte*, Bryn Mawr College Thesis, Bryn Mawr, 1929.
Taine, H. A., *L'Idealisme Anglais: étude sur Carlyle*, Paris, 1864.
Taine, H. A., *History of English Literature*, New York, 1889.
Thayer, W. R., *Throne Makers*, "Carlyle," pp. 163-92, Boston, 1899.
Thrall, Miriam M. H., *Rebellious Fraser's*, Columbia Univ. Press, New York, 1934.
Trevelyan, G. M., "Carlyle as an Historian," *Living Age*, Vol. 223, pp. 366-75.
Vaughan, C. E., "Carlyle and His German Masters," *English Association: Essays and Studies*, Oxford, 1910.
Wilson, D. A., *Carlyle*, 6 vols., 1923-34.
Young, Norwood, *Carlyle, His Rise and Fall*, New York, n.d.

BIBLIOGRAPHY

ADDITIONAL SOURCES

Acton, John E. Dahlberg, Lord, *Lectures on the French Revolution*, London, 1910.
Acton, J. E. Dahlberg, Lord, *Lectures on Modern History*, London, 1906.
Barnes, H. E., *History and Social Intelligence*, New York, 1926.
Barnes, H. E., *The History of History Writing*, Univ. of Okla. Press, Norman, Okla., 1937.
Barnes, H. E., *The New History and the Social Studies*, New York, 1925.
Beard, Charles A., *The Discussion of Human Affairs*, New York, 1936.
Becker, Carl, "Presidential Address," *Am. Hist. Review*, Vol. 37, Jan. 1932, pp. 221-36.
Becker, Carl, "What Are Historical Facts?" *Am. Hist. Review*, Jan. 1927.
Benn, Alfred W., *History of English Rationalism in the 19th Century*, London, 1906.
Berdyaev, Nicolas, *The Meaning of History*, New York, 1936.
Black, J. B., *The Art of History: A Study of Four Great Historians of the 18th Century*, New York, 1926.
Brown, Philip A., *The French Revolution in English Literature*, New York, 1924.
Burke, Edmund, *Works*, 12 vols., Boston, 1881.
Bury, J. B., *Selected Essays*, ed. H. Temperley, Cambridge, 1930.
Bury, J. B., *The Idea of Progress*, New York, 1912.
Cheyney, Edward P., *Law in History*, New York, 1927.
Coleridge's Miscellaneous Criticism, ed. T. M. Raysor, London, 1935.
Coleridge, S. T., *Table Talk*, ed. T. Ashe, London, 1896.
Coleridge, S. T., Unpublished Letters of, ed. E. L. Griggs, London, 1932.
Coleridge, S. T., Letters of, ed. E. H. Coleridge, 2 vols., London, 1895.
Colvin, Thos., *Life and Writings of Friedrich Schiller*, New York, 1902.
Croce, Benedetto, *Historical Materialism and the Economics of Karl Marx*, tr. by P. M. Meredith, London, 1922.

Croce, Benedetto, *History, Its Theory and Practice,* tr. by Douglas Ainslee, New York, 1921.
Dewey, John, *Art as Experience,* New York, 1929.
Downey, June E., *Creative Imagination,* London, 1929.
Emerson, R. W., *Complete Works—Centenary Edition,* Boston, 1903.
Emerson, R. W., *Journals,* Boston, 1909-1914.
Engelbrecht, H. C., *Johann Gottlieb Fichte,* Columbia Univ. Press, New York, 1933.
Ergang, Reinhold R., *Herder and the Foundations of German Nationalism,* New York, 1931.
Fichte, Johann Gottlieb, *Popular Works,* 2 vols., trans. by Wm. Smith, London, 1848.
Flint, Robert, *The Philosophy of History in France and Germany,* London, 1874.
Freeman, Edward A., *Historical Essays,* 2nd series, 3rd ed., London, 1889.
Froude, James A., *Short Studies on Great Subjects,* 1st series, "The Science of History," New York, 1864. Second series, "Scientific Method Applied to History," London, 1871.
Fueter, Eduard, *Histoire de l'Historiographie Moderne,* Paris, 1914.
Gibbon, Edward, *Autobiography,* ed. John Murray, London, 1896.
Gibbon, Edward, *History of the Decline and Fall of the Roman Empire,* with intro. by J. B. Bury, 2nd ed., London, 1929.
Gooch, George P., *Germany and the French Revolution,* London, 1920.
Gooch, George P., *History and Historians in the 19th Century,* London, 1913.
Hearnshaw, F. J. C., *Social and Political Ideas of the Revolutionary Era,* London, 1931.
Hegel, Georg Wilhelm Friedrich, *The Philosophy of History,* tr. by J. Sibree, New York, 1900.
Herder, J. G., *Ideen zur Geschichte der Menschheit,* Leipzig, 1869.
Hume, David, *Enquiries Concerning the Human Understanding and Concerning the Principles of Morals,* ed. by L. A. Selby-Bigge, Oxford, 1894.
James, Henry, Literary Remains of, ed. Wm. James, Boston, 1885.
Lamprecht, K., *Old and New Tendencies in the Science of History,* Berlin, 1896, p. 18.

Langdon, Ida, *Milton's Theory of Poetry and Fine Art*, Yale Univ. Press, New Haven, 1924.

Langlois and Seignobos, *Intro. to the Study of History*, tr. by S. S. Berry, New York, 1909.

Lecky, Wm. E. H., *Historical and Political Essays*, New York, 1908, "Thoughts on History" and "Carlyle's Message to His Age."

Lowes, J. L., *The Road to Xanadu*, New York, 1927.

Lyall, Sir Alfred, *Studies in Literature and History*, London, 1915.

Macaulay, T. B., *Complete Works*, Temple Bar Edition, 8 vols., New York, n.d.

Maccunn, John, *Political Philosophy of Burke*, London, 1913.

Maurois, André, *Poets and Prophets*, New York, 1935.

McLaughlin, Robert W., *The Spiritual Element in History*, New York, 1926.

Merz, John T., *A History of European Thought in the 19th Century*, 4 vols., London, 1914.

Mill, John Stuart, The Letters of, ed. by Hugh G. R. Elliot, 2 vols., London, 1910.

Morley, John, *Diderot and the Encyclopedists*, new ed. in 1 vol., New York, 1878.

Morley, John Viscount, *Edmund Burke: A Historical Study*, London, 1867.

Morley, John Viscount, *Notes on Politics and History*, New York, 1914.

Murray, R. H., *English Social and Political Thinkers of the 19th Century*, 2 vols., Cambridge, 1929.

Nicolson, Harold, *Development of English Biography*, New York, 1928.

Nordau, Max, *The Interpretation of History*, tr. M. A. Hamilton, New York, 1910.

Peardon, T. P., *The Transition in English Historical Writing, 1760-1830*. Columbia Univ. Press, New York, 1933.

Poincaré, Henri, *Foundations of Science*, tr. by G. B. Halsted, New York, 1929.

Pollard, A. F., *Factors in Modern History*, London, 1907.

Pringle-Pattison, A. S., "The Philosophy of History," *Proceedings of the British Academy*, Vol. XI, London, 1924.

Richards, I. A., *Coleridge on Imagination*, New York, 1935.

Robertson, J. S., *The Genesis of Romantic Theory*, Cambridge, 1923.
Robinson, J. H., "Newer Ways of Historians," *Am. Hist. Review*, Vol. 35, pp. 245-55.
Robinson, J. H., *The New History*, New York, 1912.
Robinson, J. H., *The Mind in the Making*, New York, 1921.
Ruskin, John, *Complete Works*, Library Edition, 31 vols., London, 1903.
Schiller, Friedrich, *Prose Works*, 2 vols., Philadelphia, 1870.
Schlegel, Frederick von, *The Philosophy of History*, tr. by James Burton Robinson, London, 1890.
Sée, Henri, *Economic Interpretation of History*, tr. M. M. Knight, New York, 1929.
Seignobos, see Langlois.
Shotwell, James T., *An Introduction to the History of History*, New York, 1923.
Singer, Edgar A., *On the Contented Life*, New York, 1936.
de Staël,-Holstein, Mme, *Germany*, 2 vols., tr. by O. W. Wight, New York, 1859.
Stephen, Leslie, *History of English Thought in the 18th Century*, 2 vols., London, 1876.
Stubbs, Wm., *Lectures in Medieval and Modern History*, Oxford, 1886.
Stubbs, Wm., Letters of, W. H. Hutton, London, 1904.
Tacitus, *Histories*, Loeb Classical Library, London, 1925.
Teggart, J. F., *The Theory of History*, Yale Univ. Press, New Haven, 1924.
Trevelyan, G. O., *Life and Letters of Lord Macaulay*, 2 vols., New York, 1875.
Vaughan, C. E., *Studies in the History of Political Philosophy*, Manchester Univ. Press, Manchester, 1925.
Vaughan, C. E., *Romantic Revolt*, New York, 1907.
Welch, Livingston, *Imagination and Human Nature*, London, 1937.
Windelband, W., *A History of Philosophy*, New York, 1898, tr. by J. H. Tufts.
Wordsworth, Wm., *Prose Works*, Vol. II, ed. Grosart, London, 1876.

INDEX

Acton, Lord, 49, 124
Art, function of, 60, 93ff
   biographic purport of, 97ff, 106ff
Aulard, A., 136-37

Beard, C. A., 6
Becker, C., 182-83
Berdyaev, N., 180
Boswell, J., 106, 123, 151
Buchanan, G., 79-80
Buckle, T., 4, 5, 180-81
Burke, E., 4, 28, 43, 45, 47-48, 55-56, 63ff, 80, 83, 87
Burns, R., 39, 55, 82, 84, 86, 102, 148-49
Byron, Lord, 43

Calvinism, 25, 57, 79ff
Carlyle, J. W., 14, 16-17, 29, 117, 120
Carlyle, T. C., early reading of, 8-10
  works cited,
    "Biography," 106ff, 149
    "Boswell's Life of Johnson, 113
    "Cagliostro," 79, 95, 132-33, 141
    "Characteristics," 65, 68, 75, 139
    Cromwell, 3, 71, 73, 104, 116, 125-27, 135, 137, 140, 143, 158, 167-69
    "Diamond Necklace," 79, 95, 113, 118, 133, 141, 161
    "Diderot," 112
    "Dr. Francia," 88
    Frederick, 3, 71, 73, 127, 135, 137, 140, 146, 160, 164-65, 168
    French Revolution, 2, 3, 44, 55, 70-71, 73ff, 83, 90, 113, 125, 127, 135-37, 140, 142-43, 156, 160, 167-68, 177, 179-80
    Heroes and Hero Worship, 82ff, 128
    Historic Survey of German Poetry," 61
    "Joanna Baillie," 31-34, 55
    Life of Schiller, 20, 28-32, 55, 101, 103, 141
    Life of Sterling, 3, 50, 131, 168
    Two Notebooks, 24, 26, 30, 33-34, 36, 39, 66, 81
    "On History," 105ff, 155
    "On History Again," 107ff
    Past and Present, 123-25, 151, 160, 162-63, 168
    Reminiscences, 16-17
    Sartor Resartus, 7, 29, 33, 44, 55, 57, 59, 61-62, 68, 70, 91, 95, 141, 160-61
    "Sir Walter Scott," 40
    "Signs of the Times," 58
    "Wotton Reinfred," 95
Cazamian, L., 83, 87, 141, 167
Clarendon, Earl of, 5, 7, 150-51
Coleridge, S. T., 8, 29, 38, 42-43, 50, 52, 55, 69, 114
Comte, A., 55, 180-81
Coulanges, Fustel de, 54
Cousin, V., 63
Croce, B., 8

Dryasdust, 2, 4, 96, 115-16, 168, 170-71

Emerson, R. W., 3, 93, 99, 100, 113, 115, 118, 132, 143, 148, 151, 154, 156, 159, 161, 167, 179, 185

Fichte, J. H., 23-26, 49, 55, 60, 66, 83, 87, 112-13
Flaubert, G., 153ff
Fletcher, C. R. L., 2
Fueter, E., 2
Froude, J. A., vii, 175

Gibbon, E., 1, 7-8, 11ff, 26, 33, 182
Goethe, J. W. von, 22-28, 55-57, 68, 78, 79, 83, 86, 99, 102, 111, 129, 148-49
Gooch, G. P., viii, 1-2, 177
Guizot, F., 180-82

Hallam, H., 13, 176
Harrison, F., 182
Harrold, C. F., viii, 137
Hegel, G., 25, 55-58, 89
Herder, J., 15, 20-28, 35-37, 45-47, 55, 60-79
Herodotus, 5, 7, 10, 52, 72, 185
Heroes, theory of, 23, 78, 81ff
"Historic sense," 6-7, 51, 118
Historiography, rationalist, 11ff, 39; romantic, 15-20, 27, 39-42, 60-61, 88-89
History, method of writing, 5-8, 63, 95ff, 110ff, 119ff, 149-60; related to poetry, 5-6, 54, 95ff, 100ff
Homer, 7, 99, 118, 148, 155
Hume, D., 8-20, 36, 50, 55, 63, 67, 176

Imagery, use of, 154ff
Irrationalism, 21-22, 63
Irving, E., 29-30

James, H., 7, 56, 91, 93

Kant, I., 7, 24-25, 32-35, 55, 66, 87-89
Klopstock, F., 21, 24, 28
Knox, J., 79

Lessing, G., 166
Lyall, Sir A., 169

Macaulay, T. B., 1, 3, 13, 42, 120, 175ff, 185
Marx, K., 4, 180-81
Mazzini, G., 54
Michelet, J., 137
Mill, J. S., 8, 56, 58, 96-97, 115, 133-34, 177
Milton, J., 110-12
Mommsen, T., 5
Montesquieu, 12, 16, 45
Morley, Lord, 43, 47, 172, 176ff, 181, 185

Niebuhr, B., 3, 181
Nietzsche, F., 87
Novalis, 24-26, 55, 59, 62

Poincaré, H., 152, 53
Periodicity, theory of, 67ff
Plutarch, 5, 10, 27
Puritanism, 119, 125ff, 146

Ranke, L. von, 1, 4, 67, 180-82
Revolution, morality of, 78ff; theory of, 69ff
Richter, J., 24, 26, 55, 59
Robertson, W., 11-14, 121-22
Roe, F. W., 111
Romanticism, 4, 10, 39, 43ff, 55, 60
Rousseau, J., 20-26, 35, 45, 66, 76, 84

Saintsbury, G., 6-7, 131
Sallust, 10, 20
Schelling, F., 25, 55-57, 60
Schiller, F., 1, 4, 22, 24ff, 36, 41-43, 49, 55, 59-60, 64, 69, 71, 82, 89, 112-13, 119-20, 138, 166
Schlegel, A. and W., 24-25, 55, 57
Scott, Sir W., 4, 7, 27, 55, 111

Shaftesbury, W., 64-65
Shakespeare, W., 7, 65, 99, 111, 130, 148, 155
Shelley, P., 43
Smollett, T., 8, 121
Social organism, theory of, 23ff, 45ff, 63ff, 84
Southey, W., 43-48
Spinoza, B., 55, 57, 86-87
Staël, Mme de, 28-30
Sterling, J., 3, 91, 93, 104, 117, 143, 145, 161, 166, 178
Strachey, L., 5
Stubbs, W., 174ff
Subjectivism, historical, 26-31, 41, 124, 144

Tacitus, 3, 5, 7, 10, 17, 52, 72, 77, 94, 177-78, 182
Taine, H., 43, 137
Thackeray, W., 3, 179
Thayer, W., 7
Thiers, L., 97, 137
Thrall, M., 96
Thucydides, 5, 10, 52, 128, 177
Tieck, J., 24-26, 55
Transcendentalism, 49, 52-57, 82, 87, 89
Trevelyan, G. M., 184-85
Turgot, 12, 75

Voltaire, 11-12, 18-20, 50, 85, 103, 111, 181
Vico, 21-22, 46, 55, 67

Wilson, D. A., 10, 95
Wordsworth, W., 43-44, 48, 111-12

Date Due

MAY 31 '97			

BRODART, INC.   Cat. No. 23 233   Printed in U.S.A.